Structured
Programming
with
True BASIC

Little, Brown Computer Systems Series

CHATTERGY, RAHUL, AND UDO W. POOCH
    Top-down Modular Programming in FORTRAN with WATFIV

COATS, R. B., AND ANDREW PARKIN
    Computer Models in the Social Sciences

CONSTABLE, ROBERT L., AND MICHAEL J. O'DONNELL
    A Programming Logic, with an Introduction to the PL/CV Verifier

CONWAY, RICHARD, AND JAMES ARCHER
    Programming for Poets: A Gentle Introduction Using BASIC

    Programming for Poets: A Gentle Introduction Using FORTRAN with WATFIV

CONWAY, RICHARD, JAMES ARCHER, AND RALPH CONWAY
    Programming for Poets: A Gentle Introduction Using Pascal

FINKENAUER, ROBERT G.
    COBOL for Students: A Programming Primer

FREEDMAN, DANIEL P., AND GERALD M. WEINBERG
    Handbook of Walkthroughs, Inspections, and Technical Reviews, Third Edition

GAUSE, DONALD C.
    Are Your Lights On?

GREENFIELD, S. E.
    The Architecture of Microcomputers

    The Architecture of Microcomputers, Volume I: Fundamentals

LEMONE, KAREN A., AND MARTIN E. KALISKI
    Assembly Language Programming for the VAX-11

MILLS, HARLAN D.
    Software Productivity

MONRO, DONALD M.
    Basic BASIC: An Introduction to Programming

MORRILL, HARRIET
    Structured Programming with True BASIC

MOSTELLER, WILLIAM S.
    Systems Programmer's Problem Solver

NICKERSON, ROBERT C.
    Fundamentals of FORTRAN 77 Programming, Third Edition

    Fundamentals of Programming in BASIC, Second Edition

    Fundamentals of Structured COBOL

PARIKH, GIRISH
    Techniques of Program and System Maintenance

PARKIN, ANDREW
    Data Processing Management

    Systems Analysis

PIZER, STEPHEN M., WITH VICTOR L. WALLACE
    To Compute Numerically: Concepts and Strategies

REINGOLD, EDWARD M., AND WILFRED J. HANSEN
    Data Structures

    Data Structures in Pascal

SAVITCH, WALTER J.
    Abstract Machines and Grammars

SHIVA, SAJJAN G.
    Computer Design and Architecture

SHNEIDERMAN, BEN
    Software Psychology: Human Factors in Computer and Information Systems

WALKER, HENRY M.
    Introduction to Computing and Computer Science with Pascal

    Problems for Computer Solutions Using BASIC

    Problems for Computer Solutions Using FORTRAN

WEINBERG, GERALD M.
    Rethinking Systems Analysis and Design

    Understanding the Professional Programmer

WEINBERG, GERALD M., AND DENNIS P. GELLER
    Computer Information Systems: An Introduction to Data Processing

Structured
Programming
with
True BASIC

HARRIET MORRILL

LITTLE, BROWN AND COMPANY

Boston
Toronto

Library of Congress Cataloging-in-Publication Data

Morrill, Harriet.
    Structured programming with true BASIC.

    (Little, Brown computer systems series)
    Includes index.
    1. BASIC (Computer program language)   2. Structured
programming.   I. Title.   II. Series.
QA76.73.B3M668   1986   005.1'13   85-19903
ISBN 0-316-58406-1

Library of Congress Catalog Card No. 85-19903

ISBN 0-316-58406-1

9 8 7 6 5 4 3 2 1

MV

Published simultaneously in Canada
by Little, Brown & Company (Canada) Limited

Printed in the United States of America

Designed and produced by Newcomer/Muncil Associates

IBM is a registered trademark of International Business Machines Corporation.

Preface

Structured Programming with True BASIC is a computer textbook with two goals:

1. To explain how to write computer programs using True BASIC.
2. To teach the principles of structured programming.

It carries students, step by step and regardless of their mathematics background or computing experience, through the rudiments of programming to the use of structured programming techniques, disk files, and graphics. It includes numerous sample programs and over 100 chapter exercises. The accompanying instructor's guide provides an answer key and notes on teaching techniques.

True BASIC

True BASIC is a portable version of BASIC. The True BASIC Language System is available for the IBM PC, IBM PCjr, IBM XT, IBM AT, and the Apple Macintosh computers. True BASIC programs written and compiled on one type of computer will run on other types of computers that also have the True BASIC Language System. Because True BASIC conforms to the standards proposed by the American National Standards Institute (ANSI) Committee on BASIC in July 1984, the range of computer types that can run True BASIC programs is likely to increase over time.

This is not to say that using True BASIC is the same for all types of computers. Programmers must work with the keyboards and devices that make up their computer system. IBM PC programmers, for example, use function keys to control editing processes. Macintosh programmers accomplish editing functions by manipulating a mouse. The True BASIC Language System provided for each computer type includes a *True BASIC User's Guide* that details everything the user needs to know in order to run True BASIC on that particular microcomputer.

Structure and Focus

Structured Programming with True BASIC focuses on True BASIC language statements and structured programming techniques. It assumes that you are familiar with the computer system being used and have access to the machine-dependent information in the *True BASIC User's Guide*. In the occasional references made to machine-dependent functions, the examples given are for the IBM PC.

The text embodies the fruits of my years of teaching, and incorporates my philosophy that the most effective learning is active learning. It begins with a hands-on session using True BASIC. The book encourages students to enter the example programs that appear throughout each chapter into the computer and to observe how they work. Students have tested the examples and exercises on the high school level at The Hotchkiss School in Lakeville, Connecticut, and on the university level at Wesleyan University in Middletown, Connecticut.

Structured Programming with True BASIC also draws on my experience working for IBM as a programmer/writer. Superimposed on the how-to aspect of this book is the theory of structured programming. Chapter 2 explains what structured programming is; the remainder of the book uses that presentation as a frame of reference. The subsequent explanations of how to use each True BASIC statement illustrate and amplify the concepts set forth in Chapter 2.

Thus, this book applies to students wishing to focus on the details of True BASIC. It is equally valuable for students wishing to gain a theoretical understanding of modern programming techniques.

Acknowledgment

This book exists because of my husband, James M. Morrill, who provided the wisdom, perseverance, and good humor necessary to take an idea and give it life.

Harriet Morrill
Lakeville, Connecticut

Contents

Introduction   **xiii**

1   **A sample programming session**   **1**

Invoking True BASIC   1
Selecting Display Screen Colors   2
Splitting the Screen   3
Entering a Program   3
Running a Program   4
Editing a Program   5
Giving Commands   6
Looking at Your Computer System   8
Looking at the True BASIC Language System   10
Summary   12
Review Questions   13

2   **Structured programming**   **14**

Defining a Problem   15
Designing a Program from the Top Down   17
Module Design   19
Desk-Checking   23
Summary   24
Review Questions   24

3   **The PRINT, REM, and END statements in a program module**   **25**

The Program Module   25
The Sequential Control Structure   26

The PRINT statement   26
The REM Statement and Line Comments   29
The Program Prologue   30
The Program Format   30
Editing a Program   32
The Finished Program Module   33
Summary   33
Review Questions   34

4   **Computer calculations**   **36**

Arithmetic Operations   37
Numeric Functions   39
The RANDOMIZE Statement   42
True BASIC Numbers   42
Summary   45
Review Questions   45

5   **The LET, INPUT, READ, and DATA statements**   **47**

The LET Statement   47
The INPUT Statement   53
The INPUT PROMPT Statement   56
The LINE INPUT and LINE INPUT PROMPT Statements   56
The READ and DATA Statements   57
The RESTORE Statement   61
Summary   62
Review Questions   62

6   **Decisions: The IF and SELECT CASE statements**   **66**

The True-False Control Structure   66
The IF Statement   67
The Case Control Structure   77
The SELECT CASE Statement   78
Summary   82
Review Questions   82

7   **Loops: The DO and FOR loops**   **85**

The DO and LOOP Statements 86
The EXIT DO Statement 91
The DATA, File, and Keyboard Tests 91
Nested DO Loops 93
The FOR and NEXT Statements 95
Nested FOR Loops 99
The EXIT FOR Statement 100
Combining FOR and DO Loops 101
Summary 102
Review Questions 102

8   **Subscripts and matrices**   **105**

The DIM Statement 106
Related Lists 108
Sorting Lists 109
Using Subscripts 109
The MAT PRINT Statement 115
The MAT READ Statement 117
The MAT INPUT Statement 119
The MAT LINE INPUT Statement 120
The MAT LINE INPUT PROMPT Statement 121
Redimensioning 121
Matrix Arithmetic 123
Built-in Matrices 125
Built-in Matrix Manipulation Functions 127
Summary 128
Review Questions 128

9   **Subroutines and functions**   **130**

Overview of Programming with Subroutines 130
The SUB and END SUB Statements 134
Overview of Programming with User-Defined Functions 136
The FUNCTION and END DEF Statements 139
The DECLARE DEF Statement 140
String Functions 140
Internal Subroutines and User-Defined Functions 142
One-Line Functions 143

The EXTERNAL Statement   143
The LIBRARY Statement   144
Summary   145
Review Questions   146

---

10   **Trapping errors**   **148**

The WHEN EXCEPTION IN, USE, and END WHEN
   Statements   148
True BASIC Error Codes and Messages   150
Correcting a Run-Time Error   151
Nesting Exception Handlers   152
Percolation   152
The CAUSE EXCEPTION Statement   154
Summary   156
Review Questions   156

---

11   **Fine-tuning printed output and string input**   **158**

Formatted Printing   158
The PRINT TAB Statement   159
The PRINT USING Statement   161
String Functions   166
Summary   169
Review Questions   170

---

12   **Colors, cursors, keys, sounds, and songs**   **172**

Using Color   172
The SET COLOR and SET BACKGROUND COLOR
   Statements   173
The CLEAR Statement   175
Controlling the Cursor   175
Key Codes and the GET KEY Statement   177
The KEY INPUT Statement   179
The SOUND Statement   180
The PLAY Statement   180
Summary   182
Review Questions   182

---

13   **Graphics: Lines, boxes, windows, and pictures**   **184**

The SET WINDOW Statement   184
The PLOT POINTS: Statement   186

The PLOT LINES: Statement   187
The PLOT AREA: Statement   187
The PLOT TEXT, AT X,Y: Statement   188
The GET POINT: Statement   188
Animating Displays with the BOX Statements   189
The BOX LINES Statement   190
The BOX AREA Statement   190
The BOX CLEAR Statement   191
The BOX CIRCLE and BOX ELLIPSE Statements   191
The FLOOD Statement   191
Working with Many Screens   192
The OPEN #n: SCREEN Statement   192
The WINDOW #n Statement   193
The CLOSE #n Statement   194
Using Graphics Subroutines   194
The DRAW Statement   195
The PICTURE, END PICTURE, and EXIT PICTURE
   Statements   196
Summary   199
Review Questions   199

14   **File processing concepts**   **201**

The Computer "Worldview"   201
Computer Processes   202
Programming Tasks   204
The OPEN Statement (programming tasks 1, 2, and 3)   204
Transferring Data (programming task 4)   206
The CLOSE Statement (programming task 5)   206
File Design: Files, Records, and Fields   206
The ASK Statement   209
The SET Statement   210
The ERASE Statement   210
The UNSAVE Statement   211
Summary   211
Review Questions   212

15   **Text files**   **213**

Writing into a Text File   213
The PRINT #n: Statement   214
The PRINT #n, USING: Statement   215
Reading from a Text File   216

The INPUT #n: Statement   217
The LINE INPUT #n: Statement   217
Updating a Text File   218
Appending Data to a Text File   219
Summary   221
Review Questions   221

16   Record files   **224**

Designing a Record File   225
Writing into a Record File   226
Reading a Record File   227
Updating a Record File   230
Appending Data to a Record File   231
Summary   232
Review Questions   233

17   Byte files   **235**

Designing a Byte File   235
Writing into a Byte File   236
Reading a Byte File   238
Updating a Byte File   239
Appending Data to a Byte File   240
Transferring Raw Data   241
Reading Data from a Foreign File   242
Summary   244
Review Questions   245

Appendix A   The binary number system and computer codes   **246**

Binary vs. Decimal   246
Binary Codes   247
ASCII Codes   248

Appendix B   The extended ASCII code for the IBM PC   **249**

Appendix C   Solutions to selected chapter exercises   **253**

Index   **297**

Introduction

It was a glorious Saturday morning in the Spring of 1984 that Tom Kurtz, Chairman of the Dartmouth College Graduate Program in Computer and Information Sciences, introduced me to True BASIC. We met that day in the office suite of True BASIC Inc., one flight up from the college-town bustle of Hanover's main street. Clearly, the moving-in was still in progress. The stream of sunlight through the large, unadorned windows exaggerated the spacious newness of the scene. The walls were a freshly painted white. Telephone wires snaked across the bare floors. A few people sat on folding chairs and worked on bare tables. The only things that seemed to have found a permanent home were the books and the computers.

I had made the trek from New York to New Hampshire to find out what truth there was to the rumor that Kurtz, along with his colleague, Dr. John Kemeny, past president and Professor of Mathematics at Dartmouth, had, indeed, created a new version of the BASIC programming language they invented 20 years before. It was said that this new BASIC provided the functions demanded by the growing body of BASIC programmers and quelled criticisms from structured-programming advocates who had turned from BASIC to PASCAL, a more formal language.

Professor Kurtz spoke with quiet enthusiasm. He harkened back to the Spring of 1964 when he and Kemeny introduced the Beginner's All-Purpose Symbolic Instruction Code that was to become known as BASIC. Their purpose was to provide a computer language that was so similar to ordinary English that it would make learning to program quite easy. Then, the theory went, BASIC programmers would quickly be able to learn the more complex and abstract languages of the real computing world.

Since that time the use of BASIC has gone beyond the classroom. Over the years, it seems, experienced programmers have preferred to embellish BASIC rather than to switch to a completely new language. By 1984 numerous versions of BASIC that were more powerful than the original had become available. Most of the improvements had occurred in response to advances in computer equipment. Instructions to make use of the color display screens, for example, were incorporated into many of the follow-on BASICs.

In Kurtz's view, and in the view of many others, the rise of the numerous versions of BASIC had disadvantages as well as advantages. One problem was "portability." Programs written on one type of computer using its version of BASIC would not work on another computer driven by a different version of the language.

Another problem was "function." Programmers who had "grown up" on BASIC began to use it for professional programming projects, and the available

L. to R.: Dr. Thomas E. Kurtz, Vice Chairman of True BASIC Inc., and Dr. John G. Kemeny, Chairman of True BASIC Inc.

versions of BASIC were not up to the job. Projects like managing a company payroll, for example, involve numerous subtasks (reading and updating a data file, calculating sums, printing reports) and require complicated logic. But the BASICs of the time included instructions capable of only simple logic and did not have the capability to segment sections of large projects into discrete, independent, manageable modules. As a consequence, enormous unstructured BASIC programs strangled in their own code.

For Kurtz, ironically, the most serious problem of all was the negative effect the stream of easy-to-use, machine-dependent BASICs had on computer programming education. Teachers, like professional programmers, frequently acted as though programming in BASIC was all one ever needed to learn to become a "professional." They did not always go beyond the intentionally fundamental lessons imparted by learning BASIC to teach the more formal discipline of the professional programmer's craft.

To be used effectively, programming languages, like any other language, require adherence to principles. Additionally, in the increasingly complex programming world, the principles themselves have become a universal language that allows the community of programmers to understand and support each other's work. By 1984 it was no longer sufficient to be able to make the computer do what needed to be done. It also mattered that one wrote programs in a way that was readily understandable to future generations of programmers.

Educators who felt as Kemeny and Kurtz did about the plethora of BASIC languages took various measures. Many, recognizing the pitfalls of the freedoms allowed by BASIC, turned to PASCAL, a language that forces the programmer to follow a structure that incorporates many principles of good programming. In fact, in 1982 the College Entrance Examination Board in Princeton, New Jersey, recognized PASCAL as the only acceptable language for high school students seeking placement in advanced computer courses in college. PASCAL became the computer language of the Advanced Placement Examination in Computer Science.

Others sought to set standards for the various versions of BASIC. The American National Standards Institute (ANSI) set up a committee on BASIC, with the mission of developing standards for this language, just as previous committees had developed standards for other widely used languages (ANSI COBOL, ANSI FORTRAN). From 1974 to 1984 Tom Kurtz served as the chairman of the ANSI committee on BASIC. (As of mid-1985 the proposal standard was working its way through the formal approval process.)

True BASIC was born from this history. As its name implies, True BASIC attempts to incorporate all the features that professional programmers and computer educators believe a language should have. The following list of notable True BASIC attributes is a long one. If you are new to programming you may not understand all of the issues these features address. Still, you can see that they are aimed at the three goals of portability, function, and adherence to standards.

True BASIC Attributes:

- Retains the ease of use and ease of learning of the original BASIC.
- Follows the American National Standards Institute (ANSI) standard. True BASIC programs will run on any machine that has the True BASIC system. The True BASIC system makes machines that are actually quite different act as though they were identical.
- Supports sophisticated instructions:
    The SELECT CASE, IF/THEN/ELSE, and DO LOOP control structures
    Subroutines identified by name rather than by number
    Parameters passed among modules
    Optional (and not recommended) line numbers
- Allows user-created program libraries in order to share routines among several different programs.
- Includes statements that perform matrix operations and matrix input and output.
- Includes easy-to-use graphics statements.
- Includes powerful error recovery features and allows user-defined error messages.
- Includes built-in graphics transformations allowing programmers to concentrate on the graphics design rather than on complicated computer instructions.
- Makes it possible to divide a single display screen into several "windows" — each performing its own task.
- Programs execute very quickly.
- Programs make economical use of the computer's memory.
- Handles very large numbers and long strings of characters.
- Includes an editing capability that makes it easy to enter, debug, and update programs.
- Automatically gives programmers two display windows — one for editing a program, and one for watching what happens as it runs.

Eventually, Professor Kurtz turned his gaze from the colorful True BASIC displays to the world outside the windows. Birds were building a nest on the edge of a sill. A corner of the Dartmouth campus was visible. "True BASIC will stun the world," he concluded.

I thought of you, the reader of this book. You are the world.

Structured
Programming
with
True BASIC

## Chapter 1

A sample programming session

The best way to learn programming is to pick up your book, find a computer with a True BASIC system disk, and begin experimenting. Combine your reading and computing by typing in the program examples that appear throughout and see what they do. Modify them and see if you can predict what effect your changes will have.

This chapter introduces you to programming in this hands-on way. It assumes you have a True BASIC disk prepared according to the instructions in the *True BASIC User's Guide* for your computer and that you are ready to insert it in the system disk drive and begin your life as a programmer.

As a programmer you are part of a team that consists of yourself, your programming language, and your computer. Your job is to enter programs into the computer that are made up of True BASIC statements. The statements tell the computer what steps to take and the order in which to take them. As you work you also give True BASIC commands that tell the computer what to do with the programs you write: run them, modify them, or store them. True BASIC's job is to translate your statements and commands into the electronic code that the computer understands. The computer's job is to execute each instruction.

During this first computer session you will gain an overview of the programming process. First, you will practice doing your part: entering, running, and editing a program. Then, you will be asked to stand back and take a closer look at the jobs done by the rest of your computing team: your computer and the True BASIC Language System.

Invoking True BASIC

Begin your programming session by turning on your computer with a True BASIC disk containing the computer operating system in the system disk drive. Respond to the operating system prompt by entering a simple

```
hello
```
                                                                              (press enter)

True BASIC becomes active and divides your screen into two sections, or windows. The upper window is for entering and editing programs. The lower window is for giving commands and observing the computer's responses; this is the window where you see what is produced as your program runs. Switch control from one window to the other by pressing the appropriate key.

Which key is appropriate depends upon the type of computer you are using, and is given in the *True BASIC User's Guide* for your type of computer. On the IBM PC, for example, key F1 sends control to the upper window and key F2 sends control to the lower window. Figure 1–1 lists these and the other True BASIC keys for the IBM PC.

Figure 1–1. True BASIC keys for the IBM PC

Key name	*Key function*	*Key*
Edit	Move cursor to edit window	F1
Command	Move cursor to command window	F2
Find (characters)	Search edit window for next occurrence of the characters (cursor must be in edit window)	F3
Mark	Highlight (mark) the line	F4
Copy	Edit window: copy marked lines Command window: copy current line to command line On command line: copy last line entered	F5
Move	Move marked lines	F6
Delete	Delete a character or a line	Del
Undelete	Reverse the effect of last delete	F7
Insert line	Insert a new line	Enter
Insert	Insert characters in a line	Ins
RUN	Execute the program in the edit window	F9
Help	Brief explanations of True BASIC	F10
Foreground color	Change the foreground color	CTRL and F
Background color	Change the background color	CTRL and B
Edge color	Change the border color	CTRL and E

Selecting display screen colors

Notice the key combinations: CTRL and F, CTRL and B, and CTRL and E. If your computer system includes a color display, you can use these to select colors for the typed characters (foreground), the background, and the border of each window. Each time you hold down the CTRL key and press B you will see the background become one of the available colors. Press CTRL and B again and you will see the background become another color. Try changing the foreground and border in the same manner until you have a foreground, background, and border that please you.

With these key combinations you set the colors for the window currently displaying the cursor. Use F2 or F1 to move the cursor to the alternate window and finish preparing your screen.

Later on you will learn how to set display screen colors by means of True BASIC statements in the programs you write. Such program-driven screen colors override the "CTRL – letter" settings while the program runs. But when the program ends, the original colors reappear; they remain in effect until you key new ones or until you shut the computer off.

Splitting the screen

True BASIC sees the screen as having 24 lines, numbered from 1 at the top to 24 at the bottom. By default, it splits the screen at line 18 so that there are 17 lines in the edit window and 5 usable lines in the command window. You can change the size of the windows by using the *split* command to move the line that separates them. Enter the *split* command in response to the Ok. prompt in the command window and indicate where the line should appear. For example,

```
Ok. split 13
```

redraws the line across the middle of the screen. Both windows are 12 lines long. The command

```
Ok. split 0
```

completely removes the edit window from view and makes the entire screen a command screen. This is one way True BASIC allows you to make the whole screen available for the output of a program.

You cannot entirely eliminate the command screen from view with the *split* command. *Split 24* leaves a one-line command window.

Aside from the *split* command, True BASIC includes statements that control the display from within a program. Later chapters explain how to use them.

Before you know it, the use of the True BASIC windows will become second nature to you. Keep in mind that each window functions independently, just as though you are working with two separate display screens. The work you do in one window does not affect the work going on in the other.

Entering a program

The Ok. prompt in the command window tells you the computer is set for True BASIC. The location of the blinking cursor tells you which window is in control. At the outset, the cursor blinks in the command window.

The NEW command

To enter a program, type the command NEW at the cursor and press *enter*. In the command window you see:

```
Ok. new
```

The computer responds by switching control to the upper (edit) window. In the edit window you see a small, solid box:

■

This box is a "line tag," which indicates where to type a line in your True BASIC program. The line itself is empty, waiting for you to enter a True BASIC statement. If, for example, you want the computer to calculate how long it took Charles Darwin to circumnavigate the globe in the H.M.S. Beagle, enter the program of Figure 1–2. Use any combination of capitals and lowercase letters. Remember to press *enter* at the end of each line. This moves the cursor to a new line and creates a new line tag.

Figure 1–2. Entering a True BASIC program

```
[Edit window]

■ PRINT "The H.M.S. Beagle"                      (press enter)
■ PRINT "sailed in 1831 and returned in 1842."   (press enter)
■ PRINT "It took"                                (press enter)
■ PRINT 1842 - 1831                              (press enter)
■ PRINT "years to circle the globe."             (press enter)
■ END                                            (press enter)
```

```
    True Basic here.
    Ok. new
    Ok.

[Command window]
```

Running a program

Switch control to the next Ok. prompt in the command window (on the IBM PC, you press F2) and enter the RUN command. The computer will begin by obeying the first instruction in your program; then it will follow the sequence of the True BASIC statements. The results of your program appear at the bottom of your screen in the command window. Figure 1–3 shows what you will see.

Figure 1-3. Running a True BASIC program

```
▌ Print "The H.M.S. Beagle"                          (press enter)
▌ Print "sailed in 1831 and returned in 1842."       (press enter)
▌ Print "It took"                                     (press enter)
▌ Print 1842 - 1831                                   (press enter)
▌ Print "years to circle the globe."                  (press enter)
▌ End                                                 (press enter)
```

```
Ok. run
The H.M.S. Beagle
sailed in 1831 and returned in 1842.
It took
 11
years to circle the globe.
Ok.
```

Once the run of your program is complete, another Ok. prompt appears in the command window. You can give another command if you wish or transfer control to the upper window and modify your program and then RUN it again.

Editing a program

The edit window is where you modify the programs you write. If your program becomes larger than the window, you can scroll forward or back to see the lines that follow or precede.

Chapter 3 gives details on the powerful editing features of True BASIC. For now, you can correct a line by retyping it. Place the cursor over any erroneous characters and retype, delete, or insert new characters as you wish. If your H.M.S. Beagle voyage dates are incorrect, retype the numbers and then RUN your program, as shown in Figure 1-4. When you RUN the new program the results will differ according to the changes you have made.

Figure 1-4. Correcting a True BASIC program

```
▌ PRINT "The H.M.S. Beagle"                          (press enter)
▌ PRINT "sailed in 1831 and returned in 1836."       (press enter)
▌ PRINT "It took"                                     (press enter)
▌ PRINT 1836 - 1831                                   (press enter)
▌ PRINT "years to circle the globe."                  (press enter)
▌ END                                                 (press enter)
```

```
Ok. run
The H.M.S. Beagle
sailed in 1831 and returned in 1836.
It took
 5
years to circle the globe.
Ok.
```

Giving commands

The lower window is for giving commands and observing the results. It is also known as the "history window" because it keeps a record of your computing session. Throughout your computing session you can scroll forward or back in this window to see all of the commands you have given as well as all of the responses you have received.

Figure 1–5 lists all of the commands that you can *enter in response to the Ok. prompt in the command window*. You have already used the NEW and SPLIT commands, and you will probably find that you only need a few others for most of the work you do. The sections that follow describe the other most useful True BASIC commands.

Figure 1–5. True BASIC commands given in response to the Ok prompt.

Command	Function
Break	Create a breakpoint, that is, a place where program execution stops
Bye	End True BASIC session and return to operating system
Change	Change characters in program (edit window)
Compile	Compile the program in the current window
Continue	Continue program execution at the most recent breakpoint
Copy	Copy part of a program to another part (edit window)
Delete	Delete part of a program (edit window)
Do Format	Reformat current program according to proper programming style
Do Num	Add line numbers to program in edit window
Do Page	Format output
Do Renum	Assign new line numbers to program in edit window
Do Unnum	Remove line numbers from program in edit window
Edit	Edit only part of a program
Find	(F9 IBM PC) prompts you to give an item to be found in edit window
Files	Display the directory of saved disk files
Include	Include saved program in current program (edit window)
Keep	Delete all but part of a program (edit window)
Key	Assign new meaning to a key
List	Print program listing on the printer
Locate	Display all occurrences of a word or phrase (edit window)
Move	Move lines within a program (edit window)
New	Clear edit window, prepare first program line tag
Old	Copy program from disk to edit window
Replace	Copy changed program from edit window back to disk
Save	Copy program from edit window to disk
Split n	Separate the edit and command windows at line n
Try	Change with verification (edit window)
Unsave	Delete a saved program from the disk

The SAVE command

If you are satisfied with the way your program works and wish to save a permanent copy of it on the disk, think of a name for it — like BEAGLE — and respond to the Ok. prompt by entering the command

```
save beagle
```

The computer will copy the program in the edit window onto the disk in the system drive under the name *beagle.tru*. The *.tru* extension tells you and the computer that the program is written in the True BASIC language.

The OLD command

When you want to retrieve the beagle program, respond to the *Ok.* prompt by entering

```
old beagle
```

Soon, a copy of the beagle program will appear in the edit window, replacing whatever has been there.

The REPLACE command

You can run or modify a saved program as you wish. None of the changes will become permanent until you enter the command

```
replace
```

Then, the new version of the program will replace the previous version on the system disk.

The LIST command

If your computer system includes a printer, you can get a printed copy of the program currently in the edit window by typing the command

```
list
```

Abbreviated commands

You can save yourself time by abbreviating commands and entering several on one line. Abbreviate a command by using only its first three letters. Type *rep,* for example, rather than *replace*. Combine commands by separating them with semicolons. One useful combination is

```
old beagle;run
```

which commands the computer to copy the beagle program from the disk into the edit window and to then run it for you.

Finish a programming session by turning off the computer and storing your disks in a safe place. But before you leave your computer, take a little time to consider the other partners in the computing process: your computer and True BASIC.

Looking at your computer system

The term *computer system,* rather than *computer,* best describes the equipment you are using, for the equipment is really a *network* of components and concepts that have emerged from technological history. The combination of devices that comprise the computer system is known as *hardware.* The combination of concepts that control the devices is known as *software.*

Hardware

The devices that make up the computer system you are using are the culmination of three strands of human history:

1. The search for a fast calculating machine
2. The need to store vast amounts of data
3. The desire to calculate and store data automatically

Calculations are performed in the *central processing unit (CPU),* a small device also known as the *microprocessing unit (MPU)* or *microprocessor.* Today, millions of calculations can be done in one second, although they still must be done one at a time. The CPU uses a temporary storage place to hold partial and final results, along with the currently running program with the next instruction to be processed. *Random access memory (RAM),* or *main storage,* is the term for the circuitry that provides this temporary storage. Computers are frequently compared as to the amount of RAM each has. Programs that create graphics designs need more RAM than those that do text processing. Many computer systems also include *read-only memory (ROM),* where the circuits are permanently set to represent a particular program. Programs in ROM are available whenever the computer is on.

No matter how large the RAM may be, this storage is not designed to hold large files of information. For this reason, and because the RAM is erased every time the power is shut off, computer systems include devices for *long-term storage* of programs and data files. Usually, magnetic tapes or disks serve this purpose. Tapes are less expensive, but disks are faster and more reliable.

Computers act automatically because of computer *programs.* Once a program has been copied into RAM and set into operation, data processing and problem solving can continue without intervention.

Program writers and program users communicate with the computer system through *input and output (I/O) devices.* Keyboards and light pens are examples of input devices. Display screens and printers are output devices. Differences in these devices on the various computer systems give rise to differences in the way you perform some True BASIC functions. For example, as you have seen, the IBM PC recognizes ten function keys that other computers don't have. Such system-

Figure 1-6. Components and connections of a computer system

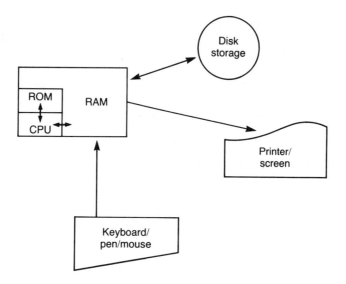

dependent considerations are described in the *True BASIC User's Guide* for your type of computer.

Look at Figure 1-6 to identify the components of the computer system you are using. Your work as a programmer will be much easier if you can visualize where each component is and how it connects with other components. Notice the position of the RAM. This is the traffic center of the system. All input passes through the RAM to its destination in the CPU or long-term storage. All output passes from the CPU or storage device, through RAM, to its destination on the screen or printer.

Software

The calculating and other miracles accomplished by computers occur because computers use speedy and precise electrical circuits to express numbers and characters rather than the cumbersome marks of a pen, the beads of an abacus, or the mechanical gears of the various devices used by preceding generations. The genius of computer scientists has been to combine the properties of electrical energy with the notion of the binary number system.

The *binary number system* is the link between the world of humans and the world of machines that makes computing possible. This number system is so fundamental to computing that if you are not familiar with it, take time to review the explanation in Appendix A.

Computer codes. Building on the idea that one electrical impulse should signal one binary digit (known as a *bit*), computer scientists have created sophisticated electric computer codes that are the smoke signals and talking drumbeats of modern civilization. Known as software, over the years, these codes have become so sophisticated that they are considered whole languages.

True BASIC, the language we are talking about, is one of several high-level languages. FORTRAN (FORmula TRANslation), a science-oriented programming language, was the first high-level language. COBOL (COmmon Business Oriented

Language), which is used for business data processing, is one of the world's most widely used computer language. PASCAL, a formal language, is popular in academic communities.

To represent numbers, computer scientists group binary digits (bits) in multiples of eight, called *bytes,* and set arbitrary limits as to the number of bytes a particular language will reserve for representing a number. These limits determine both the range of available numbers and the number of significant digits by which a number is represented in any particular system.

True BASIC reserves eight bytes for storing a number. However, numbers are packed into the eight bytes according to a variation of the Institute of Electrical and Electronic Engineers (IEEE) format, which does such things as eliminate zeros in order to compress many significant digits. Thus, in True BASIC, eight bytes can store a number far greater than can be represented by 64 bits in the binary number system, that is, any number in the range -1×10^{99} to 1×10^{99}. True BASIC computes each number with a precision of at least ten significant digits.

ASCII codes for representing characters.   To greatly expand the binary code's usefulness and create high-level languages, scientists developed a code known as the American National Standard Code for Information Interchange (ASCII), which gives letter and character equivalents for the numbers 0 through 127. Each of these numbers can be expressed in one byte. Actually, in spite of the attempt at standardization, this character code varies from computer to computer, and True BASIC recognizes the code established for the computer system on which it runs. Appendix B gives the ASCII code equivalents for the IBM PC.

Looking at the True BASIC Language System

As a computer language, True BASIC has three primary goals:

1. Ease of use
2. Power
3. Speed

To achieve these goals, True BASIC actually includes a network of programs that work together and are known as the True BASIC Language System. Figure 1–7 portrays how these programs relate to one another as they translate a program.

The True BASIC control program

The control program is the part of True BASIC with which you communicate when you enter True BASIC commands. It recognizes what you want to do and sends control to the programs that can service your requests. If you make an error in a True BASIC command, the control program recognizes this and gives you information to help you correct it.

Figure 1–7. The True BASIC Language System

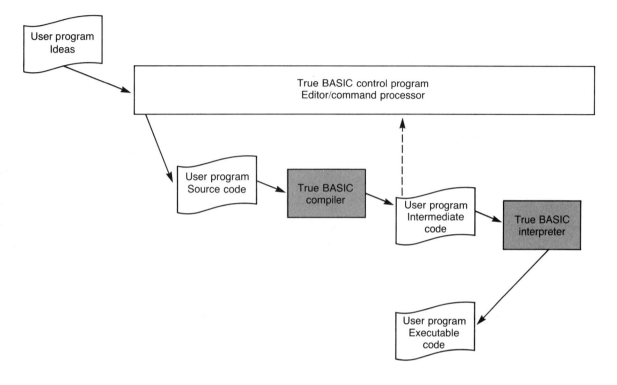

The True BASIC editor

The editor is the program with which you communicate when you enter programs into the edit window. This program makes it possible to insert, delete, copy, move, or otherwise manipulate whole sections of program code. It is actually a word processing program built into the True BASIC Language System.

The True BASIC compiler

The compiler makes it possible for True BASIC language statements to be English-like phrases rather than combinations of binary digits. Once you give the RUN command, the compiler translates the True BASIC statements for you. As it translates, the compiler recognizes syntax errors in your program statements and assists you in correcting them by halting processing and by printing an explanatory message. It also points out the erroneous statement by sending the cursor to the error's position in the edit window.

The True BASIC interpreter

Actually, the compiler stops working when it has translated your program into an intermediate code not quite readable by the computer. It is the interpreter that does the final translation into executable code and triggers the actual execution of each program statement. If a processing error occurs, such as an attempt to use a printer that is not turned on, the interpreter halts execution and prints an explanatory, run-time message.

The operating system

The True BASIC Language System works hand-in-hand with the operating system programs that come with each type of computer. These programs govern the computer system operations by performing such tasks as transmitting keyboard input, activating the True BASIC Language System, writing data onto disks, and locating and storing the programs you write. The operating system programs usually reside on the disk with True BASIC and are the first ones loaded into RAM when the power comes on.

Summary

As a programmer your job is to enter programs made up of True BASIC statements into the computer. These statements tell the computer what steps to take and the order in which to take them. As you work you also give True BASIC commands that tell the computer what to do with the programs you write. True BASIC's job is to translate your statements and commands into the electronic code that the computer understands. The computer's job is to execute each instruction.

Programming skills

Invoking True BASIC
Entering a program
Running a program
Editing a program

Computer concepts

Hardware

Central processing unit (CPU)
Random-access memory (RAM)
Read-only memory (ROM)
Input/output devices (I/O)
Storage devices

Software

Bit
Byte
ASCII
Source code
Compiler
Interpreter
Executable code
Operating system

Review questions

1. Display the directory of programs saved on your True BASIC disk. Run one of the demonstration programs (indicated with .tru extension to the program name).
2. Enter, run, and save a program that prints the following:

```
    True BASIC Commands
NEW - clears the edit window
SAVE - stores the program on the disk
OLD - retrieves the program from the disk
RUN - runs the program in the edit window
```

3. Enter, run, and save a program that prints the following:

```
    True BASIC Keys on the IBM PC
F1 - sends cursor to the edit window
F2 - sends cursor to the command window
F4 - marks a line
F5 - copies marked lines
F6 - moves marked lines
F9 - runs the program in the edit window
```

4. Split the True BASIC screen so as to have the largest possible command window. Run a program. Return the screen to split settings that show at least 10 lines of each window.
5. If your computer is equipped with a color display, set up the True BASIC display so that the edit window has a different background color than the history window.
6. Draw a hardware diagram of a computer system. Label the components and show how they are related.
7. Draw a software diagram of a computer system running True BASIC. Label the components and show what effect each has on a user's program.
8. Explain what is meant by the following statement.

   The binary number system is the link between the world of humans and the world of machines that makes computing possible.

9. What three components of a computer system represent the solution to what three strands of technological history? Set up your answer in a table such as the following.

Component	*Historical Reason*
_____	_____
_____	_____
_____	_____

10. Define the following terms:
    a. Bit
    b. Byte
    c. ASCII
    d. Source code
    e. Intermediate code
    f. Executable code
    g. True BASIC editor
    h. True BASIC compiler
    i. True BASIC interpreter
    j. Operating system

Chapter 2

Structured programming

In the Foreword to David A. Higgins' *Programming Design and Construction,** Ken Orr makes the statement that, with programming: "It is better to be obviously wrong than obscurely right." He argues that "if you are obviously wrong, someone will probably tell you; if you are obscurely right, you may never know if you are getting the right answers." What is more, if you are obscurely right and the time comes, as it inevitably will, for someone to modify your program, they may be unable to understand what you have done and thus be unable to proceed. Your program will die an early death.

Being obvious (whether right or wrong) is what structured programming is all about. Simply stated, *structured programming* means writing a program in such a way that its structure, logic, and flow of control are patently clear. Laying-out city streets in a gridlike pattern, for example, is structured urban development. Establishing a government with executive, legislative, and judicial branches is structured civil development.

Not every structure that seems good to you will do. Over the years programmers have made enough mistakes and witnessed enough successes so that one structure that works for all programs has emerged. This is the top-down design. As David Higgins writes later in his book:† "Data processing people will tell you that top-down design is the best way to design. It is not. It is the only way."

A *top-down design* shows the overall solution to the problem at the top; each lower level gives greater detail as to how the solution is achieved. Figure 2–1 portrays a top-down design for a chocolate chip cookie baking project.

Each module in a top-down design has a clearly defined structure of its own. For computer programs, modules are made from the five universally understood design elements listed below. Known as control structures, these design elements direct the flow of computer processing according to preset patterns. Experience shows that any problem can be solved by using them in various combinations.

---

* David A. Higgins, *Programming Design and Construction* (Englewood Cliffs, N.J.: Prentice-Hall, 1979), p. x.
† Ibid., p. 33.

Figure 2-1. Example of top-down design: chocolate chip cookie project

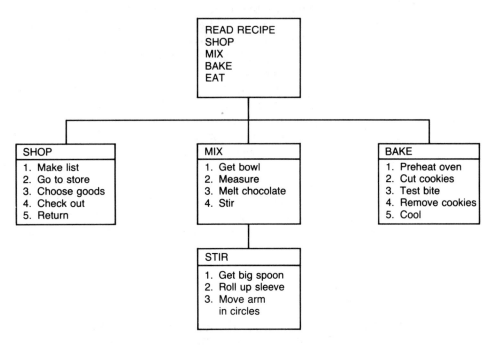

Control Structures

1. **Sequential.** Processing tasks in order—doing first things first.
2. **True-False.** Testing a condition and taking one path if the condition is false, or taking another path if the condition is true.
3. **Case.** Testing a condition and taking a path that depends on which of several alternatives matches the condition.
4. **Leading Decision Loop.** Testing for a terminating condition and ending the process if the condition has occurred; repeating the process if it has not.
5. **Trailing Decision Loop.** Performing the process and then testing for the terminating condition; if it has not yet occurred repeating the process.

This chapter describes what goes on at the programmer's drawing board. It shows how to apply your understanding of structured programming to the task of turning a problem statement into a top-down design. The rest of the book shows how to turn your design into a structured True BASIC program. It explains the True BASIC way of creating and connecting the various control structures.

Defining a problem

The first task in programming is the most difficult. This is the task of translating whatever problem statement you are given into a useful problem definition. Such a problem definition must answer some fundamental questions:

1. **What output is required?** If you can, get a sample of the chart, the paycheck, or whatever display the computer is expected to produce. If one

does not yet exist, sit down and draw one so that you and everyone else can agree upon the goal of your program.

2. **What input will be available?** You need to know whether your input will be data from a disk file, the keyboard, or another device and whether it will be numeric data or character data.

3. **What procedure is required?** For instance, if your output is a bar graph comparing dollar amounts for the first quarter of the year, and your input is the number of buttons sold in that period, what does your program have to do to make the transition from buttons to dollars? Your problem statement should include any formula needed or any relevant data, such as price per button.

If you have few details about the correct procedure, you may need more information, or you may need to put your thinking cap on. Your genius may be what you have to rely upon in getting from "there" to "here" in your programming project. Regardless of its source, be sure you know what procedure to use before you begin to write your program.

The computer dating problem

Examine the following problem statement to see if you can break it down into the three essential components of a problem definition: output, input, and procedure.

Write a computer dating program that finds the ideal partner for a Computer Dating Service customer. The customer will answer a questionnaire provided by the Society for Better Friends and receive a printed list of the five people most likely to be compatible.

The computer will display the questionnaire on the screen and accept responses from the keyboard. It will select possible partners from disk files containing other individuals' questionnaire responses. The philosophy guiding selection will be "opposites attract."

The *expected output* is clear: (1) Provide display prompts of the survey questions for the customer. (2) Provide a printed list of five names.

The *anticipated input* is less clearly presented in this problem statement. It will come from two sources, the customer's keyboard and disk data files, and it will be composed of responses to a questionnaire. You need to find out what form the responses will take. Will they be numbers on a scale from 1 to 10? true or false notations? or some other type of answer?

The *procedure* of this problem statement is also ill defined. To program the computer, you need something more than the guideline that opposites attract; you need a detailed sequence of steps to follow in order to actually select partners according to this criteria. (At this stage in your project there is no need for a one-to-one correspondence between each step in the procedure and each computer statement you write, although the closer you come to such a correspondence, the easier your job will be later on.) Since the problem statement does not provide the details you need, you have to do some investigating and make some decisions.

Figure 2–2 includes a sample of a complete problem definition you might prepare once your research is done. In actuality, there is never only a single correct problem definition for a project. What is important is that you take the time to think things through in terms of output, input, and procedure.

Defining your problem gets you off to a good start on a programming project.

Figure 2-2. Problem definition: input, procedure, output

Input

Data will be integers in the range from 1 to 10, representing answers to survey questions. The data will come from two sources:

1. The keyboard accepting replies from the current client.
2. The Dating Service disk file containing replies given previously by potential partners.

Procedure

1. Accept responses from the keyboard.
2. Total the score for the keyboard input.
3. Open the appropriate male or female disk file as a source of partners.
4. Read each disk file score.
5. Compare each disk file score with the client's score; find the absolute value of the difference between the client's score and each disk file score.
6. Select the disk file partner with the greatest score difference.
7. Repeat the search to find the next-most-different score.
8. Repeat the search five times.

Output

1. Display "Better Friends Survey Questions" for the customer.
2. Print the report heading: "Computer Dating Service Report."
3. Print the list of five selected names.

The problem definition becomes the outline that directs your program design. Remember, however, that a problem definition is not cast in concrete. As you work you will discover new information and you will refine the problem definition. It will become part of the package that explains what your program does and how it works.

Designing a program from the top down

Program design determines which modules will work together to function as the complete program. Generally speaking, even the smallest project has at least four modules: at least one for each of the input, output, and procedure phases of the problem definition, and one that governs the flow of control among the modules. This last is the *main routine*. Figure 2-3, which diagrams the program design for the computer dating service project, shows each of the modules and indicates by lines which modules are controlled by another module. It does *not* show the sequence of events.

The design structure of Figure 2-3 is a top-down design. Not only does each level give greater details, but each level also represents a stage in the hierarchy of the control of modules. At the top level, the main routine calls each of the second-level routines, which in turn may call other, third-level modules. Third level works only for the second-level module that calls it. In the dating project, the routine that finds

Figure 2–3. Example of a top-down design diagram: computer dating program

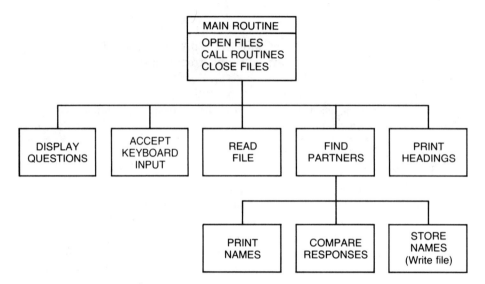

partners calls another routine to keep track of the top five names as they are discovered.

There can be only one line into a module. If, for some reason, two second-level modules needed the third-level, name-storing routine, the design would have to be redrawn as in Figure 2–4, in which the connecting circle joins the two lines before they enter the name-storing routine.

Lines in program designs cannot cross one another. If your design contains lines that cross, reconsider your design. Chances are you have a module that does too much and should be divided into smaller components.

Any time spent fussing with your program design diagram is time well spent. The diagram will help you as you write your program modules and will eventually become another part of your final program package.

Figure 2–4. Two modules controlling a third module: computer dating program

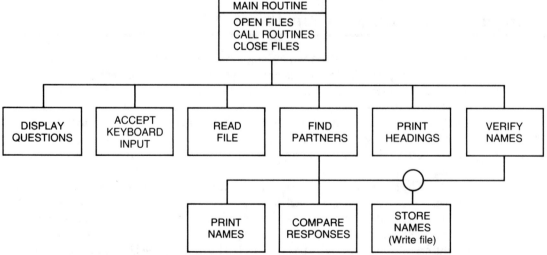

Module design

Once your design diagram is completed you are ready to plan the modules that make up your program. You need to chart the flow of control from the beginning to the end of a module, including all the possible digressions in between. These charts will be your guide when you code your program using True BASIC statements. The sections that follow describe two types of module plans, flowcharts and pseudocode, and show how to use them in coding your program.

Drawing a flowchart

One way to illustrate how a module works is to draw a flowchart that presents pictorially the flow of control. Well-done flowcharts demonstrate the truth of the adage that "A picture is worth a thousand words." Flowcharts also become an important part of the final programming package.

In flowcharts, special symbols and connecting lines illustrate each step and the order in which they should be taken. Figure 2–5 shows the standard flowchart symbols adopted by both the International Organization for Standardization (ISO) and the American National Standards Institute (ANSI). If a program module is accompanied by flowcharts using these symbols, people not familiar with the program's computer language can still understand how it works.

Any problem solution can be illustrated with a flowchart. One common problem and its solution are shown in Figure 2–6. This flowchart uses the standard symbols according to the following flowchart rules:

Flow Chart Rules

1. Use straight lines, either vertical or horizontal.
2. Make sure that all lines lead to a symbol.
3. Make sure that each symbol has only one line leading to it.
4. Make sure that lines do not cross one another; use circles as connectors.
5. Use arrowheads on connecting lines to show the direction of flow.
6. Include words like YES or NO at decision points to clarify when the flow should take a particular direction.
7. Keep it simple. Not every step of a solution is needed in a flowchart. Include only the ones that make it clear how the problem is being solved.

Read through the snowman flowchart of Figure 2–6 again to see how it exemplifies the flowchart rules.

The flowchart of Figure 2–6 is a *descriptive* flowchart, one that includes explanatory text within the flowchart symbols. Programmers normally use *symbolic* flowcharts, with brief notations such as $X = 6$ within the flowchart symbols, and descriptive comments keyed in the margin with dashed lines. Figure 2–7 is a symbolic flowchart. It charts the procedure for averaging the course grades for 20 students in a class in which not all students took the same number of tests.

Writing pseudocode

Writing pseudocode is an alternative to flowcharting. It has the same purpose as writing flowcharts: to illustrate what your program module does and how it does it.

Figure 2–5. Standard flowchart symbols

Symbol	Description	Example
	Terminus: the start or any stopping point in the program	START
	Input-Output: READ, INPUT, PRINT operations as well as reading and writing disk or tape files	INPUT Y
	Decisions: any operation that determines which one of two paths to follow	X = Y YES NO
	Processing: operations that change the value or form of information	X = X + 1
	Subroutine processing	X = X + 1 RETURN
	Data	DATA20.30.40
	Preparation: set initial values, open files, set dimensions	DIM A(50)
	Connection: exit to or entry from another part of chart	2
	Off-page connection: exit to another part of chart on separate page	4

Pseudocode consists of English phrases representing programming statements. The pseudocode mimics real program statements, or program code, quite closely. Many programmers find that writing pseudocode is a more natural way of showing how a program works and is easier to translate into True BASIC code.

Figure 2–8 uses pseudocode to document the grade averaging program. In this example, the DO and LOOP lines correspond to True BASIC statements that

Figure 2-6. Flowchart for building a snowman

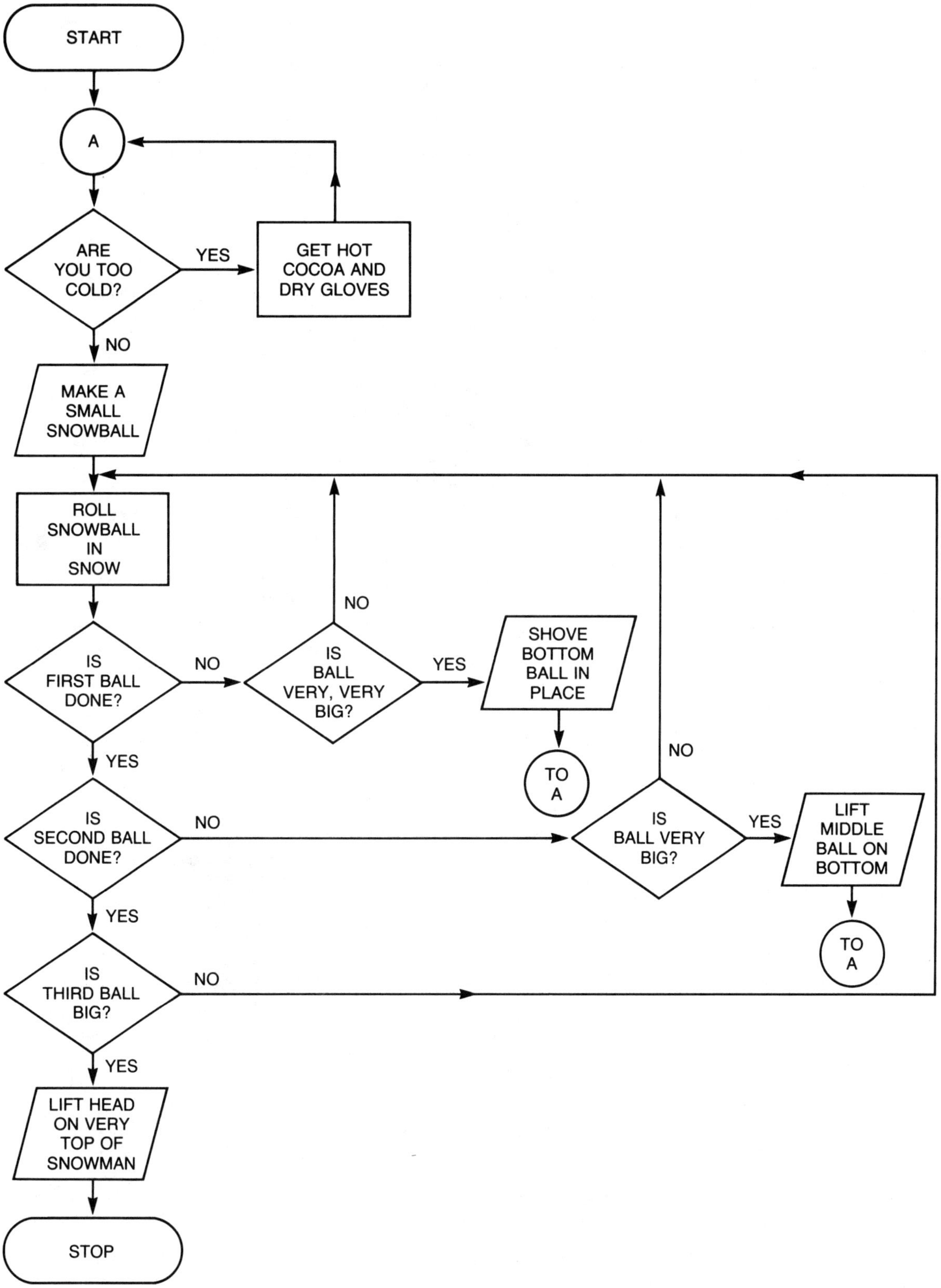

Figure 2–7. Flowchart for grade averaging program

```
        ┌─────────────────┐
        │     START       │
        └─────────────────┘
                │
                ▼
        ╱─────────────────╲
        │   Do while       │ ─ ─ ─ ─ ─ ─ ─ ─    Do the following job for 20
        │   0 < X < 20     │                    students.
        ╲─────────────────╱
                │
                ▼
        ╱─────────────────╱
        │    READ N        │ ─ ─ ─ ─ ─ ─ ─ ─    Read the scores, one at a time.
        ╱─────────────────╱
                │                                101 indicates the last score for
                ▼                                a student has been read.
        ◇─────────────────◇    NO   ┌────────────────┐
        │    N = 101       │ ──────▶ │  S = S + N     │ ─ ─ ─ ─    Add the score to the sum of the
        ◇─────────────────◇         │  G = G + 1     │            previous scores for this
                │                    └────────────────┘            student.
              YES
                │                                                  Add 1 to the count of scores.
                ▼
        ┌─────────────────┐
        │    A = S/G       │ ─ ─ ─ ─ ─ ─ ─ ─    Determine the average for this
        └─────────────────┘                    student.
                │
                ▼
        ╱─────────────────╱
        │    PRINT A       │
        ╱─────────────────╱
                │
                ▼
        ╱─────────────────╲
        │    S = 0         │
        │    G = 0         │ ─ ─ ─ ─ ─ ─ ─ ─    Return the sum and number of
        │    X = X + 1     │                    scores to zero and begin
        ╲─────────────────╱                    again. Increment counter.
                │
                ▼
    YES ◇─────────────────◇
   ◀──── │     LOOP         │ ─ ─ ─ ─ ─ ─ ─ ─    After 20 students, end the
        ◇─────────────────◇                    program.
                │
               NO
                ▼
        ┌─────────────────┐
        │     STOP         │
        └─────────────────┘
```

Figure 2–8. Pseudocode for grade averaging program

```
Start
DO 20 times
    read the score
    IF the score = 101
        THEN
            average the student's grade
            print this student's average
            sum = 0
            count = 0
        ELSE
            add this score to the sum of scores
            add 1 to the count of scores
    END IF
LOOP
Stop
```

cause the computer to repeat a series of instructions a specified number of times. The IF-THEN-ELSE and END IF statements are also similar to True BASIC statements that make decisions.

Write pseudocode in the same format as true code. Use indentations to highlight routines that occur within larger structures. In this example, the entire averaging routine occurs within a structure that repeats 20 times, and within the averaging routine the IF-THEN-ELSE statement decides when to stop adding to the sum of scores and take an average.

Desk-checking

Once your flowchart or pseudocode is written you are almost, but not quite, ready to write your program. Take time to desk-check the logic of your module diagram. With sample input data at your side, your flowchart in front of you, and paper and pencil nearby, run through your program. Using sample data, follow your flowchart and write down the output that it indicates will appear. If the output is not what you expect, go back to the drawing board. If the output *is* what you expect, try again using more unusual, but possible, input data. As you desk-check, consider any events that are likely to occur, such as a file with no data, negative scores, or unanswered survey questions, and see if your program can handle them. When all of these variations have been planned for, code your program into True BASIC. Then desk-check your True BASIC code just as you have desk-checked your flowchart.

Finally, enter your program into the computer. You will be pleased at how smoothly your module fits in its place in the program structure.

Test each module before including the next. Use program "stubs," or dummy statements, to represent modules that are not yet written. Send control to them and have each one respond with its own cheery greeting to let yourself know you have sent control along the correct programming paths.

When your program works as you intend, give it a final real-world system test. Have people unfamiliar with your project run your program. If they uncover variations that you have not considered, you will need to refine the code once again.

The program development process is a long one. It requires planning, charting, desk-checking, module testing, program testing, and real-world testing. However, having followed these procedures, you can be confident that you have done a professional job of creating a truly useful program.

Summary

Being obvious is what structured programming is all about. Simply stated, structured programming means writing a program in such a way that its structure, logic, and flow of control are patently clear.

Programming skills

Defining a problem in terms of input, process, and output
Drawing a top-down design diagram
Drawing a flowchart
Writing pseudocode
Desk-checking

Computer concepts

Structured programming
Control structures

Review questions

1. Define structured programming.
2. List the five control structures, and give a definition of each.
3. What three questions must a problem definition answer?
4. What does a top-down design diagram illustrate?
5. Select a project that interests you (like baking cookies).
   a. Write a problem definition.
   b. Draw a design diagram that has at least four modules.
6. How do flowcharts and pseudocode differ from top-down design diagrams?
7. List the seven flowchart rules.
8. Draw a flowchart of the process of selecting and watching a TV show. Remember that commercials can signal either the end of the show or time to take a quick break.
9. What is meant by *desk-checking*?
10. List at least six steps in the program development process.

## Chapter 3

The PRINT, REM, and END statements in a program module

You are ready to write structured programs. Now all you need to learn is how to use the True BASIC statements that make the computer do what your design says needs to be done and how to put them together to create a program module. This chapter starts you out and has two goals:

1. To show you how to use the PRINT statement to write to the screen or printer.
2. To show you how to use REM and END statements to create a program module that conforms to structured programming standards

It also completes the explanation of the True BASIC editing features begun in Chapter 1. Taking some time to become familiar with them now will make your future programming sessions more pleasant and productive.

The program module

```
END
```

Like the H.M.S. Beagle program in Chapter 1, the Brooklyn Bridge program in Figure 3-1 is a complete, though sketchy, True BASIC program module. This program represents a complete program module because it has the following characteristics:

1. It is built according to a control structure (sequential).
2. It uses True BASIC statements that follow the general form of:

   True BASIC keyword — optional program data.

   The True BASIC statements that this program illustrates are the PRINT statement, which tells the computer to print data on the display

Figure 3-1. A True BASIC program

```
▌ PRINT "The Brooklyn Bridge"
▌ PRINT "started in 1870 and finished in 1883."
▌ PRINT "It took"
▌ PRINT 1883 - 1870
▌ PRINT "years to build."
▌ END
```

```
The Brooklyn Bridge
started in 1870 and finished in 1883.
It took
 13
years to build.
Ok.
```

screen, and the END statement, which tells the computer where the program ends.
3. It ends with an END statement.

The sequential control structure

If there are no countermanding instructions, the computer executes each instruction in a sequential control structure sequentially, from program start to program finish. The sequence of events in the Brooklyn Bridge program, for example, is: print, print, print, print, print, and end.

Main routines that function to pass control from one program module to another use this structure. They call module 1, and when control returns they call module 2, and so on until the last module returns and they execute the END statement. Figure 3-2 depicts sequential processing for a main routine that calls one module, calls another and another, and then ends.

The PRINT statement

PRINT

As you can see from the Brooklyn Bridge program, the PRINT statement is a powerful tool. It tells the computer to print messages such as "THE BROOKLYN BRIDGE" or it tells the computer to do calculations such as the subtraction 1883 − 1870.

Even more, a single PRINT statement can do several of these jobs. The program of Figure 3-3 shortens the Brooklyn Bridge program by combining the calculation with the last two lines of text.

The semicolons tell the computer that there is more than one field of data to be printed. They also direct the computer to print the successive fields one right after another on the same line. Notice the position of the number 13. True BASIC prints numbers with a leading space (in case there is a minus sign) and a trailing space.

Figure 3-2. Sequential control structure

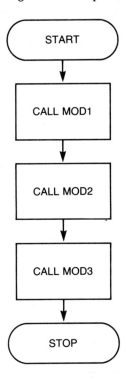

Figure 3-3. Semicolons in the PRINT statement

```
▋ PRINT "The Brooklyn Bridge"
▋ PRINT "started in 1870 and finished in 1883."
▋ PRINT "It took"; 1883 - 1870; "years to build."
▋ END
```

```
Ok. run
The Brooklyn Bridge
started in 1870 and finished in 1883.
It took 13 years to build.
Ok.
```

If the last line of this program were

```
PRINT "It took", 1883 - 1870, "years to build."
```

that is, with commas instead of semicolons, a RUN would look as follows:

```
Ok. run
The Brooklyn Bridge
started in 1883 and finished in 1870
It took          13              years to build.
Ok.
```

The computer sees a line of printing as 80 characters wide and divided into print zones of 16 characters each. Commas in the PRINT statement tell the computer to print the next item of data beginning in the next print zone.

Use commas to set up tables of information with neat-looking columns, as in Figure 3–4. Notice the second line; it is a PRINT statement with the key word, alone, and no specific data, called a *null print* statement. A null print statement causes the computer to print a blank line in order to separate the heading from the rest of the table.

PRINT statements that end with a comma or a semicolon tell the computer that the next printing to occur in the program should appear on the current print line. If your PRINT statement ends with a comma, the printing occurs in the next zone beyond the last one used. If it ends with a semicolon, the printing appears in the next character position. The program statements of Figure 3–5 take advantage of the trailing semicolon to combine two words into a new one.

Figure 3–4. Commas in the PRINT statement

```
■ PRINT "Name", "Phone"
■ PRINT
■ PRINT "F. Bacon", "332-1321"
■ PRINT "G. Chaucer", "786-3300"
■ PRINT "J. Milton", "657-1542"
■ END
```

```
Ok. run
Name                Phone

F. Bacon            332-1321
G. Chaucer          786-3300
J. Milton           657-1542
Ok.
```

Figure 3–5. Trailing semicolons in the PRINT statement

```
■ PRINT "type";
■ PRINT "writer"
■ PRINT
■ PRINT "birth";
■ PRINT "day"
■ PRINT
■ PRINT "grand";
■ PRINT "mother"
■ END
```

```
Ok. run
typewriter

birthday

grandmother
Ok.
```

Line length and zone width

You can change line length and print zone width to any setting, from 1 to whatever you need as your program runs. Include the statement

```
SET MARGIN 72
```

to change the line length from the default value of 80 characters to 72 characters. Use the statement

```
SET ZONEWIDTH 12
```

to change the zone width from the defaulted value of 16 characters to 12. Be sure that your margin setting allows for at least one zone width.

Using the printer

If you want to print your program results on your computer system printer, you must first open a channel to the printer and then use the channel number in your PRINT statement. The program statements of Figure 3–6 will cause the list of phone numbers to be printed on the printer rather than displayed in the screen command window. In the OPEN statement, the channel number can be any number from 1 to 1000 preceded by a # sign. Be sure to use the same number in the PRINT statements directed to the system printer.

Figure 3–6. PRINTing on the printer

```
▌ OPEN #1: PRINTER
▌ PRINT #1: "Name", "Phone"
▌ PRINT #1:
▌ PRINT #1: "F. Bacon", "332-1321"
▌ PRINT #1: "G. Chaucer", "786-3300"
▌ PRINT #1: "J. Milton", "657-1542"
▌ END
```

```
Ok. run
```

The REM statement and line comments

REM

Chapter 2 states that "being obvious is what structured programming is all about." Being obvious includes more than using control structures within modules and including modules in a top-down design; it also means adding English-language remarks and following a format that clearly indicates what is going on.

True BASIC provides the REM (remark) statement and the comment (!) symbol that make it possible to add explanatory comments to your program. It also allows you to use capitalization, indentation, and blank lines to create a readable program format. These devices do not affect the output of your program but appear in the list of program statements. They provide the finishing touch that make your programs truly structured.

Line comments are appended to a statement by an exclamation point (!). You can use them to clarify what a particular program statement does. Some programmers feel that every single line of a program should have a comment. Others feel that statements such as END are self-explanatory and can stand alone. Regardless of what you choose to do, remember your goal is to make the logic of your program perfectly clear.

REM statements stand alone as a True BASIC statement. Use them preceding a block of lines to explain what the following program segment does. Figure 3–7 uses line comments and REM statements to bring the Brooklyn Bridge program closer to good programming style.

The program prologue

The introductory block of REM statements in Figure 3–7, often called the *program prologue,* begins every program. It includes as much essential information as exists about the production, maintenance, and operation of the program. This example provides only the bare essentials, such as who wrote the program, in what version of the language, on what type of computer, and on what date. Real-life prologues are usually much longer.

Figure 3–7. REM statements and line comments

```
REM ******************************************
REM   Title: Brooklyn Bridge Calculator      *
REM   Date: May 9, 1999                       *
REM   Programmer: H. Morrill                  *
REM   Environment: IBM PC 256KB               *
REM   Language: True BASIC Version 1.0        *
REM   Input: none                             *
REM   Output: screen                          *
REM ******************************************

Print "The Brooklyn Bridge"                      !print the title
PRINT "started in 1870 and finished in 1883."    !print the problem
Print "It took"                                  !print conclusion
Print 1883 - 1870                                !print calculation
PRINT "Years to build."                          !Print time span
End                                              !stop program run
```

Ok.

The program format

Notice that the revised Brooklyn Bridge program employs formatting techniques to clarify what the program does as well as documentation devices. Some of the most useful of these formatting techniques follow.

1. **Use uppercase and lowercase.** You can use uppercase and lowercase for True BASIC keywords as well as for your own data. Use them, as you would in normal English, to clarify what your statement does.

2. **Use spaces.** You cannot separate the characters in a True BASIC keyword, but you can space as liberally as you wish between keywords and other statement components. Use spaces to clarify the typing on a line.

3. **Use blank lines.** Notice in the program in Figure 3–7 how the prologue is separated from the main routine by a blank line. Such blank lines appear, of course, only in the list of program statements, not in the output of the program.

4. **Indent lines.** You will soon discover that some True BASIC statements require more than one line of typing. If you indent the additional lines that complete these statements, they are easy to read, even though long.

5. **Use the True BASIC format program.** If it is too tedious to write with the format of your program in mind, use the format program included on the True BASIC system disk — it does your work for you. Type:

```
Ok. DO Format
```

and you will soon see the program in the edit window transformed into True BASIC format.

True BASIC also includes features that can detract from the clarity of your program. It is up to you to avoid them or to use them with care:

Abbreviations.   You can, for example, abbreviate the True BASIC statement PLOT LINES: to the more simple PLOT. However, PLOT LINES: makes it very clear that the statement draws lines. PLOT leaves room for question.

Abbreviating the True BASIC commands that manipulate your programs during a programming session is, of course, a different matter. These commands are your personal tools that need not be shared with others. Use them in whatever working style suits you.

Line numbers.   For compatibility with older versions of BASIC, True BASIC lets you begin each statement with a line number. This makes it easy to transfer control from one section of your program to another. If your program has line numbers, you can write a statement like

```
50 GO TO 100
```

and the computer will pass control from the current line 50 to line 100.

Unfortunately, the problem with transferring control by means of such line numbers is that the computer will know what to do but fellow programmers will have to struggle to discover what's happening on line 100 and why this program branch occurs.

You can transfer control without line numbers by using a name, rather than a number, for a program segment. If you write a statement like

```
CALL quiz
```

the computer will pass control from this CALL statement to the quiz routine. Both the computer and your friends will readily understand what your program is up to.

Editing a program

Now is the time to write your own program. Remember to enter the NEW command on the command screen line. NEW clears the edit window of any previous work, places the first line tag for you, and switches control to the edit window.

Enter your program line by line. As your program grows, take advantage of the powerful editor built into the True BASIC Language System. Use it to edit a single line or whole blocks of code.

Editing lines

Use the line tags and the True BASIC keys listed in Chapter 1 (Figure 1–1, p. 2) when you want to perform an edit function on a whole line or block of lines. If you want to delete a line, for example, place the blinking cursor on the line tag for that line and press the *delete* key. If you want to insert a line, place the blinking cursor on the line tag and press *enter;* a blank line will appear above the cursor's line.

Editing blocks of lines

You can copy, move, or delete a block of lines by marking the block and pressing the appropriate True BASIC key. To mark the block, move the cursor to the line tag for the first line in the group of lines and then press the *mark* key. The line tag will become bright, indicating that you have "marked" the line for the computer. Then place the cursor on the line tag for the last line of the group of lines and press the *mark* key again. This line tag and all of the line tags in between will become bright, meaning that you have marked the entire block of lines.

If you then press the *delete* key, the marked block of lines will be deleted. If you move the cursor to a distant line tag and press the *move* key, the marked block will be inserted just above the cursor's line and will disappear from its previous position in the sequence of lines. If you move the cursor to a distant line and press the *copy* key, a copy of the marked block will appear just above the cursor's line. The original block of lines will also remain in its original place.

Figure 3–8 experiments with the use of the *mark* and *copy* keys. The highlighted line tags indicate the marked lines of the H.M.S. Beagle program. When you place the cursor on the line tag for the END line and press the *copy* key, the marked lines reappear just ahead of the END line. When you RUN the new, longer program, the output of the duplicated statements appears at the end as well as the start of the program run.

Undelete

If you delete a line or a character by mistake, you need not despair, for True BASIC includes an undelete key to rescue you. You can retrieve a character by pressing

Figure 3-8. Copying a block of lines

```
▌ PRINT "The H.M.S. Beagle"                           (press enter)
▌ PRINT "sailed in 1831 and returned in 1836."        (press enter)
▌ PRINT "It took"                                      (press enter)
▌ PRINT 1836 - 1831                                    (press enter)
▌ PRINT "years to circle the globe."                   (press enter)
▌ PRINT "The H.M.S. Beagle"                            (press enter)
▌ PRINT "sailed in 1831 and returned in 1836."         (press enter)
▌ END
```

```
Ok. run
The H.M.S. Beagle
sailed in 1831 and returned in 1836.
It took
 5
years to circle the globe.
The H.M.S. Beagle
sailed in 1831 and returned in 1836.
Ok.
```

undelete while the cursor is still on the same line as the deleted character. You can retrieve an entire line by moving the cursor to the line following the one you wish to restore and pressing the *undelete* key. The line you had mistakenly erased will then reappear in its original place. *Undelete* works only for the very last deletion you made; nevertheless you may find it quite handy.

The finished program module

Once you are satisfied with your program code, switch control to the command window. Type RUN to see your program work. Finally, enter a short name, like VICTORY, and give the *save* command to store this first, original program on the system disk.

You can use your program again, tomorrow or next week or whenever you choose. Just make sure the disk on which it is stored is in the computer. Then enter:

```
old victory; run
```

(You don't need the *.tru* extension.) The computer will load a copy of the program into memory and proceed to do whatever you have programmed it to do.

Summary

You are ready to write structured programs. Now all you need to learn is how to use the True BASIC statements that make the computer do what your design says needs to be done. Then you can put them together to create a program module.

Programming skills

> The PRINT statement
> The PRINT # statement
> The REM statement
> Line comments
> Editing lines

Computer concepts

> Sequential control structure
> Program module
> Program prologue
> Program format

Review questions

1. Enter the program of Figure 3–1 and change it to report the construction time of the George Washington Bridge, which was begun in 1927 and finished in 1931.
2. Enter the program of Figure 3–1 and change it so that it reports on the time span between the publication of Darwin's *The Origin of Species* and confirmation of Einstein's general theory of relativity. Darwin's book was published in 1859 and the general theory was proven in 1922.
3. Print out a name tag that includes the person's name and home town. To make the tag more readable, separate the name from the town by a blank line and enclose all of the printing in a box made from asterisks.
4. Determine whether each of the following True BASIC statements is correctly entered. If it is, write "correct" on your answer sheet. If not, rewrite it correctly. Consider each statement separately. These statements are *not* part of the same program.
   a. ■ PRINT A; "is correct."
   b. ■ PRINT "Y"; is not the solution."
   c. ■ PRINT #1:
   d. ■ DO FORMAT
   e. ■ PRINT Your age
   f. ■ OK END PRINT
   g. ■ "PRINT YOUR ANSWER"
   h. ■ RUN
   i. ■ REM "This is a number averaging program"
   j. ■ PRINT X; is the solution.
5. Write a program to calculate and print out the age of Mickey Mouse the year you were born. Mickey was "born" in 1929. Save your program on the disk.
6. Write a program that produces the following table of English–metric conversions. Save it on the disk.

English	Metric
1 inch	2.54 centimeters
1 mile	1.609 kilometers
1 pound	453.6 grams

7. The race around the lake started at noon. Have the computer calculate and print the times of the first three finishers. They finished at 12:21, 12:23, and 12:42, respectively. Label your output. Save your program on the disk.

8. Jimmy sent away for Boy Scout camp gear. The items cost $42.50 plus $6.38 sales tax and $1.80 postage. Have the computer calculate and print the total that Jimmy must pay. Label the output. Save your program on the disk. (Do *not* enter the dollar sign, "$"; its use will be explained in Chapter 5.)

9. The high temperature for the day was 61°F. The low was 38°F. Have the computer calculate and print the extent of the temperature change during the 24-hour period. Save your program on the disk. Label the output.

10. Use the computer to tally the total income received by the Winter Ski Jump Association from the winter carnival. The proceeds from the various sources were:

Tickets	500.00
Refreshments	150.00
Programs	75.00

If the association spent 100 dollars for judges, what was its profit? Label the output. Save your program on the disk.

Chapter 4

Computer calculations

In 1202 Leonardo Pisano, also known as Leonardo Fibonacci, posed a question in his book *Liber Abbaci:*

> How many pairs of rabbits are produced from a single pair within N months time?

Assuming that each pair of rabbits produces a new pair of offspring every month, that each pair becomes fertile at the age of one month, and that rabbits never die, the answer is the Nth number in what has come to be known as the Fibonacci sequence. This sequence runs as follows:

$$F(1) = 1$$
$$F(2) = 1$$
$$F(3) = 2$$
$$F(4) = 3$$
$$F(5) = 5$$
$$\vdots$$
$$F(N) = F(N-1) + F(N-2)$$

Each number is the sum of the two preceding numbers.

Calculating the answers to problems such as these, and ones far more complex, can be a time-consuming and error-prone process for most people. By comparison, however, such calculations are a trivial exercise for computers. With your pen you can easily calculate in less than a minute the number of rabbits produced in a year; the computer can do this in less than a second. Given more time you can calculate the pairs of hares produced in 100 or even 1000 months. But you would probably balk at the prospect of determining how many rabbits will be produced in 10,000 months. Computer calculations indicate that the 10,000th Fibonacci number has 2000 digits.*

Because of their speed, precision, and reliability, computers have greatly enhanced humankind's mathematical accomplishments. This chapter introduces

* Fred Gruenberger, "Computer Recreations," *Scientific American* 250 (April 1984), p. 22.

your computer's computational facility, and presents two programming tools you will need to make use of it: arithmetic operations and numeric functions.

Arithmetic operations

In True BASIC the computer does all of the standard calculations using the following symbols.

$\wedge$ exponentiation
$*$ multiplication
$/$ division
$+$ addition
$-$ subtraction

An *arithmetic expression* consists of one or more calculations. Thus

$$2+2 \quad \text{and} \quad 5/7\wedge2$$

are each True BASIC arithmetic expressions.

When more than one calculation occurs in an expression, the computer evaluates the expression by scanning it from left to right and making calculations according to the following hierarchy of operations:

1. $\wedge$ exponentiation
2. $*$ or $/$ multiplication or division (whichever appears first)
3. $+$ or $-$ addition or subtraction (whichever appears first)

The computer evaluates the expression $5/7\wedge2$ by first doing the exponential operation, seven squared ($7\wedge2$), and then dividing 5 by the result. Similarly, the computer processes the statement

$$\text{PRINT } 4 * 2\wedge3 + 6 / 3 - 1$$

according to the following sequence:

Operation		*Intermediate result*
1. $2\wedge3$	$= 8$	PRINT $4 * 8 + 6 / 3 - 1$
2. $4*8$	$= 32$	PRINT $32 + 6 / 3 - 1$
3. $6/3$	$= 2$	PRINT $32 + 2 - 1$
4. $32+2$	$= 34$	PRINT $34 - 1$
5. $34-1$	$= 33$	PRINT 33

The computer never reveals the intermediate results, but in a flash, the final answer, 33, appears on your screen!

You can change the order of operations by using parentheses. For instance, change the expression "five divided by seven squared"

$$\text{PRINT } 5/7\wedge2$$

to "the square of five sevenths" by writing

$$\text{PRINT } (5/7) \wedge 2$$

The computer will process the operation within parentheses according to the hierarchy rules and then process the remaining parts of the expression.

Using parentheses makes a big difference. Compare the results of the expressions we have been looking at with and without parentheses:

True BASIC statement	Result
PRINT 5/7^2	0.102041
PRINT (5/7)^2	0.510204
PRINT 4*2^3+6/3—1	33
PRINT (4*2)^3+6/3—1	513

Parentheses must always be used when a fraction has a numerator or denominator that includes an expression such as

$$\frac{8 + 12}{25 + 175}$$

Compare the results of a True BASIC statement that defines the denominator and numerator with parentheses and one that does not:

True BASIC statement	Result
PRINT (8 + 12)/(25 + 175)	0.1
PRINT 8 + 12/25 + 175	183.48

Parentheses are also needed for fractional exponents like

$$6^{1/3}$$

Compare the results of a True BASIC statement that defines the exponent with parentheses and one that does not:

True BASIC statement	Operation	Result
PRINT 6 ^ (1/3)	6 raised to the 1/3 power	1.81712
PRINT 6 ^ 1/3	6 raised to the 1st power divided by 3	2

Even when parentheses may not change the result, it is a good idea to include them in long expressions. Without them, the computer may understand exactly what to do, but humans might not see clearly what the expression does. It is better programming style, for example, to write

PRINT 4 * (2^3) + (6/3) — 1

than

PRINT 4 * 2^3 + 6/3 — 1

even though the results are the same.

Numeric functions

Some programming routines composed of arithmetic operations are used so frequently that they have been included in the True BASIC language. You can activate these routines, known as *numeric functions,* by supplying the function name and the function argument made up of your specific data.

The function names are usually three-letter abbreviations, and the arguments, if required, are written in parentheses. Use functions in PRINT statements and in all the same situations you would use the usual arithmetic expressions.

Figure 4–8 (p. 44) lists all of the True BASIC numeric functions. The remainder of this chapter gives examples of some of the ones you will find most useful.

The SQR(X) function

The SQR function provides the square root of the number or expression in parentheses. In Figure 4–1 the computer calculates the square root of 25. SQR is the function name, 25 is the argument, and 5 is the function value or result.

Figure 4–1. The SQR function

```
▮ PRINT "The square root of 25 is "; SQR(25)
▮ END
```

```
Ok. run
The square root of 25 is 5
Ok.
```

The INT(X) function

The INT function rounds a number with decimals down to the nearest lower integer. It truncates any decimals in the argument.

Imagine all of the numbers in the world on a continuum that ranges from negative infinity on the left to positive infinity on the right:

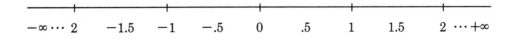

$$-\infty \cdots 2 \qquad -1.5 \quad -1 \quad -.5 \quad 0 \quad .5 \quad 1 \quad 1.5 \quad 2 \cdots +\infty$$

The INT(your number) function gives the nearest integer to the left of your number on the continuum. Look at the continuum and at the INT expressions in Figure 4–2. You will see what values the INT function gives.

Figure 4-2. The INT function

True BASIC statement	Result
PRINT INT(2)	2
PRINT INT(1.7)	1
PRINT INT(1.5)	1
PRINT INT(1.3)	1
PRINT INT(.5)	0
PRINT INT(−.5)	−1
PRINT INT(0)	0

The ROUND(X,Y) function

To round off (up) as we usually do, use the ROUND function. Specify for the first argument what number is to be rounded and for the second argument how many digits to the left or right of the decimal point you want to see. If the second argument is a positive number, you are specifying how many digits to the right of the decimal you want to see. The rightmost digit is rounded up if the next righthand digit is greater than or equal to 5. If the second argument is negative, you are specifying how many places to the left of the decimal you want rounded up. If it is zero, you are telling the computer that you want to see no digits to the right of the decimal; you are saying that you want to round up to the nearest integer. Figure 4-3 gives some examples.

Figure 4-3. The ROUND function

Number to be rounded up	True BASIC statement	Result
1.766	PRINT ROUND(1.766,2)	1.77
34.33	PRINT ROUND(34.33, − 1)	30
176	PRINT ROUND(176, − 2)	200
1.7	PRINT ROUND(1.7,0)	2
1.3	PRINT ROUND(1.3,0)	1
.5	PRINT ROUND(.5,0)	1

If you only need to round a number to the nearest integer, you can use True BASIC's single-argument ROUND function. This function rounds off the number within parentheses to the nearest integer. Thus:

$$ROUND\ (1.75)\ = 2$$
$$ROUND\ (5.301) = 5$$
$$ROUND\ (.3)\quad = 0$$

The TRUNCATE(X,Y) function

The truncate function rounds down and lets you specify how many decimal places you want to see. The first argument is the number you want rounded down and the second argument is how many places to the left or right of the decimal point you want to round to. If the second argument is a positive number, you are specifying how many digits to the right of the decimal you want to see. Any others are truncated. If it is negative you are specifying how many places to the left of the decimal you want. If the second argument is zero you are telling the computer that you want to do what the INT function does and round to the nearest integer. Figure 4–4 gives some examples.

Figure 4–4. The TRUNCATE function

Number to be rounded down	True BASIC statement	Result
1.766	PRINT TRUNCATE(1.766,2)	1.76
34.33	PRINT TRUNCATE(34.33, − 1)	30
176	PRINT TRUNCATE(176, − 2)	100
1.7	PRINT TRUNCATE(1.7,0)	1
1.3	PRINT TRUNCATE(1.3,0)	1
.5	PRINT TRUNCATE(.5,0)	0

The RND function

Unlike most True BASIC functions, RND requires no arguments. It produces a number in the range from zero up to, but not including, one. Since its exact value is unpredictable, you can use the RND function when you need a random number. Actually, RND is a pseudo-random number, since the result is produced according to a definable algorithm. Still, you and your program users will not be able to anticipate its exact value.

Although random numbers are frequently useful, random numbers that are decimals rarely are. Who wants to play a number guessing game if the correct answer is a number somewhere between 0 and 1, such as 0.56783? Fortunately, it is possible to make the True BASIC random number an integer within a range that *is* useful to you. You need to move the decimal to the right, add the lowest integer amount in your range, and truncate the remaining decimals. Figure 4–5 gives four True BASIC statements that illustrate the process of transforming a raw random decimal number into an integer within the range from 1 to 10. For purposes of illustration, each step incorporates the preceding steps. In actuality, you only need to write a statement like the fourth one, which combines all of the preceding statements. (Recall that you can truncate decimals in two ways: You can use the INT function, as in Figure 4–5, or you can use the TRUNCATE function with zero as the second argument.)

To produce an integer within any range, apply the following formula to the RND function. If HIGH is the highest number in the range and LOW is the lowest number in the range, write:

$$\text{PRINT INT((HIGH − LOW) + 1)} * \text{RND + LOW)}$$

This expression says, multiply the random decimal number by the number of numbers in the range, add the lowest number in the range to the result, and truncate the remaining decimals. Figure 4–6 uses the RND function to simulate the roll of dice. The random numbers produced all range from 1 to 6.

Figure 4–5. Converting a random decimal to an integer value

Example True BASIC Statement	*Sample random numbers*		
1. Produce a random number			
PRINT RND	0.45638	0.00099	0.99999
2. Move the decimal to the right			
PRINT RND*10	4.5638	0.00099	9.999
3. Truncate extra decimals			
PRINT INT(RND*10)	4	0	9
4. Add the lowest number in the range			
PRINT INT(RND*10) + 1	5	1	10

Figure 4–6. Using RND to roll dice

```
▮ PRINT "Dice Toss"
▮ PRINT
▮ PRINT INT((6 - 1 + 1)*RND + 1)
▮ PRINT "and"
▮ PRINT INT((6 - 1 + 1)*RND + 1)
▮ END
```

```
Ok. run
Dice Toss

 4
and
 1
Ok.
```

The RANDOMIZE statement

Without the RANDOMIZE statement, each run of your program produces the same set of random numbers. This makes testing new programs easy because it avoids the confusion created by repeatedly generating unpredictable numbers. When all is working well, however, insert the RANDOMIZE statement before the first use of the RND function. From then on, the random numbers produced will differ with each run of the program. Write the RANDOMIZE statement simply as:

```
RANDOMIZE
```

Figure 4–7 uses RANDOMIZE to ensure that a different sequence of numbers appears each time the dice toss program runs.

True BASIC numbers

All computer languages have limits as to the print format, the range, and precision of the numbers they make available. True BASIC is no exception. For most of your

Figure 4–7. Using RANDOMIZE

```
■ RANDOMIZE
■ PRINT "Dice Toss"
■ PRINT
■ PRINT INT((6 - 1 + 1)*RND + 1)
■ PRINT "and"
■ PRINT INT((6 - 1 + 1)*RND + 1)
■ END
```

```
Ok. run
Dice Toss

 6
and
 1
Ok. run
Dice Toss

 3
and
 4
Ok.
```

programming jobs this need not concern you. The True BASIC PRINT statement will print numbers as you would expect to see them and easily provide numbers in the range and precision you usually need. However, when your programming problem involves very large or very small numbers, and when calculations need extreme precision, you must be aware of the limitations of how True BASIC handles them.

Scientific notation

True BASIC prints all the digits of integers with 11 or fewer digits. It prints the digits of decimal numbers that can be rounded off in the usual fashion to six or fewer digits. But True BASIC converts all other numbers, very large and very small, to scientific notation for printing.

In using scientific notation True BASIC prints a number as a decimal with an exponent for the base number 10. The exponent tells you how many times to divide or multiply the given decimal by 10. If it is positive, multiply by moving the decimal to the right; if it is negative, divide by moving the decimal to the left. Thus,

$$1.45876E+05 \quad \text{is} \quad 145,876.0$$
because E + 05 means exponent, positive 5

and

$$1.45876E-05 \quad \text{is} \quad .0000145876$$
because E − 05 means exponent, negative 5

Figure 4–8. True BASIC numeric functions

Mathematical functions	*Result*
ABS(X)	Absolute value of X
EPS(X)	The maximum of (X − X′, X″ − X, sigma), where X′ and X″ are the predecessor and successor of X, respectively, and sigma is the smallest positive number representable
INT(X)	Largest integer not greater than X
LOG(X)	Natural logarithm of X
LOG2(X)	Logarithm, base 2, of X
LOG10(X)	Logarithm, base 10, of X
MAX(X,Y)	Maximum of X and Y
MAXNUM	Largest number available on your computer
MIN(X,Y)	Minimum of X and Y
MOD(X,Y)	X modulo Y: X − (Y * INT(X/Y))
REMAINDER(X,Y)	Remainder when X is divided by Y
RND	Pseudo-random number in the range 0 <= RND > 1.
ROUND(X,N)	X rounded to N decimal places to the right of the decimal point if N is positive
	X rounded to N decimal places to the left of the decimal point if N is negative
SGN(X)	If X is positive, SGN(X) = 1
	If X is zero, SGN(X) = 0
	If X is negative, SGN(X) = −1
SQR(X)	Square root of X
TRUNCATE(X,N)	X truncated to N places to the right of the decimal point or −N places to the left if N is less than zero

Trigonometric functions	*Result*
ANGLE(X,Y)	Counterclockwise angle between positive x-axis and (X,Y)
ATN(X)	Arctangent of X
COS(X)	Cosine of X
DEG(X)	X radians converted to degrees
PI	3.1415926 . . .
RAD(X)	X degrees converted to radians
SIN(X)	Sine of X
TAN(X)	Tangent of X

Magnitude and precision

Even if True BASIC does not print all of the digits, it computes and stores values to at least ten digits of precision. You can use the PRINT USING statement described in Chapter 11 to bypass the PRINT statement defaults and see all of these digits if you need to.

True BASIC guarantees a range of 1.0E−99 to 1.0E+99, although your particular computer may be able to provide a wider range. The True BASIC MAXNUM function gives the largest possible number your computer knows.

Summary

Because of their speed, precision, and reliability, computers have greatly enhanced humankind's mathematical accomplishments.

Programming skills

Numeric functions

SQR
INT
ROUND
TRUNCATE
RND

Computer concepts

Arithmetic operations
True BASIC numbers
Scientific notation

Review questions

1. Translate each of the following True BASIC expressions into usual arithmetic expressions:
   a. `(4^2*2^3)^.5`
   b. `22/2*4+11-3^2/.3`
   c. `(.3/.9*3-9)^1/3`
   d. `4+2/5-8+4^2`
   e. `(3*(4-2^4))^2`
   f. `2+8/4-8*3^2`

2. Write True BASIC statements that perform the following calculations and print out the result.
   a. $\dfrac{2 + 4^2}{5 \times 8}$

   b. $\dfrac{3 + 9}{8} - \dfrac{4 \times 2}{2\verb|^|2}$

   c. $\dfrac{3(6.2 + 5)}{4.5 - 2.3}$

   d. $10 \times \sqrt{25} + 11$

   e. $3.14R^2$

   f. $2W + 9L$

g. $\left(\dfrac{3+12}{Y}\right)^2$

h. $\dfrac{1}{3+\dfrac{1}{3-\dfrac{1}{3+1}}}$

i. $\dfrac{4+34\times 15-4^2}{7+8}$

j. $2X+32Y^2-4^2$

3. *Corrections.* Determine whether each of the following True BASIC statements is correctly entered. If it is, write "correct" on your answer sheet. If not, rewrite it correctly. Consider each statement separately. These statements are *not* part of the same program.

    a. ▮ `PRINT "The answer is": INT(X + .5)`
    b. ▮ `PRINT (3*X) + 4Y + Z^2`
    c. ▮ `PRINT X = C; X^2 = A; X^3 = B`
    d. ▮ `SQR(84)`
    e. ▮ `RANDOM`
    f. ▮ `PRINT TRUNCATE(6.7,-3)`
    g. ▮ `PRINT ROUND(X,2)`
    h. ▮ `PRINT INT 150.75`
    i. ▮ `PRINT INT((200-100+1)*RND + 200)`
    j. ▮ `PRINT ROUND(3.2)`

4. Write a program that takes a decimal number and prints it out rounded down to the nearest integer. Write another small program that takes the decimal and rounds it up to the nearest integer.

5. Write a program that prints the following table on the printer after it is run:

NUMBER	SQUARE	CUBE
2	4	8
3	9	27
4	16	64
5	25	125

6. Write a program that calculates the year you will retire and how many years from now you need to work before retiring.

7. Mr. Blackstone runs the bookstore but doesn't like to be bothered with change. All coins go to charity. Write a program that starts with the price of an item sold (like $1.99 for eating oranges) and prints out dollar amounts for Mr. Blackstone and the change amounts for charity.

8. The state lottery has tickets for Juvenile, Adult, and Senior divisions. The ticket numbers for each division are in the following ranges:

Juvenile   1 to 100
Adult   101 to 200
Senior   201 to 250

Use the computer to randomly select the winning ticket in each division.

9. Use the computer to determine how long a ladder is needed to rescue Purrky, the kitty, from the very top of a 20-foot tree. Keep in mind that the foot of the ladder must be set 7 feet away from the base of the tree in order not to destroy the flower beds.

10. The Internal Revenue Service is very generous with taxpayers. If the tax you owe includes some change under 50 cents, you need not send in the pennies. If the tax includes 50 cents or more in change, you are supposed to round up and send in the next highest dollar amount. Use the computer to provide the taxpayer with a printout of how much he or she should send to Uncle Sam.

## Chapter 5

The LET, INPUT, READ, and DATA statements

When the time came to take the U.S. census for 1890, officials realized that with the existing technology, the results could not be tabulated before they became obsolete. (The previous census, of 1880, was not fully tabulated until 1887.) The Census Bureau held a competition to develop new methods for processing the 1890 data. Herman Hollerith, perhaps the world's first statistical engineer, won the competition. His system using punched cards greatly reduced tabulating time. Hollerith's company eventually became a part of IBM, and his methods were absorbed into computer technology.

Because it is a fundamental reason for using computers, providing a means of storing information for later processing is an essential feature of any computer language. This chapter explains the LET, INPUT, READ, and DATA statements upon which True BASIC's data processing capability is built. These programming statements let you temporarily store limited amounts of data. Later chapters explain how True BASIC permits you to permanently store larger data files on computer disks.

The LET statement

> LET

The computer keeps track of the memory address where each item of data is stored. In True BASIC the LET statement is one way of assigning an address to a piece of information. Each time the address is referenced in a program, the information stored there is available for processing.

Variable names

True BASIC uses names, rather than actual addresses, to represent addresses. These names are known as *variables* because the values they represent can change during the run of a program.

True BASIC actually uses two types of variables: numeric variables, which represent numbers, and character-string variables, which represent letters and other characters. The rules for forming the two kinds of variables are the same, except that string variables must end with a dollar sign ($).

Although True BASIC variable names must begin with a letter, the name can include uppercase and lowercase letters, digits, and the underscore. Variable names can be up to 31 characters long. The following examples are valid variable names in True BASIC:

```
MONEY
NAME$
total
Before__tax__income
student123
Q
```

Long, descriptive variable names make your program easier to understand, but they also cause problems. It is easy to misspell a fancy variable name; and if you do, the computer will not recognize what you really mean. You may replace uppercase letters with lowercase, but otherwise all references to the same variable must appear the same. In general, variable names should be descriptive but brief.

In Figure 5–1, the variables X, Y, and Z are symbols for the memory addresses in which are stored the values 1, 3, and 5, respectively. In this program, the LET statement assigns values to a variable. The PRINT statement displays the values assigned to the variables.

Figure 5–1. LET assigns values to a variable

```
■ LET X = 1                        !storing 1 in location X
■ LET Y = 3                        !storing 3 in location Y
■ LET Z = 5                        !storing 5 in location Z
■
■ PRINT "Some odd numbers are:"
■ PRINT X, Y, Z                    !referencing the data in
■                                  !locations X, Y, Z
■ END
```

```
Ok. run
Some odd numbers are:
 1                  3                  5
Ok.
```

Calculations

The LET statement can also do calculations before assigning data to an address. When calculations are part of a LET statement, the computer evaluates the expression on the right side of the equals sign and stores the result in the memory location represented by the variable to the left of the equals sign. Figure 5–2 adds calculations to the previous program. Because of the values assigned to X, Y, and Z, the right side of the LET SUM = X + Y + Z statement has the value 9. The computer assigns this value to the memory location denoted by the variable SUM on the left side of the equals sign.

Figure 5–2. LET does calculations

```
■ LET X = 1                        !storing 1 in location X
■ LET Y = 3                        !storing 3 in location Y
■ LET Z = 5                        !storing 5 in location Z
■ LET SUM = X + Y + Z              !storing the total in SUM
■ PRINT "Some odd numbers are:"
■ PRINT X, Y, Z                    !referencing the data in
                                    locations X, Y, Z
■ PRINT "The total is:"
■ PRINT SUM                        !referencing the data in
                                    location SUM
■ END
```

```
Ok. run
Some odd numbers are:
 1                3                5
The total is:
 9
Ok.
```

The equals sign in a LET statement is not at all like the one you've seen in algebra. In True BASIC the two sides of the equals sign are not equivalent. It is not correct to say

```
LET 10 = X
```

as a replacement for

```
LET X = 10
```

Only the statement

```
LET X = 10
```

will do.

The term to the left of the equals sign must be a single variable or a group of variables, each denoting a memory address. The right side may be a single value or a complicated expression denoting the data to be stored.

If several variables are to have the same value, you can assign them their values in one statement:

```
LET X, Y, Z = 64
```

True BASIC treats these as three separate locations, all storing the value 64.

Counting

Some people may be mystified by the statement:

```
LET SUM = SUM + 1
```

This looks like an equation that is out of balance, but it is actually a valid and useful LET statement. In evaluating the right side first, the computer adds 1 to the current value of SUM. (If none has been previously assigned, the computer assumes SUM to be 0.) The new value is stored back in location SUM, since it is the variable on the left. The previous SUM value is replaced. IF SUM had been 1, now it is 2. IF the LET SUM = SUM + 1 statement is executed another time, the process repeats. The statement

```
LET SUM = SUM + 5
```

is a way to count by fives; the statement

```
LET SUM = SUM + 2
```

is a way to count by twos; and so on.

Character-string assignments and character-string variables

Compare the two similar programs of Figures 5–2 and 5–3. As we have seen, the Figure 5–2 program stores and prints numbers across the print line. The program of Figure 5–3, on the other hand, prints character data.

In True BASIC character data are known as string data because they consist of a "string" of any combination of ASCII characters: letters, digits, blank spaces, punctuation marks, and others. True BASIC stores string data differently than it stores numeric data, and the formats of the string variable and the string data item

Figure 5–3. LET stores character data

```
■ LET NAME$ = "Sam Smith"        !storing data in NAME$
■ LET STREET$ = "Elm Street"     !storing data in STREET$
■ LET PHONE$ = "542-2398"        !storing data in PHONE$
■ PRINT NAME$, STREET$, PHONE$
■ END
```

```
Ok. run
Sam Smith      Elm Street      542-2398
Ok.
```

are designed to set the character-string-handling process in motion. This is why a string variable ends with a dollar sign and why the string itself must be surrounded with quotation marks, as in "SAM SMITH".

Substrings

The LET statement allows you to assign new values to part of a string if doing so makes sense in your programming project. The program of Figure 5–4 uses this feature to change the name of the month on a string used to print report headings. The arguments within parentheses indicate the beginning and ending character positions in the previously stored string that will be replaced by the new characters. Because "Jan" comprises the nineteenth, twentieth, and twenty-first character positions in the heading "Profit report for Jan." (a blank space counts as a character), the values 19 through 21 are given as arguments in the parentheses. When the LET statement with this substring notation is executed, "Feb" replaces "Jan" in the heading.

The program of Figure 5–5 adds the word "The" to the beginning of the string with the statement

```
LET HEAD$(1:0) = "The"
```

that gives 0 for the second argument.

Figure 5–4. Assigning new values to a substring

```
▌ LET HEAD$ = "Profit Report for Jan."
▌ PRINT HEAD$
▌ LET HEAD$(19:21) = "Feb"
▌ PRINT HEAD$
▌ END
```

```
Ok. run
Profit Report for Jan.
Profit Report for Feb.
Ok.
```

Figure 5–5. Assigning new values to the start of a string

```
▌ LET HEAD$ = "Profit Report for Jan."
▌ PRINT HEAD$
▌ LET HEAD$(1:0) = "The "
▌ PRINT HEAD$
▌ END
```

```
Ok. run
Profit Report for Jan.
The Profit Report for Jan.
Ok.
```

Figure 5-6. Assigning new values to a string of unknown length

```
▌ LET HEAD$ = "Profit Report for Jan."
▌ PRINT HEAD$
▌ LET HEAD$(15:maxnum) = "for the merry month of May"
▌ PRINT HEAD$
▌ END
```

```
Ok. run
Profit Report for Jan.
Profit Report for the merry month of May
Ok.
```

Maxnum. Figure 5-6 shows that even if you do not know how many characters are in a string, you can still change characters from the middle of the string to the end. A statement like

```
LET HEAD$(15:maxnum) = "for the merry month of May"
```

gives "maxnum" for the second argument. *Maxnum* is a special True BASIC variable that stores the largest number your computer knows. When the ending value exceeds the number of characters in the string, the computer interprets that to mean the last character in the string. Thus, *maxnum* is useful in this example because it guarantees that the computer will replace all of the characters beyond character 15 in HEAD$ no matter how long HEAD$ may be.

Figure 5-7 adds a word to the end of a string with the statement

```
LET HEAD$(maxnum:maxnum) = " for the Widget Co."
```

that gives *maxnum* for both arguments. When the starting argument is *maxnum*, the computer interprets that to mean the last character in the string and appends the new characters to the end of the string.

Figure 5-7. Assigning new values to the end of a string

```
▌ LET HEAD$ = "Profit Report for Jan."
▌ PRINT HEAD$
▌ LET HEAD$(maxnum:maxnum) = " For the Widget Co."
▌ PRINT HEAD$
▌ END
```

```
Ok. run
Profit Report for Jan.
Profit Report for Jan. For the Widget Co.
Ok.
```

Figure 5–8. Replacing a substring with a longer substring

```
▮ LET HEAD$ = "Profit Report for Jan."
▮ PRINT HEAD$
▮ LET HEAD$(18:18) = " chilly "
▮ PRINT HEAD$
▮ END
```

```
Ok. run
Profit Report for Jan.
Profit Report for chilly Jan.
Ok.
```

The number of characters you are adding to the string does not have to be the same as the number you are deleting. You can create longer or shorter strings as a result of your substring manipulations. Figure 5–8 replaces the blank in character position 18 of the phrase "Profit report for Jan." with the word " chilly ." Notice that the numbers given as arguments represent character positions in the *starting* string rather than the new, longer string. In this example, since only one character is being replaced (the 18th), the starting and ending arguments are both 18.

The INPUT statement

```
┌─────────┐
│  INPUT  │
└─────────┘
```

Like the LET statement, the INPUT statement assigns a value to a variable. With INPUT, however, the data are entered while the program runs.

INPUT is why, contrary to popular myth, computers are likely to make life in our society more personal. Computer-driven manufacturing processes can adjust to individual preferences as each item is produced. Someday we may all wear custom-made clothes, since the choice of size, color, and style need not be limited to just a few predetermined ones. You might, for example, enter your measurements into the pattern-cutting program of your local clothier's computer and, even if your jacket size differs from your pants size, be able to buy a suit that needs no alterations.

Figure 5–9 illustrates how the INPUT statement works. As the program runs, the INPUT statement prints a question mark to prompt the user to enter information. The computer stops the program at the INPUT statement, waiting for something to be entered. When you enter something, processing continues. In the output of Figure 5–9 three question marks appear because there are three INPUT statements in the program. Data entered in response to a prompt are stored in the variables given in the INPUT statement. Thus, PROJECT$ becomes "The White House," and START becomes "1800," and STOP becomes "1803."

INPUT makes it possible for one program to process more than one set of data. For example, there is no need to write several programs for calculating the construction times of several projects. A single, generalized program will do. Figure 5–10 runs the program of Figure 5–9 again. New values are entered and new calculations performed using the new values. Thus, PROJECT$ becomes "The Empire State Building," START becomes "1926," and STOP becomes "1931."

Figure 5 – 9. INPUT assigns a value to a variable

```
■ PRINT "What is the project"
■ INPUT PROJECT$
■ PRINT "When was it begun"
■ INPUT START
■ PRINT "When was it finished"
■ INPUT STOP
■ PRINT PROJECT$;" took";STOP - START;"years to build."
■ END
```

```
Ok. run
What is the project
? The White House
When was it begun
? 1800
When was it finished
? 1803
The White House took 3 years to build.
Ok.
```

As with PRINT, more than one job can be done in a single INPUT statement. Figure 5 – 11 shows that several values can be accepted. A, B, and C, the three variables in this INPUT statement, are separated by commas. As the program runs, the computer pauses until you give at least one reply to match each variable.

An INPUT statement with a trailing comma as in Figure 5 – 12 tells the computer that another INPUT statement follows. The computer expects your replies for both INPUT statements to be entered on one line. If they are not, the computer gives an error message and prints another prompt. It will pause until you

Figure 5 – 10. INPUT assigns a new value to a variable

```
■ PRINT "What is the project";
■ INPUT PROJECT$
■ PRINT "When was it begun";
■ INPUT START
■ PRINT "When was it finished";
■ INPUT STOP
■ PRINT PROJECT$;" took";STOP - START;"years to build."
■ END
```

```
Ok. run
What is the project? The Empire State Building
When was it begun? 1926
When was it finished? 1931
The Empire State Building took 5 years to build.
Ok.
```

Figure 5–11. One INPUT assigns values to several variables

```
▌ PRINT "Weekend Jogging Tally"
▌ PRINT "Enter the miles for Friday, Saturday, Sunday"
▌ INPUT A,B,C
▌ PRINT "You ran a total of"; A + B + C; "miles"
▌ END
```

```
Ok. run
Weekend Jogging Tally
Enter the miles for Friday, Saturday, Sunday
? 3,5,6
You ran a total of 14 miles
Ok.
```

give enough replies for the variables in both INPUT statements. Because of the trailing comma in the first INPUT statement in this example, both INPUT statements are satisfied when the jogging distances are entered on one line.

Notice in the preceding examples that you can enter only constant values with an INPUT statement. You cannot enter expressions. String variables accept string data and numeric variables accept numbers.

The string you enter can be composed of any characters, including blanks. You need not surround a string that is a reply to INPUT with quotation marks unless the reply includes leading or trailing blanks, commas, or quotation marks. The following are all acceptable strings

Mrs. Martin
". . . ahh . . ."
457-4096

Figure 5–12. Two INPUTs assign values to several variables

```
▌ PRINT "Weekend Jogging Tally"
▌ PRINT "Enter the miles for Friday, Saturday, Sunday"
▌ INPUT A,B,
▌ INPUT C
▌ PRINT "You ran a total of"; A + B + C; "miles"
▌ END
```

```
Ok. run
Weekend Jogging Tally
Enter the miles for Friday, Saturday, Sunday
? 5,6,7
You ran a total of 18 miles
Ok.
```

For numeric variables you can enter any type of number, but you cannot enter commas, arithmetic expressions, or characters. Thus 4, 4.7, and -12332 are acceptable, but a character such as A or an expression like $30 + 51$ is not allowed.

If your INPUT prompt requires more replies than you can fit on one line, end the first line of replies with a comma and enter it. The computer will respond with a new question mark prompt and wait for you to continue with your next reply. When you continue replies onto another line, however, be sure you do not break a particular response in the middle. Insert the trailing comma after the last complete reply on the first response line.

The computer complains if your replies do not match the INPUT request in number and type. Thus, for example, if the computer expects two names and a number, you must provide two strings and a number. If there is less information, the computer will ask for more. If there is too much data, the computer will tell you it ignored the excess. If you enter a string instead of a number, the computer will complain that a number was expected and ask you to try again. If you enter a number when a string is expected, the computer will not complain; it will consider the number a text character useful for printing but not for calculations.

The INPUT PROMPT statement

> INPUT
> PROMPT

You can combine a question and the question mark input prompt to make a more natural-looking dialogue. True BASIC combines the functions of PRINT and INPUT in the INPUT PROMPT statement you see illustrated in Figure 5–13. The key words INPUT PROMPT, the quotation marks, the colon, and a variable are all required. You can make up any prompt you wish. If it is a question, you must include the question mark followed by a space within the quotes. The computer does not automatically print a question mark with the INPUT PROMPT statement. As with the INPUT statement, the variable you supply stores your response.

Figure 5–13. INPUT assigns a new value to a variable

```
■ INPUT PROMPT "How many years have you worked here? ": TERM
■ PRINT "You have earned"; TERM * 3;"days vacation."
■ END
■
```

```
Ok. run
How many years have you worked here? 23
You have earned 69 days vacation.
Ok.
```

The LINE INPUT and LINE INPUT PROMPT statements

> LINE
> INPUT

The LINE INPUT and LINE INPUT PROMPT statements accept one line of typing as the response for each variable in the statement. Use them if you expect long replies that might include commas, leading or trailing spaces, or quotation marks.

LINE
INPUT
PROMPT

Figure 5–14 illustrates how LINE INPUT accepts everything entered between the prompting question mark and the press of the *enter* key as a single reply. Notice that the variable TOPONE$ is a string variable, as any variable used with LINE INPUT must be.

Figure 5–15 uses the LINE INPUT PROMPT to combine the features of the other INPUT statements. Like INPUT PROMPT, this statement prints a leading phrase before the question mark prompt. Like LINE INPUT it assigns an entire reply line to a string variable.

Figure 5–14. LINE INPUT assigns a line-long reply to a variable

```
▌ PRINT "What are your favorite things"
▌ LINE INPUT TOPONE$
▌ PRINT "I shall buy you"
▌ PRINT TOPONE$
▌ PRINT "my child!"
▌ END
```

```
Ok. run
What are your favorite things
? trees and flowers, birds and fruits, tea and chocolate
I shall buy you
trees and flowers, birds and fruits, tea and chocolate
my child!
Ok.
```

Figure 5–15. LINE INPUT PROMPT combines all the INPUT statements

```
▌ LINE INPUT PROMPT "Tell me your favorites? ":TOPONE$
▌ PRINT "I shall buy you"
▌ PRINT TOPONE$
▌ PRINT "my child!"
▌ END
```

```
Ok. run
Tell me your favorites? furniture and house plants
I shall buy you
furniture and house plants
my child!
Ok.
```

The READ and DATA statements

READ

Like LET and INPUT, the READ and DATA combination of statements assigns data to one or more variables. The variables are listed in the READ statement; the data are listed in the DATA statement.

DATA

READ and DATA are designed to accommodate lists of data known to the programmer when the program is written such as the months of the year or the medal winners in the Olympic Games. During various phases of the program run some or all of this information will be needed. Figure 5–16 shows how READ and DATA make the data available. The statements are used in combination: DATA holds the information; READ accesses it. Think of an imaginary arrow or pointer indicating which item of data is assigned to which variable each time the computer executes a READ statement. At the outset of the program, the pointer aims at the first data item, COMPACT. This is assigned to the first variable in the READ statement, STYLE_1$. Then the pointer moves to the next data item, SPORTY, and assigns it to the second variable, STYLE_2$. Finally, the pointer moves on and LARGE is assigned to STYLE_3$.

Figure 5–16. READ assigns values to variables; DATA holds the values

```
■ READ STYLE_1$, STYLE_2$, STYLE_3$
■ PRINT "The types of cars we rent"
■ PRINT "are ";STYLE_1$;" and ";STYLE_2$;" and ";STYLE_3$
■
■ REM This is the data section of the program
■ DATA COMPACT, SPORTY, LARGE
■ END
```

```
Ok. run
The types of cars we rent
are COMPACT and SPORTY and LARGE
Ok.
```

Every time a READ statement is encountered, the computer assigns data in a sequential manner. It begins using the data where the pointer is currently positioned and continues until all of the READ variables have been assigned a value.

If there are fewer data items than variables, the computer complains by displaying "Reading past end of data" in the command window. If there are more items than variables, there is no complaint. In fact, as Figure 5–17 shows, you most probably will have more data items than you read at a particular time. These are used by other READ statements later in the program.

The first read statement in Figure 5–17 sends the data pointer from COMPACT to SPORTY to LARGE so that it finally rests at LUXURY. The second READ statement begins at the pointer, assigns LUXURY to STYLE_4$, and moves the pointer beyond LUXURY to the end of the data. Any further reading causes an error, since the pointer no longer points to any data. Figure 5–18 uses an arrow to illustrate the progress of the pointer.

DATA is a unique True BASIC statement because its location in the program does not affect the sequence of events. For the program run, it is the location of the READ statement that makes a difference. The READ statement positions the pointer and assigns values to variables. The READ statement must precede the PRINT or other statements that make use of the data being read.

String or numeric constants separated from one another by commas are the only valid items for DATA. You cannot use variables or expressions. DATA is one

Figure 5-17. Several READ statements may appear in one program

```
■ READ STYLE_1$, STYLE_2$, STYLE_3$
■ PRINT "The types of cars we rent"
■ PRINT "are ";STYLE_1$;" and ";STYLE_2$;" and ";STYLE_3$;"."
■ PRINT "But we can get"
■ READ STYLE_4$
■ PRINT STYLE_4$; " cars if you want."
■
■ REM This is the data section of the program
■ DATA COMPACT, SPORTY, LARGE, LUXURY
■ END
```

```
Ok. run
The types of cars we rent
are COMPACT and SPORTY and LARGE.
But we can get
LUXURY cars if you want.
Ok.
```

situation where you may not need quotation marks around strings. Figure 5-19 compares the data items that do and do not need quotation marks. You may want to make a habit of using them, however, because in True BASIC it is never wrong to do so. Even numeric data that will be read by numeric variables can be surrounded with quotation marks. Trying to remember the special cases when you *must* have quotes might be more trouble than its worth.

Figure 5-18. Progress of the pointer through the data

1. Before any READ statement executes
   DATA COMPACT, SPORTY, LARGE, LUXURY

2. After READ STYLE_1$,STYLE_2$,STYLE_3$
   DATA COMPACT, SPORTY, LARGE, LUXURY

3. After READ STYLE_4$
   DATA COMPACT, SPORTY, LARGE, LUXURY

Figure 5-19. DATA items that *do* need quotation marks

When quotes are needed	Example
Leading and trailing blanks	" Hi "
Strings with commas	" Hi there, big boy"
Strings with quotation marks	" Hi""big""boy" (Use 2 pairs of quotation marks for each one included in the DATA string item)
Strings with exclamation marks	" Hi!"

Figure 5 – 20 illustrates the type of READ and DATA use that is more likely to occur in your program. It uses strings, blanks, and numbers for data in a program that prints a report on some Olympic events. The example shows only the READ, DATA, and PRINT statements, but you can assume they are part of a longer program that returns control to them over and over again in order to read and print about several events. Assume also that there are many lines of data with information on many more contests. The first time the READ and PRINT routine receives control, it reports on the results of the water polo event. Since this is a team sport, no names are available. The data item read by NAME$ is a blank and is represented by

Figure 5 – 20. A routine that READs and PRINTs data items

```
PRINT "OLYMPIC GOLD MEDAL WINNERS"
PRINT



READ EVENT$
PRINT EVENT$;":"
READ NATION$, NAME$, SCORE
PRINT NATION$, NAME$, SCORE
PRINT

     !control returns to READ


REM Olympic Results for Water Sports
DATA WATER POLO,YUGOSLAVIA, "" , 7
DATA KAYAK,NEW ZEALAND, FERGUSON, "4.6"
DATA CANOE,CANADA,CAIN,22

           !more data

END
```

```
True BASIC here.
Ok. run
OLYMPIC GOLD MEDAL WINNERS

WATER POLO:
YUGOSLAVIA                    7

KAYAK:
NEW ZEALAND     FERGUSON      4.6

CANOE:
CANADA          CAIN          22
 .
 .
Ok.
```

quotation marks that surround nothing. The next time control passes to the READ and PRINT routine it reports on the Kayak event. Nations, names, and times are available, and all of this information is printed. Each time control returns to this routine new values are assigned to the READ variables and new information is printed.

Notice that SCORE, a numeric variable, reads and prints the numeric data. This is so even though these data are surrounded by quotation marks. Notice also the position of the DATA statements in the program. They are set apart by a REM statement just before the END statement. Since DATA has no effect on the sequence of events, setting DATA apart is possible. It is also a good programming practice. Not only can everyone easily see what information you are working with, but they can also read without distraction the other statements that produce the logic of your program.

The RESTORE statement

RESTORE

As you use the READ and DATA combination, the pointer moves forward through the data. It never moves backward. RESTORE is a statement that moves the pointer back to the beginning of the data. Any subsequent reading starts again from the beginning of the data. For example, you might want to use the Olympic reporting program to make an alphabetical listing of the winners. You can reuse the data with a RESTORE statement that sets the pointer back to the first data item in the program module. Then, you can pass control to a routine that READs and sorts names.

Although it is usually used in longer programs, Figure 5 – 21 uses RESTORE to retrieve the first data item after it has once been read.

Figure 5 – 21. RESTORE returns the pointer to the beginning of data

```
READ MINUTE
PRINT "The first place time was"; MINUTE;"minutes."
READ MINUTE
PRINT "The second place time was"; MINUTE;"minutes."
READ MINUTE
PRINT "The third place time was"; MINUTE;"minutes."
RESTORE
READ MINUTE
PRINT "The winner broke the record by"; 9-MINUTE;"minutes."
DATA 7,11,13
END
```

```
Ok. run
The first place time was 7 minutes.
The second place time was 11 minutes.
The third place time was 13 minutes.
The winner broke the record by 2 minutes.
Ok.
```

Summary

Providing a means of storing data for later processing is an essential feature of any computer language. The LET, INPUT, and READ statements let you temporarily store limited amounts of data.

Programming skills

The LET statement
The INPUT statement
The INPUT PROMPT statement
The LINE INPUT statement
The LINE INPUT PROMPT statement
The READ, DATA, and RESTORE statements

Computer concepts

Variables
Counting
Strings
Substrings

Review questions

1. *Corrections.* Determine whether each of the following True BASIC statements is correctly entered. If it is, write "correct" on your answer sheet. If not, rewrite it as it should be. Consider each statement separately. These statements are *not* part of the same program.

   a. ■ `INPUT 1,2,3`
   b. ■ `DATA 4 + 5, 8, "station #1", 1 + 2,2, "station #2"`
   c. ■ `INPUT "Enter your name and address";NAME$,ADDRESS$`
   d. ■ `LET N = "Jones"`
   e. ■ `LET TON$ = "4550"`
   f. ■ `LET Y$ = "A very, very long line of instructions."`
   g. ■ `RESTORE 40`
   h. ■ `READ "MY NAME"`
   i. ■ `LET W,E,S,T,U,V = 45`
   j. ■ `LET GRAPH$(MAXNUM,MAXNUM) = "with all the data."`
   k. ■ `INPUT PROMPT "What is your age and name?" AGE,NAME$`
   l. ■ `LINE INPUT PROMPT "What favorite pets?":PET$1,PET$2,PET$3`
   m. ■ `DATA ""boy"",his!!,Marcy,4,5,Jim`
   n. ■ `PRINT A$ = "Mary"`
   o. ■ `LINE INPUT HODGE$`

2. *Programs to Read.* What will be printed when each of the following programs is run? If input from the keyboard is needed, show some sample input that would fit with the program.

   a. ■ `READ A,X,B`
       ■ `PRINT A,X`

```
▮ DATA 12
▮ DATA 4,5
▮ END
```

b.
```
▮ READ A,X,B
▮ PRINT A,B
▮ DATA SUE,9,20
▮ END
```

c.
```
▮ READ ADD,ADD2,ADD3
▮ PRINT ADD2
▮ DATA 12, 3
▮ END
```

d.
```
▮ READ CAT$,X
▮ PRINT CAT$,X
▮ DATA HENRY,"6",5
▮ END
```

e.
```
▮ LET A = 12
▮ PRINT A
▮ READ D,B
▮ PRINT A + B
▮ DATA 8,10
▮ END
```

f.
```
▮ READ A
▮ READ B
▮ DATA 4,5,6,7,8,9
▮ RESTORE
▮ READ X,Y
▮ PRINT X;" PLUS ";Y;
▮ PRINT " IS ";X + Y
▮ END
```

g.
```
▮ LET R$ = "MELANIE"
▮ LET X = 21
▮ PRINT "IS"
▮ PRINT R$
▮ PRINT X
▮ PRINT R$;" IS "; X
▮ END
```

h.
```
▮ PRINT "SALES OF MILK"
▮ PRINT
▮ READ A$,A,B$,B,C$,C,D$,D,E$,E
▮ PRINT A$,A
▮ DATA MONDAY,TUESDAY,WEDNESDAY, THURSDAY, FRIDAY
▮ DATA 25,26,32,42,38
▮ END
```

i.
```
▮ READ M$
▮ READ B$
▮ DATA SHE
▮ RESTORE
▮ READ F$,J$,L$
▮ READ X$,Y$,Z$
▮ DATA "IS"," THE",WRITER
▮ READ P$,Q$,R$
▮ DATA NOT, "THE", " TYPE"
▮ DATA " HERE"
```

```
█ DATA ANYMORE
█ PRINT J$;L$;P$;X$;Q$
█ END
```

j.
```
█ LINE INPUT PROMPT "LIST 3 OF YOUR FAVORITE FOODS ":FOODS$
█ LET AGE1$,AGE2$,AGE3$ = "AGED"
█ READ AGE1,AGE2,AGE3
█ READ NAM1$,NAM2$,NAM3$
█ PRINT NAM2$;" ";AGE1$;AGE1
█ PRINT NAM1$;" ";AGE3$;AGE1
█ PRINT NAM3$;" ";AGE2$;AGE3
█ PRINT "ALL LIKE ";FOODS$
█ DATA 12,25,26,JIM, MARTY, LARRY
█ END
```

3. To reduce the federal deficit, social welfare programs will be cut by $15,275.80 each. The original budgets are:

Health	$42,756.99
Education	84,546.50
Welfare	92,250.00

Use the computer to print out the new budget amounts and the total reduction in funds for these social programs. (Remember to omit the commas when entering these numbers.)

4. You are pursuing one of America's favorite pastimes, reading the label on your breakfast cereal box. It says:

Percentage of U.S.
Recommended Daily Allowances

1 ounce of Dream Flakes

Protein	2
Vitamin A	25
Vitamin C	35
Iron	8

You have eaten 2 ounces of Dream Flakes this morning. Use the computer to figure out what percentage of these nutrients you still need to consume today. Practice using the LET statement.

5. Write a program that asks for the year you were born. Have the computer print out the year you will retire and how many more years you must work before that date arrives.

6. Show how friendly the computer can be: Write a program that addresses the user by name. Ask the user to enter one adverb, one noun, one adjective, and one verb. Print out a silly sentence using these words.

7. Write a program that stores the following data, reads them, and prints out the total of points scored for each hockey player, along with his name. Print out the total points scored by the group.

Player's Name	Points per Period		
Marvin	1	0	0
Peter	2	2	1
Fred	1	1	1
Alan	2	0	1
Bill	0	1	1

8. Every registered voter in Democracy has been asked to phone two adults in his or her precinct to ask them to register to vote in the upcoming election. Write a program that stores the following numbers of callers in each precinct and have it print out the total calls made in each. Also, print out the grand total of phone calls.

Precinct	Registered Voters
A	5,600
B	10,890
C	7,806
D	55,090
E	43,567

9. Mr. Jones and Mr. Smith each decided to buy the sailboat that was recently marked down from $1100 to $1000 for the Labor Day sale. Mr. Jones borrowed the purchase price and agreed to pay it back in one year with 14% interest. Mr. Smith decided not to borrow money but to save his pennies each month and purchase the boat outright at the end of the year. In so doing he lost the advantage of the sale price and was victimized by inflation that raised the regular price of the boat by 10%.

   Use the computer to determine how much more Mr. Smith paid for his sailboat. Express the difference as the amount as well as the percent increase over Jones's expense.

10. Swifty Spritz is training for the Olympics as a freestyle swimmer. She swims 3 hours before breakfast and 2½ hours each evening during the week. On Saturdays, she swims for 6 hours and on Sundays she takes a complete rest. Every minute she swims four lengths in the 25-yard pool, and each half-hour she burns 250 calories.

    Use the computer to determine how many calories Swifty must add to her weekly diet in order not to lose weight during this period in her life. Also, calculate how many miles she swims each week.

11. Use the computer to express your age in terms of years, months, and days. Assume the average month has 30.4167 days.

Chapter 6

Decisions: The IF and SELECT CASE statements

Computers are automatons that do whatever they are told, whenever they are told, for however long they're told to work. In this diligence they far surpass human beings. They don't take coffee breaks or holidays or even a nap. They never get angry or fall in love, but, rather, give single-minded attention to the most tedious chores.

Yet computers are as dumb as they are diligent. If you set them in operation and never tell them to stop, they won't stop. This ability to proceed automatically is, indeed, a fundamental reason for the existence of computers as we know them, but it must be channeled to produce meaningful solutions to real problems.

There are two control structures that allow the computer to vary from working line-by-line from first program instruction to last: "true-false" and "case." These control structures change the direction of control according to preset or even spontaneously created conditions. In some sense, they enable the computer to make decisions, thus making the computer far more powerful than calculators or than mere automatons working repetitiously at a single set of tasks. In some sense, they make the computer a thinking machine.

This chapter describes these two control structures and explains how to use the two True BASIC statements that implement them: the IF statement, which evaluates one or a series of expressions and branches accordingly, and the SELECT CASE statement, which tests the value of a single variable or expression and chooses among several alternative branches.

The true-false control structure

The true-false structure sends control along one particular path if a condition is true, and along another path if the condition is false.

In our daily lives, we frequently function according to a similar decision-making structure. For instance, IF it is snowing, THEN wear boots; ELSE (if it is not snowing) wear shoes. Figure 6-1 illustrates the flow of control through an if-then-else structure. There are two paths of control through this structure: the true path and the false path. Control enters into the decision diamond, the test is made, and, depending upon the result, control follows the true or the false path. Finally, control flows out of the structure.

Figure 6-1. True-false control structure

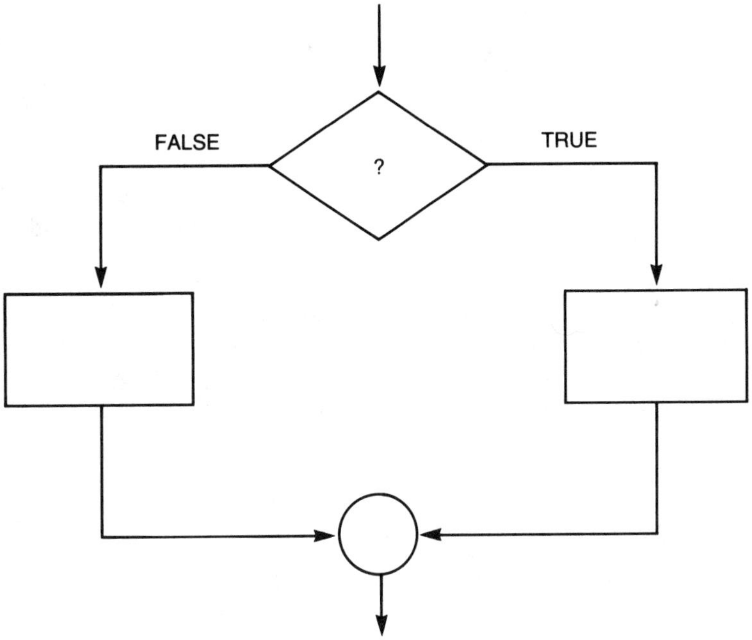

The IF statement

IF

The IF statement is the True BASIC equivalent of the true-false control structure. It tests for a condition and, depending on the result, channels control into one of two paths: the true path or the false path. Regardless of which path is executed, when processing along the path is complete, control returns to the line following the END IF statement. Figure 6-2 uses the IF statement to determine whether or not zero has been entered at the keyboard. The IF statement asks a question and makes a choice. It asks if DENOM is 0. If that is "true," it sends control to the line following THEN, and the computer prints messages rejecting the denominator and refusing to do any arithmetic. If the answer is "false" (DENOM is a number other than zero), the IF statement bypasses the true path and sends control to the routine following the ELSE statement. In this example the computer responds politely and performs the division. When processing of either the true or the false path is complete, the computer prints the farewell message and the program ends.

Figure 6-3 presents a flowchart of this program which makes its relationship to the true-false control structure clear. Control enters at the IF statement

Figure 6-2. The IF statement

```
INPUT PROMPT "What is the numerator ":NUMER
INPUT PROMPT "What is the denominator? ":DENOM
PRINT
IF DENOM = 0 THEN
    PRINT "Denominator invalid"
    PRINT "No division possible"
ELSE
    PRINT "Thank you"
    PRINT NUMER;"divided by";DENOM;"is";NUMER/DENOM
END IF
PRINT
PRINT "Here ends today's lesson."
END
```

```
Ok. run
What is the numerator 5
What is the denominator? 0

Denominator invalid
No division possible

Here ends today's lesson.
Ok. run
What is the numerator 5
What is the denominator? 2

Thank you
 5 divided by 2 is 2.5

Here ends today's lesson.
Ok.
```

check, branches in the true or false direction, and returns to the main line to exit from the structure.

Relational operators

Aside from equals, there are several other relations that the IF statement can evaluate. The numeric relations and their signs are listed in Figure 6-4.

The program of Figure 6-5 sorts out those youngsters who are old enough to vote (age 18 years or older). Notice that it is unnecessary to write an IF statement to check for any age below 18. Knowing how the relational operator works in the IF statement, you know that if control ever reaches the ELSE path, the computer has proven the age is less than 18. There is no need to check again.

You can use variables, constants, or arithmetic expressions in a relational expression. The computer evaluates the arithmetic expressions first and then compares them. All of the following IF statements have valid relational expressions:

Figure 6–3. The IF statement structure

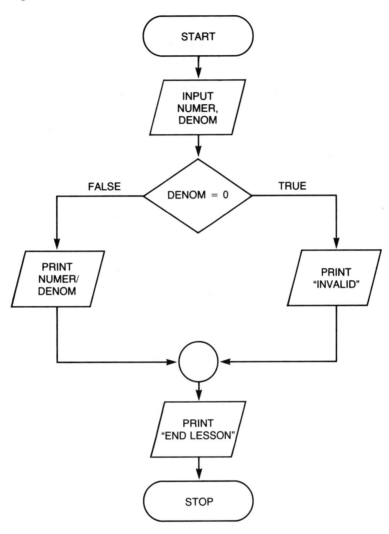

Figure 6–4. Numeric relational operators

Sign			Relation
$=$			equal to
$>$			greater than
$<$			less than
$>=$	or	$=>$	greater than or equal to
$<=$	or	$=<$	less than or equal to
$<>$	or	$><$	not equal to

String comparisons in IF statements

Facts as well as numbers can be evaluated and used to direct the computer. This occurs when you make relational comparisons of character-string data. Figure 6–6 lists the relational signs that have meaning for string comparisons.

Figure 6-5. Relational operators in the IF statement

```
INPUT PROMPT "How old are you? ":AGE
PRINT
IF AGE >=18 THEN
    PRINT "You may vote."
ELSE
    PRINT "You are too young."
    PRINT "You must wait"; 18 - AGE;"years."
END IF
PRINT "Thank you. You are a good citizen."
END
```

```
Ok. run
How old are you? 12

You are too young.
You must wait 6 years.
Thank you. You are a good citizen.
Ok. run
How old are you? 23

You may vote.
Thank you. You are a good citizen.
Ok.

IF price + tax > budget THEN
.
.
ELSE
.
.
END IF

IF time - 2 = workday THEN
.
.
ELSE
.
.
END IF

IF 16^3 = C/3 THEN
.
.
ELSE
.
.
END IF

IF distance >= time THEN
.
.
ELSE
.
.
END IF
```

Figure 6–6. String relational operators

Sign	Relation	Character meaning
=	equal to	Identical, with no trailing or leading blanks
<	less than	Closer to the beginning of the alphabet, identical but shorter
>	greater than	Closer to the end of the alphabet, identical but longer
<> or ><	not equal to	

The program of Figure 6–7 sends ticket holders to their seats. The theater manager has decided that all people whose names come before M in the alphabet must sit in the balcony; the other patrons must sit in the orchestra. The IF statement relational expression asks whether the name stored in NAME$ is closer to the beginning of the alphabet than is the letter M. Depending upon the answer, the computer sends control along one path or the other. When *Smith* is entered and stored in LNAME$, the relational comparison proves false, because *Smith* comes after M in the alphabet. Control jumps to the ELSE path and the message "Sit in the orchestra" appears. When *Banks* is entered, the comparison is true. *Banks* goes up to the balcony.

Figure 6–7. String relational operators in the IF statement

```
▌ INPUT PROMPT "What is your last name? ":LNAME$
▌ PRINT
▌ IF LNAME$ < "M" THEN
▌     PRINT "Sit in the balcony."
▌ ELSE
▌     PRINT "Sit in the orchestra."
▌ END IF
▌ PRINT
▌ PRINT "Welcome to the Bijou!"
▌ END
```

```
Ok. run
What is your last name? Smith

Sit in the orchestra.

Welcome to the Bijou!
Ok. run
What is your last name? Banks

Sit in the balcony.

Welcome to the Bijou!
Ok.
```

The computer is really making numerical comparisons when it processes character data in relational expressions. It compares the ASCII code equivalents for the characters and branches accordingly. This means that the computer considers lowercase letters that have a higher ASCII value to be greater than capital letters. Thus, the comparison

```
"a" > "D"
```

is true.

One great advantage of using character data is that doing so humanizes computing. Still, you must proceed somewhat cautiously. Programs that manipulate strings are more likely to come up against human inconsistencies than programs that process only numbers.

When it comes to language, humans are capricious, but computers never are. For example, a programmer might type the "M" in the Figure 6–7 program as " M" or "M "—that is, with leading or trailing blanks. However, in accepting responses to INPUT, True BASIC always trims leading and trailing spaces. Thus, the computer would compare the M entered that has no trailing or leading space with the programmer's string that includes a space. The computer would consider *(space)* M to be less than M, and M *(space)* to be greater than M.

String comparisons are based on the first character of each character string. If the first characters are the same, the second characters are compared and so on. If entire strings are identical, the comparisons are based on the length of the strings. In the first instance above, a blank space has a lower numeric equivalent than M. In the second instance, the blank space appended to M makes it a longer string than M alone. If all else is equal, longer strings are greater than shorter ones.

True BASIC includes many string-handling functions that help check for and accommodate such inconsistencies. In later chapters you will see that, with meticulous programming, you can use string functions to create appropriate computer responses.

Logical operators

You can form logical expressions in True BASIC by using the logical operators AND, OR, and NOT. Before you begin experimenting, take a minute to look at Figure 6–8 to remind yourself of the truth tables for the logical operators available in True BASIC.

Figure 6–8. True BASIC AND, OR, NOT logical operators

a	b	a AND b	a OR b	NOT a
true	true	true	true	false
true	false	false	true	false
false	true	false	true	true
false	false	false	false	true

The True BASIC logical expressions are formed by combining relational expressions with the logical operators. Some True BASIC logical expressions are:

```
6 > X OR S < X

6 > X AND S < X

NOT COST = 0
```

The OR and AND operators must be flanked on either side by a relational expression. The computer evaluates each expression and then evaluates the logical operation. The logical expression

```
2+3 > 4 OR 3^2 = 7
```

is evaluated according to the following sequence.

Operation	Intermediate result
1. $2+3 > 4 \rightarrow$ true	true OR $3^2 = 7$
2. $3^2 = 7 \rightarrow$ false	true OR false
3. true OR false	true

As a result of this evaluation, a program such as

```
IF 2+3 > 4 OR 3^2=7 THEN
    PRINT "strange, but true"
ELSE
    PRINT "just plain strange"
END IF
```

would follow the true path and print "strange, but true."

The NOT operator takes one relational expression. If the result of the relational expression is true, the result of the NOT logical expression is false. If the result of the relational expression is false, the result of the NOT logical operation is true. Thus a NOT expression in the statement

```
IF NOT 3^2=7 THEN
    PRINT "strange, but true"
ELSE
    PRINT "just plain strange"
END IF
```

would also produce the message "strange, but true." The expression $3^2 = 7$ is false. Logically the expression "NOT false" means true.

True BASIC evaluates logical expressions as it does arithmetic ones. Figure 6–9 shows the True BASIC hierarchy of logical operators.

With respect to the logical operators, the statement

```
IF 10 > 4 AND NOT 10>6       THEN
    PRINT "10 is within range."
ELSE
    PRINT "10 is not usable."
END IF
```

follows the sequence

Operation	Intermediate result
1. 10>16 $\rightarrow$ false	$10 > 4$ AND NOT false
2. NOT false $\rightarrow$ true	$10 > 4$ AND true
3. 10>4 $\rightarrow$ true	true AND true
4. true AND true	true

and prints "10 is within range."

Figure 6–9. True BASIC hierarchy of logical operators

highest priority	NOT
	AND
lowest priority	OR

One-line IF statements

True BASIC allows you to simplify and write a complete IF statement on one line. All you need to do is append a complete True BASIC statement after the THEN, as shown in Figure 6–10. Notice that the construction is really an if-then-else structure, with a null, or empty, false path.

Figure 6–10. Simple IF statement

```
▪ INPUT PROMPT "What month is it? ": MONTH$
▪ PRINT
▪ IF MONTH$ = "May" THEN PRINT "Spring is here!"
▪ PRINT "I love Springtime!"
▪ END
```

```
Ok. run
What month is it? September

I love Springtime!
Ok. run
What month is it? May

Spring is here!
I love Springtime!
Ok.
```

Though Figure 6–10 may seem easy to follow, one-line IF statements often are difficult to read. For this reason, structured programming requires that you stick to the complete IF statements except in the most straightforward situations. Using a null ELSE (or THEN) clause that has no programming statements also documents the fact that you have considered the null path and chosen to not use it. Thus, although it takes more typing, the program of Figure 6–11 is an example of better programming style than the simpler program of Figure 6–10. Its logic is unmistakably clear. This program shows that if the IF-statement test results send control on a null path, nothing happens and control continues right along to the line following END IF. If *January* is entered, for example, control falls to the ELSE path, which is null, and then exits the loop. The message "I love Springtime" appears.

True BASIC even allows you to write complex IF statements on one line. Figure 6–12 illustrates this situation. Both paths in the if-then-else structure exist in the one line. The computer performs the same as with a structured IF statement.

Figure 6-11. A structured simple IF statement

```
▌ INPUT PROMPT "What month is it? ":MONTH$
▌ PRINT
▌ IF MONTH$ = "May" THEN
▌    PRINT "Spring is here!"
▌ ELSE
▌ END IF
▌ PRINT "I love Springtime!"
▌ END
```

```
Ok. run
What month is it? January

I love Springtime!
Ok. run
What month is it? May

Spring is here!
I love Springtime!
Ok.
```

When the test result is true the statement following THEN executes, and control falls to the line following the IF statement. HIGH takes the value *A* and this value is printed. When the test result is false control falls to the statement following ELSE and then to the line following the IF statement. HIGH takes the value *B* and this value is printed. Structured programmers prefer, of course, to write this program as seen in Figure 6-13.

Figure 6-12. A complex one-line IF statement

```
▌ PRINT "Enter two numbers."
▌ INPUT A,B
▌ If A>B THEN LET HIGH = A ELSE LET HIGH = B
▌ PRINT "The highest number entered was"; HIGH
▌ END
```

```
Ok. run
Enter two numbers.
? 23,55
The highest number entered was 55
Ok. run
Enter two numbers.
? 45,8
The highest number entered was 45
Ok. run
Enter two numbers.
? 450,78
The highest number entered was 450
Ok.
```

Figure 6-13. A structured IF statement

```
PRINT "Enter two numbers."
INPUT A,B
IF A>B THEN
    LET HIGH = A
ELSE
    LET HIGH = B
END IF
PRINT "The highest number entered was"; HIGH
END
```

```
Ok. run
Enter two numbers.
? 23,55
The highest number entered was 55
Ok. run
Enter two numbers.
? 45,8
The highest number entered was 45
Ok. run
Enter two numbers.
? 450,88
The highest number entered was 450
Ok.
```

The ELSE IF clause

Frequently you need to choose between more than two alternatives. Structured IF statements with ELSE IF clauses make this possible. In these statements the computer checks a series of relational expressions each of which has an associated block of statements to execute when true. If none of the tests prove true, the structure provides a false (ELSE) path. Figure 6-14 uses this structure to find the largest of three numbers.

This IF statement has two "true" paths and one "false" path that is shared by both IF decisions. When stripped of the number-checking logic, the statement looks something like

```
IF A> B THEN
      [true path]
ELSE IF C> B THEN
      [true path]
ELSE
      [false path]
END IF
```

Control falls to the ELSE IF check when the first IF statement check proves false. IF both the first IF check and the ELSE IF check prove false, then control falls to the

Figure 6-14. An IF statement with ELSE IF

```
PRINT "Enter three numbers."
INPUT A,B,C
IF A>B THEN
    IF A>C THEN
        LET HIGH = A
    ELSE
        LET HIGH = C
    END IF
ELSE IF C>B THEN
    LET HIGH = C
ELSE
    LET HIGH = B
END IF
PRINT "The highest number entered was";high;"."
END
```

```
Ok. run
Enter three numbers.
? 34,56,1
The highest number entered was 56 .
Ok. run
Enter three numbers.
? 67,23,90
The highest number entered was 90 .
Ok.
```

ELSE path. Once processing is complete along any of the paths, control jumps out of the IF statement to the next line of the program.

In these IF, ELSE IF combinations you may have as many ELSE IF clauses as you wish. Although True BASIC lets you leave out the ELSE path, with statements that use ELSE IF it is particularly important to take time to put in the null ELSE. Then anyone reading the program knows you have considered the "false" path and chosen not to use it.

The case control structure

The case structure makes it possible to select which of several forms of an item or expression is true and to send control along an appropriate program path. For any given situation it says: If alternative 1 does not apply, try alternative 2. If that does not apply, try the next. And so on. Weary travelers use case processing every day: "If today is Monday, we must be in Portugal," they sigh. "If today is Tuesday, we must be in France."

Figure 6-15 flowcharts the case structure. Control enters the structure by defining the item or expression to be evaluated. It passes from one case check to another, comparing the item or expression with alternative values until a match, or "true" test, occurs. Then control follows the programming path associated with the

Figure 6–15. Case control structure

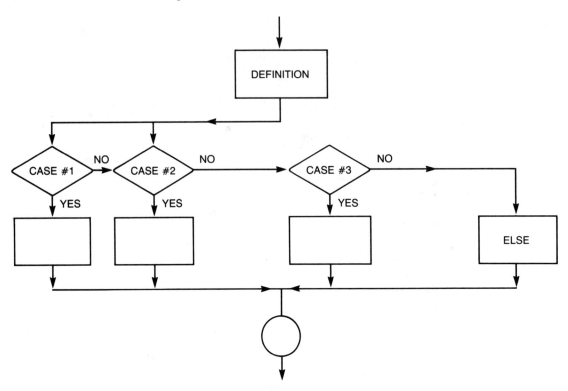

"true" case and, when that processing is complete, it passes out of the structure. If none of the alternative cases are true, the case structure provides an *otherwise* clause to handle the exceptional situation.

The SELECT CASE statement

```
SELECT
CASE
```

The SELECT CASE statement is True BASIC's implementation of the case control structure. It provides an efficient way to take a look at a string or numeric variable or expression and see, during the run of the program, if it has attained any one of several possible values. A common programming practice, for example, is to give a value to a variable (setting a flag) in one module and passing the flag on to the next module in the sequence of program control. The receiving module begins by testing the flag and taking action dependent on the result. The SELECT CASE statement makes flag testing easy.

Figure 6–16 uses the SELECT CASE statement to check a flag set by a module whose job is to read and validate a data file record. The flag gives the receiving module the information it needs in order to proceed.

The flag settings in Figure 6–16 are entered during the program run. In real

Figure 6-16. The SELECT CASE statement

```
■ PRINT "Enter the flag setting."
■ INPUT FLAG
■ SELECT CASE FLAG
■ CASE IS = 4
■       PRINT "Seniors dine in Commencement Hall."
■ CASE IS = 3
■       PRINT "Juniors dine in the Pub."
■ CASE IS = 2
■       PRINT "Sophomores eat in the Fast-Food Factory."
■ CASE IS = 1
■       PRINT "Freshmen are often very hungry."
■ CASE IS = 0
■       PRINT "Insufficient data, can't proceed."
■ END SELECT
■ PRINT "Flag checking completed."
■ END
```

```
Ok. run
Enter the flag setting.
? 0
Insufficient data, can't proceed.
Flag checking completed.
Ok. run
Enter the flag setting.
? 3
Juniors dine in the Pub.
Flag checking completed.
Ok.
```

life, as later chapters explain, flag settings are passed internally from one module to another. The possible flags settings are:

Flag setting	Meaning
4	Senior
3	Junior
2	Sophomore
1	Freshman
0	Invalid record

The CASE clause

In the SELECT CASE statement, the CASE clauses check the variable or expression against all possible values, or cases. If a match occurs, control falls to the appropriate statement or block of statements and then jumps to the line following END SELECT.

Figure 6-17 provides a flowchart of the SELECT CASE example. Notice that it matches the case control structure picture in Figure 6-15.

Figure 6–17. The SELECT CASE statement structure

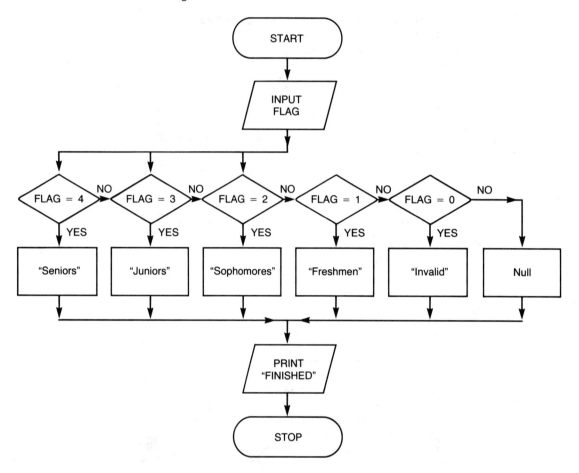

The CASE ELSE clause

The SELECT CASE statement includes a CASE ELSE clause, which sends control to the block of code that is executed if no match is found among the cases. Use of CASE ELSE is optional, but it is often dangerous not to include it. Unlike if-then-else, failure to find a "true" CASE or CASE ELSE match causes a True BASIC run-time error that stops your program. Once the CASE ELSE clause is executed, control exits to the line following END SELECT.

SELECT CASE tests

The tests made by the CASE clause can be one of five types:

Case tests	Sample CASE clause
a constant	"Monday"
group of constants	2,4,6,8
low to high (numeric)	1 TO 100
low to high (string)	"A" to "Z"
IS (operator) constant	IS >= 18

Figure 6–18 uses the SELECT CASE statement to evaluate an expression according to a low-to-high test. It calculates the semester grade and then prints a report card.

Figure 6–18. The SELECT CASE statement

```
INPUT PROMPT "What is the student's name? ":STUDENT$
INPUT PROMPT "What are the three test scores? ":A,B,C
PRINT
PRINT "Report Card for: ";STUDENT$
PRINT
SELECT CASE ROUND ((A+B+C)/3)
CASE 90 TO 100
     PRINT "** A **"
CASE 80 TO 89
     PRINT "** B **"
CASE 70 TO 79
     PRINT "** C **"
CASE 60 TO 69
     PRINT "** D **"
CASE 1 TO 59
     PRINT "** F **"
CASE ELSE
     PRINT "Incomplete"
END SELECT
PRINT "BIOLOGY 101"
END
```

```
Ok. run
What is the student's name? Jones
What are the three test scores? 80,83,90

Report Card for: Jones

** B **
BIOLOGY 101
Ok. run
What is the student's name? Smith
What are the three test scores? 0,0,0

Report Card for: Smith

Incomplete
BIOLOGY 101
Ok.
```

Any of the problems solved by the SELECT CASE statement can be solved using other True BASIC statements. This statement is really an organizational tool. Because of this it is an excellent aid to structured programming. As you plan your code, consider using SELECT CASE whenever you can. The combination of computing power and organizational structure it provides will make your programs easy to write, maintain, and understand.

Summary

The computer's ability to vary from working line-by-line from the first program instruction to the last enables it to make decisions.

Programming skills

The IF statement
One-line IF statements
The SELECT CASE statement

Computer concepts

True-false control structure
Relational operations
Logical operations
Case control structure

Review questions

1. *Corrections.* Determine whether each of the following True BASIC statements or programs is correct. If it is, write "correct" on your answer sheet. If not, rewrite it correctly. Consider each statement or program separately. These exercises are not part of the same program.

   a. ▮ `IF Y = 76 THEN PRINT "Soda Crackers."`

   b. ▮ `IF FOOD$ = "Grapefruit" AND "Apples" THEN`
      ▮ `     PRINT "Grocery Department"`
      ▮ `ELSE`
      ▮ `     PRINT "Meat Department"`
      ▮ `END IF`

   c. ▮ `IF A > B THEN LET Y = Y + 3 ELSE PRINT Z`

   d. ▮ `INPUT AGE`
      ▮ `SELECT CASE FLAG`
      ▮ `CASE IS >= 18`
      ▮ `    PRINT "You may drive."`
      ▮ `CASE ELSE`
      ▮ `    PRINT "You are too young to drive."`
      ▮ `END SELECT`

   e. ▮ `IF "end" > N$ THEN PRINT "finished."`

   f. ▮ `IF A > B AND NOT A<C THEN`

   g. ▮ `PRINT "The matrix has triple subscripts." THEN GOTO 40`

   h. ▮ `IF MEM$ = Memorial Day THEN LET P = P + 5`

   i. ▮ `IF INT 23.5 = Y THEN`

   j. ▮ `IF AT = 45 AND ET = 55 AND MT = 23 OR LT = 24 THEN`

2. *Programs to Read.* What will be printed when each of the following programs is run? If input from the keyboard is needed, show some sample input that would fit the program.

   a. ▮ `LET H = 1`
      ▮ `PRINT H + H^2`
      ▮ `LET H = (H + 1)^2`
      ▮ `IF H>=10 THEN`
      ▮ `    PRINT "You have exceeded the limit."`

```
■ ELSE
■     PRINT "You are under the limit. Proceed."
■ END IF
■ END
```
b.
```
■ INPUT PROMPT "Enter your final score: ":SCORE
■ PRINT "Your adjusted score is: "
■ SELECT CASE ROUND((SCORE*2 + SCORE*1.677)/3.677)
■ CASE 0 TO 60
■     PRINT "NOT SO HOT!"
■ CASE 60 TO 80
■     PRINT "BETTER"
■ CASE 80 TO 90
■     PRINT "MUCH BETTER"
■ CASE ELSE
■     PRINT "SUPERIOR"
■ END SELECT
■ END
```
c.
```
■ LET TO = 24
■ LET TE = 20
■ IF TO > TE OR NOT TE <= 3^5 THEN
■     PRINT "You may move on to the next round."
■ ELSE
■     PRINT "You are required to play this one again."
■ END IF
■ END
```
d.
```
■ READ A$,B$
■ IF A$ = "-1" THEN
■     PRINT "That's all folks."
■ ELSE
■     RESTORE
■     READ Q$
■ END IF
■ IF Q$ = "-1" THEN
■     READ A$,B$
■ ELSE
■     PRINT Q$
■ END IF
■ PRINT A$
■ DATA "The duck family"
■ DATA -1, Huey, Looey, Duey
■ END
```
e.
```
■ LET T = 23
■ IF " Christmas" <= "christmas" THEN
■     LET T = T + 3
■ ELSE
■     LET T = T + 15
■ END IF
■ PRINT T^2
■ END
```

3. To attract new business, a snack bar is offering sodas at a nickel per can, with a limit of six cans per customer. Write a program that monitors the quantity sold to each customer and prints a warning if the customer tries to buy too many.

4. Write a computer program that asks a person for her age. If she is 18 or over, tell her she is old enough to drive. Otherwise, tell her how long she must wait.

5. Write a program that asks the U.S. Olympic cross-country skiing coach for the time, in minutes and seconds, of the gold, silver, and bronze medalists in the 30-kilometer event. If anyone is less than a second faster than the next-slowest time, have the computer print THIS WAS REALLY A TIE FOR THE _____ MEDAL.

6. Use the SELECT CASE statement to send ticket holders to their seats. As the tickets are shown, have the patrons enter their first names, and send everyone whose name

comes before "M" to sit in the balcony and everyone else to sit in the orchestra. Allow for special people with the name Fred; send them to sit in the Royal Boxes.

7. Use the SELECT CASE statement to toss a coin and declare either "Heads, you win" or "Tails, you lose."

8. Use the SELECT CASE statement to sort bathing suits by size and price. When a customer enters the size she wishes, the computer reports its price. Use the following chart:

Size	Price
2, 4, 6	$32.50
8, 10, 12	34.50
14, 16, 18	36.50

9. Use the SELECT CASE statement to inform wrestlers of the weight class they'll be in today. Have the team member enter today's weight and have the computer print out the wrestler's class based on the following chart:

Weight Range	Wrestling Class
121–130	Bantam
131–140	Light
141–150	Middle
151–160	Heavy
161 and up	Unlimited

10. Use the SELECT CASE statement to simulate the use of the bar code by grocery stores. Each unique combination of binary digits represents a grocery item. Depending upon the bar code combination received as input, the computer prints out the item's name, size, and current price. If, for example, the bar code produces the binary digits "01110," the computer prints: Chocolate Candy, 6 oz., $.45. The computer also uses the entered amount of the item to calculate how much the customer must pay. If, for example, 12 oz. of chocolate candy is purchased, the computer prints: You must pay $.90. Ask the user to enter the bar code and the quantity of the item purchased, in ounces. Assume a two-digit bar code in which the combination "00" indicates the customer has no more purchases.

## Chapter 7

Loops: The DO and FOR loops

If computers did nothing more than repeat tasks efficiently and tirelessly, as they do when they are under the control of a programming loop, they would still have revolutionized the way we process information. The capability to automatically carry on with a job is one of the fundamental contributions computers have made to the problem of coping with enormous amounts of information and data.

True BASIC provides two pairs of statements that create loop control structures: DO and LOOP statements and the FOR and NEXT statements. The DO-LOOP combination provides controls by testing relational operations. The FOR-NEXT combination provides controls by testing the progression of arithmetic values. Both kinds of loop are powerful tools for writing structured code. This chapter illustrates loop control structures and then explains how to use the statements that create them.

The leading decision loop. A loop is a sequence of program statements that executes over and over again. An endless loop must be ended by aborting the run of a program. Other loops are ended as the result of tests.

With a *leading decision loop* the test for exit is made before the job of the loop is done even once. Depending on the test result, the loop may be either entered or bypassed completely. If it is entered, the job is done and the test repeated.

Many of us enter a kind of leading decision loop when we wake up in the morning. We ask, for example, "Is it 7:15 yet?" If the answer is no, we doze, and then a little later we ask again, "Is it 7:15 yet?" When, finally, the answer is yes, we hop out of bed. One thing is sure: We ask the question before setting even one foot on the floor. We are functioning in a leading decision loop. Figure 7–1 depicts the flow of control in such a leading decision loop.

The trailing decision loop. Some days we function in a trailing decision loop. We work for a while and then ask, "Is it 5:00 PM yet?" If the answer is no, we go back to

Figure 7-1. Leading decision loop control structure

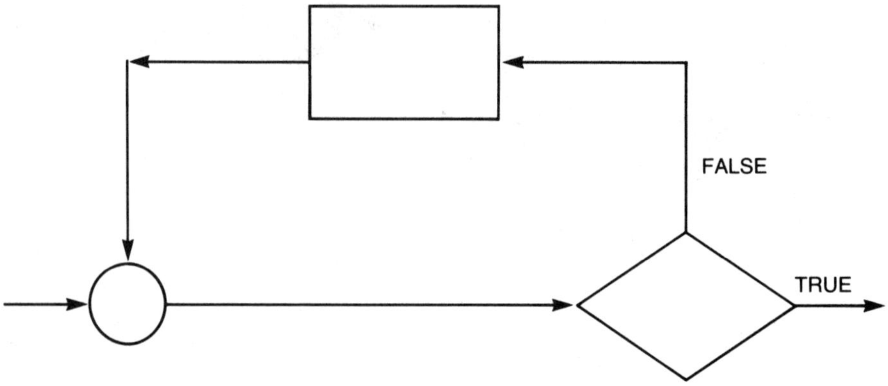

the job, and then a little later we ask, "Is it 5:00 PM yet?" When the answer is yes, the repetition ends and we leave the loop. Figure 7-2 illustrates the structure of a trailing decision loop.

The DO and LOOP statements

The DO statement tells the computer to begin a loop. The LOOP statement marks the end of the loop. All of the programming statements between these two statements form the body of the loop and define the job that is to be repeated. Control passes from the DO statement and through the body of the loop, until the LOOP statement is reached. LOOP returns control to the DO statement, which starts the loop again, and the process repeats.

Figure 7-3 shows a loop that prints a greeting to newcomers over and over again. Notice the format of the routine. The body of the loop is indented in order to make clear exactly what the loop does. This example DO loop has no mechanism for stopping. It is an *infinite loop* that can only be halted by aborting the run of the program.

Sometimes such endless loops are useful. Usually, however, you need to create a loop that completes when an existing condition ceases or when a previously nonexistent condition finally occurs. Just as some runners keep on running *while*

Figure 7-2. Trailing decision loop control structure

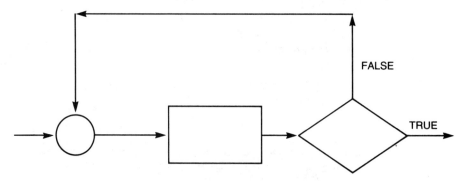

Figure 7-3. An infinite DO loop

```
■ DO
■
■      PRINT "How DO you DO?"
■      PRINT "You LOOP DO you?"
■
■ LOOP
■ END
```

```
Ok. run
How DO you DO?
You LOOP DO you?
How DO you DO?
You LOOP DO you?
How DO you DO?
       .
       .
       .
```

there is no pain and others keep on running *until* they reach the finish line, your program loops can continue WHILE a condition exists or UNTIL a condition becomes true. In True BASIC the DO and LOOP statements have WHILE and UNTIL modifiers that control the number of times a loop repeats by making such checks on changing conditions.

The DO WHILE and DO UNTIL loops

Loops with WHILE or UNTIL modifying the DO statement are leading decision loops. At the outset of the loop, the computer checks for the condition that would end the looping. Depending upon the result of the WHILE or UNTIL test on the DO statement, the computer either proceeds with the loop or bypasses it and sends control to the line following the LOOP statement.

Figure 7-4 gives a program loop that keeps track of the number of guesses required until the correct answer is entered. It is a leading decision loop. GUESS$, the variable whose value controls exit from the loop, is set to an initial value of "Unknown." This ensures passage through the loop at least one time. The DO statement checks the value of GUESS$, and if it is not equal to *Victoria*, the correct answer, control falls into the loop. Once a new GUESS$ is entered and the COUNT incremented, the LOOP statement sends control back to the DO statement. The DO WHILE combination checks again to see if GUESS$ has been set equal to *Victoria*. When GUESS$ finally does have the value *Victoria*, control jumps past the loop to the PRINT statement, which is the next executable statement following the LOOP statement.

You can replace the DO WHILE statement with DO UNTIL if you wish. As Figure 7-5 shows, when you do so, the programming result is the same.

Whether to use DO WHILE or DO UNTIL depends upon how you prefer to phrase the question that ends the looping process. Use DO WHILE if you prefer to proceed while a condition is true and exit when it becomes false. If you prefer to

Figure 7-4. A DO WHILE loop

```
■ LET COUNT = 0
■ LET GUESS$ = "Unknown"
■ PRINT "What is the capital of British Columbia?";
■ DO WHILE GUESS$ <> "Victoria"
■     INPUT GUESS$
■     LET COUNT = COUNT + 1
■ LOOP
■ PRINT "You took";COUNT;"guesses."
■ END
```

```
Ok. run
What is the capital of British Columbia? Quebec
? Victoria
You took 2 guesses.
Ok.
```

proceed when a condition is false and exit when it becomes true, use DO UNTIL. In general, use the DO statement modifier that presents your program most clearly.

The flowcharts in Figure 7-6 compare loops controlled by DO WHILE and DO UNTIL checks. Both loops require an initialization step, a leading decision, and a process. DO WHILE loops continue when the decision results are true; DO UNTIL loops continue when the test results are false. Keeping these pictures in mind will help you decide which kind of loop is more appropriate to your particular programming problem.

Figure 7-5. A DO UNTIL loop

```
■ LET COUNT = 0
■ LET GUESS$ = "Unknown"
■ PRINT "What is the capital of British Columbia?";
■ DO UNTIL GUESS$ = "Victoria"
■     INPUT GUESS$
■     LET COUNT = COUNT + 1
■ LOOP
■ PRINT "You took";COUNT;"guesses."
■ END
```

```
Ok. run
What is the capital of British Columbia? Calgary
? Victoria
You took 2 guesses.
Ok.
```

Figure 7-6. Leading decision loops

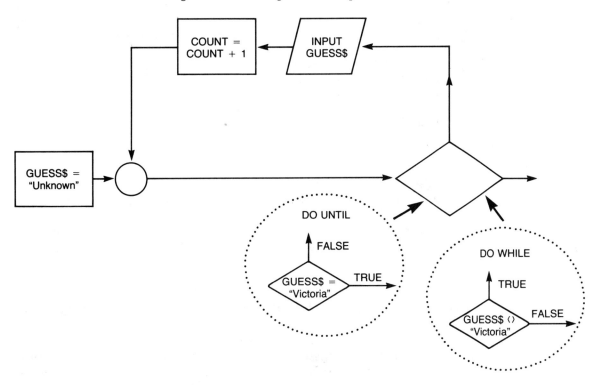

The LOOP WHILE and LOOP UNTIL combinations

Loops with WHILE or UNTIL modifying the LOOP statement are trailing decision loops. The computer does the job of the loop at least one time and then makes the WHILE or UNTIL check when control reaches the LOOP statement. Figure 7-7 performs the same function as the preceding examples; it loops to allow new guesses until the correct answer is entered and counts how many guesses it took to get the correct answer.

The overall logic and the results of the DO (WHILE, UNTIL) and the LOOP (WHILE, UNTIL) loops are the same. Each answer is input, counted, and evaluated. The value of the GUESS$ variable determines whether the loop ends. The *difference* is that, with the LOOP (test) structure, there is no need to initialize GUESS$ before the loop begins in order to be sure that the loop will be executed at least once. The first guess is sure to be made, since control passes to the INPUT statement before the LOOP statement.

Whether you use LOOP modifiers or DO modifiers to control a loop depends upon the problem at hand. For the guessing-game problem, the LOOP WHILE combination is most appropriate. This is because evaluating INPUT is a trailing decision problem, and LOOP WHILE creates a trailing decision loop. You can also use LOOP UNTIL instead of LOOP WHILE, again depending upon how you wish to phrase the exit test. Figure 7-8 illustrates with flowcharts the structure of these loops. There is no initialization step, the body of the loop executes, and the trailing decision is made. If the decision is a WHILE test, the loop continues when the result

Figure 7–7. A LOOP WHILE loop

```
■ LET COUNT = 0
■ PRINT "What is the capital of British Columbia?";
■ DO
■     INPUT GUESS$
■     LET COUNT = COUNT + 1
■ LOOP WHILE GUESS$ <> "Victoria"
■ PRINT "You got it in";COUNT;"guesses."
■ END
```

```
Ok. run
What is the capital of British Columbia? Vancouver
? Toronto
? Victoria
You got it in 3 guesses.
Ok.
```

is "true." If the decision is an UNTIL test, the loop continues when the result is "false."

As the example programs show, you can solve the same problem with any type of loop; the programming steps differ only slightly. You may prefer to always use one style of loop — DO WHILE, for example — and adjust it to suit the problem, or you may prefer to change loop formats as your problem changes. As always, your main concern is what loop structure and exit test is most likely to be understood by others.

Figure 7–8. Trailing decision loops

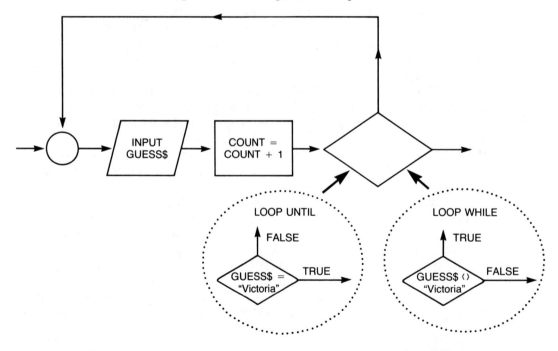

The EXIT DO statement

EXIT
DO

The EXIT DO statement interrupts normal DO-loop processing. It transfers control out of the body of a DO loop and passes it to the line following the LOOP statement. The program of Figure 7–9 determines the highest of a group of scores entered into the computer. It combines EXIT DO with an IF-THEN statement to exit from the loop after all scores have been entered. The end of the scores is signaled by entering −1.

Figure 7–9. An EXIT DO loop

```
LET HIGH = 0
PRINT "ENTER -1 TO STOP"
DO
    INPUT SCORE
    IF SCORE = -1 THEN EXIT DO
    LET HIGH = MAX(HIGH,SCORE)
LOOP
PRINT "The highest score is ";HIGH
END
```

```
Ok. run
ENTER -1 TO STOP
? 90
? 75
? 60
? -1
The highest score is 90
Ok.
```

EXIT DO is actually a type of GO TO statement. Usually, structured programming avoids the use of GO TO because it obscures the flow of control through a program. Therefore, use EXIT DO sparingly — that is, only when doing so simplifies your program without detracting from the clarity of your logic. The example of Figure 7–9 uses EXIT DO wisely — it provides the only exit from the loop.

Even if you never used EXIT DO, you could still solve problems quite easily. Figure 7–10 solves the same problem as the previous example without using EXIT DO. A LOOP UNTIL statement controls exit from the loop. Actually, this routine is shorter than the one using EXIT DO. But, more importantly, it is also easier to understand.

The DATA, file, and keyboard tests

True BASIC includes special tests for controlling loops that process data. These tests, listed in Figure 7–11, check whether data have been entered from the keyboard, a disk file, or a DATA statement. (Don't worry if you don't understand the file tests now; they will make sense after you've had experience with data files.) You can use these tests with the WHILE or UNTIL modifiers to make data processing routines easy to program and understand.

Figure 7-10. A structured loop exit

```
█ LET HIGH = 0
█ DO
█      INPUT SCORE
█      LET HIGH = MAX(HIGH,SCORE)
█ LOOP UNTIL SCORE = -1
█ PRINT "The highest score is ";HIGH
█ END
```

```
Ok. run
? 50
? 80
? -1
The highest score is 80
Ok.
```

Figure 7-12 contains a loop that searches the DATA statement to find whether the name entered matches one in the list. In order to read the data without running past the end if no match is found, the MORE DATA test is used. This test recognizes the end of the data and passes control to the line following the LOOP statement. You could also rewrite the DO statement as DO UNTIL END DATA and achieve the same result.

When you read data from disk files, use DO WHILE MORE #n and DO UNTIL END #n in order to control loops. Chapters 14-17 of this book give more details on how to read True BASIC data files.

To find out when a key has been pressed at the keyboard, you can use KEY INPUT with a DO statement. If you start with the statement

```
DO UNTIL KEY INPUT
```

your program loop continues, perhaps making displays or keeping track of time, until a key is pressed at the keyboard. Then control jumps to the line following the LOOP statement. The routine in Figure 7-13 uses KEY INPUT to keep track of how long the players take to answer a trivia game question. Before the loop begins, START takes the value of TIME, a True BASIC function that gives the time since midnight, in seconds. As the loop progresses the new time is stored in STOP so that as soon as a key is pressed the computer can calculate how much time has passed. Then the game proceeds.

Figure 7-11. True BASIC tests for data

Test	The test is "true" when:
MORE DATA	Some data in a DATA statement have not yet been read
END DATA	There are no data in a DATA statement waiting to be read
MORE #n	Some data in the file on channel #n have not been read
END #n	The file pointer on channel #n is at the end of the file
KEY INPUT	A key has been pressed at the keyboard

Figure 7-12. The MORE DATA test

```
INPUT PROMPT "What is the name of the employee? (enter in capital letters) ":EMPLOYEE$
LET Z$ = "Not Found."
DO WHILE MORE DATA
    READ NAME$
    IF NAME$ = EMPLOYEE$ THEN
        LET Z$ = "Found."
    ELSE
    END IF
LOOP
PRINT Z$
DATA ABLE,BAKER,CHARLES,GROVER,KING
END
```

```
Ok. run
What is the name of the employee? (enter in capital letters) SMITH
Not Found.
Ok.
```

Nested DO loops

Frequently you want to have one loop within another loop. For example, you might want to use the loop in Figure 7-7, page 90, which keeps track of how many guesses it takes to answer a question, as part of a larger program loop that controls how many questions make up a complete quiz. Figure 7-14 shows a program that tests knowledge of the capitals of seven Canadian provinces. It includes one loop to read and print questions and another loop to accept each guess and keep track of how many are needed.

Figure 7-13. The KEY INPUT test

```
PRINT "Press the space bar when you are ready to answer."
LET START = TIME
DO UNTIL KEY INPUT
    LET STOP = TIME
LOOP
LET WAIT = STOP - START
PRINT "Your team waited";WAIT;"seconds."
    .
    .          (Rest of game occurs)
    .
END
```

```
Ok. run
Press the space bar when you are ready to answer.
Your team waited 9.5 seconds.
Ok.
```

Figure 7‑14. Nested DO loops

```
DO WHILE MORE DATA
    LET COUNT = 0
    READ QUESTION$,ANSWER$
    PRINT "What is the capital of ";QUESTION$
    DO
        INPUT GUESS$
        LET COUNT = COUNT +1
    LOOP WHILE GUESS$ <> ANSWER$
    PRINT "You got that one in ";COUNT;" guesses."
    PRINT
LOOP
DATA "British Columbia", Victoria
DATA Alberta, Edmonton
DATA Saskatchewan, Regina
DATA Manitoba, Winnipeg
DATA Ontario, Toronto
DATA Quebec, Quebec
DATA Newfoundland, St. John's
END
```

```
Ok. run
What is the capital of British Columbia
? Winnipeg
? Victoria
You got that one in 2 guesses.

What is the capital of Alberta
? Winnipeg
? Calgary
? Edmonton
You got that one in 3 guesses.

What is the capital of Saskatchewan
?
```

The technique of including one loop within another is known as *nesting*. It has the important requirement that the inner loop must run to completion during a single iteration of the outer loop. In Figure 7‑14, the entire process of accepting and evaluating guesses for one question is completed before a new question is read and printed. Figure 7‑15 diagrams the structure of nested loops.

When they are properly nested, all of the loops have a chance to run to completion. If the proper LOOP statement is not matched with the proper DO statement, the results will be confusing and you will have a hard time figuring out what has gone awry. Indenting the loops as in Figure 7‑15 helps you keep track of what you are doing as much as it helps your readers. Have as many loops within one another as you like, but be sure to nest them like paper cups in a stack — one inside another.

Figure 7-15. The structure of nested DO loops

```
DO WHILE MORE DATA
.
.
.
    DO
      .
      .
      .
    LOOP WHILE GUESS$ <> ANSWER$
.
.
.
LOOP
```

The FOR and NEXT statements

FOR

NEXT

The FOR and NEXT statements control looping by means of a counter that increments with each pass through the loop. Use them when you know beforehand exactly how many times you want a loop to repeat or when you want a succession of values that begins where you specify, ends where you specify, and increases or decreases at a regular interval that you specify.

FOR loops are leading decision loops. The FOR statement tells the computer that a loop is beginning and makes the test to see if the loop is complete. The NEXT statement is the last one in the loop. It returns control to the start. All of the statements in between form the body of the loop, which may range from a few short lines to a lengthy program module.

The program of Figure 7-16 uses the FOR-NEXT combination to print a greeting to newcomers three times. INDEX, the loop control variable, is a numeric variable that stores the value used to determine when to exit from the loop. This value is incremented with each iteration. The FOR and NEXT statements work together to control exit from the loop, a decision they make by incrementing and checking the value of the loop control variable with each pass through the loop. The FOR statement sets the starting and ending values of the control variable and, as the loop progresses, keeps track of whether this variable has gone beyond its ending limit. If it has, there is no more looping, and control jumps to the line following the

Figure 7-16. A FOR loop

```
■ FOR INDEX = 1 TO 3
■     PRINT "Welcome to True BASIC!"
■ NEXT INDEX
■ PRINT "Another job well done."
■ END
```

```
Ok. run
Welcome to True BASIC!
Welcome to True BASIC!
Welcome to True BASIC!
Another job well done.
Ok.
```

NEXT statement. If the control variable has not exceeded its limit, the loop repeats another time. The NEXT statement adds 1 to the value of the control variable at the end of each pass through the loop and then sends control back to the FOR statement. In this example, INDEX starts at 1 and progresses to 3. A greeting appears each time. At the end of the third pass through the loop, the NEXT statement raises INDEX from 3 to 4 and returns control to the FOR statement for checking. When FOR discovers that INDEX exceeds 3, control falls out of the loop and the message "Another job well done" is printed. INDEX retains the value 4; the loop is completed.

Using the control variable

The control variable has many more uses than just storing the incremental values of the loop. It is useful within the loop as well. The FOR-NEXT statements in Figure 7–17 give the loop control variable, CONTROL, a succession of values from 1 to 5. The program uses these control variable values to produce a table of the squares and cubes of the numbers in the succession.

Figure 7–17. Using the control variable within the loop

```
■ PRINT "NUMBER","SQUARE","CUBE"
■ PRINT
■ FOR CONTROL = 1 TO 5
■     PRINT CONTROL, CONTROL^2,CONTROL^3
■ NEXT CONTROL
■ END
```

```
Ok. run
NUMBER      SQUARE      CUBE

  1           1           1
  2           4           8
  3           9           27
  4          16           64
  5          25          125
Ok.
```

In fact, you can use this same loop to do any job requiring a succession of values from 1 to 5. Figure 7–18 uses a succession of values from 1 to 5 for the control variable, METRIC, in order to produce a table that converts kilometer distances to their equivalent English distances.

Using the control variable within the loop is clearly very handy. But you must be careful *not* to change the control variable *within* the loop. This must be done by the NEXT statement only, or the loop will not follow the plan set out in the FOR statement. In Figure 7–19 a mistakenly included LET statement drastically changes the outcome of the routine. By the time control reaches the NEXT statement, METRIC has been changed to 50, far beyond the limit of 5 set forth in the FOR statement. So, the computer, which never questions the wisdom of an instruction, terminates the loop.

Figure 7–18. Using the control variable for metric-to-English conversions

```
▮ PRINT "KILOMETERS"," FEET"," YARDS"," MILES"
▮ PRINT
▮ FOR METRIC = 1 TO 5
▮     PRINT TAB(5);METRIC,METRIC*3281,METRIC*1093.6,METRIC*.6214
▮ NEXT METRIC
▮ END
```

```
Ok. run
KILOMETERS    FEET      YARDS      MILES

    1        3281      1093.6     .6214
    2        6562      2187.2    1.2428
    3        9843      3280.8    1.8642
    4       13124      4374.4    2.4856
    5       16405      5468      3.107
Ok.
```

Figure 7–19. Mistakenly changing the control variable

```
▮ PRINT "KILOMETERS"," FEET"," YARDS"," MILES"
▮ PRINT
▮ FOR METRIC = 1 TO 5
▮     LET METRIC = 50
▮     PRINT TAB(5);METRIC,METRIC*3281,METRIC*1093.6,METRIC*.6214
▮ NEXT METRIC
▮ END
```

```
Ok. run
KILOMETERS    FEET      YARDS      MILES

   50       164050     54680      31.07
Ok.
```

The STEP modifier

The control variable need not always start with a value of 1 and go up in units of 1 to whatever limit is set. It can start at any value and go up or down by any amount that is useful to the problem at hand. The STEP modifier on the FOR statement provides the means to specify how the control variable will change as the loop proceeds. Use any STEP amount that suits your problem: 2, 5, 100, or even −1.

Figure 7–20 uses STEP 2 to print a list of even numbers. STEP 2 tells the computer to increment the control variable by 2 each time the NEXT statement executes. The computer keeps looping back until the control variable is greater than the limit of 10. INDEX starts at 0 and goes up by 2, and when it reaches 12, control is sent to the line following the NEXT statement and the program ends.

Figure 7-20. The STEP modifier

```
▪ FOR INDEX = 0 TO 10 STEP 2
▪      PRINT INDEX
▪ NEXT INDEX
▪ END
```

```
Ok. run
 0
 2
 4
 6
 8
 10
Ok.
```

If you wish to count down, use a negative STEP and be sure the starting value for the control variable is greater than the ending value. The statement

```
FOR INDEX = 100 TO 1 STEP -1
```

causes INDEX to start at 100 and decrease by 1 with each pass through the loop.

The FOR loop is quite flexible. You can use numeric variables to represent the starting, ending, and STEP values. Figure 7-21 prints numbers at whatever STEP interval is entered, beginning with whatever starting value is entered and ending at whatever end value is entered. During this sample run the computer uses an interval of 5, a starting value of 40, and an ending value of 60.

Figure 7-21. Using variables to control a FOR loop

```
▪ INPUT INTERVAL
▪ INPUT START
▪ INPUT STOP
▪ FOR INDEX = START TO STOP STEP INTERVAL
▪      PRINT INDEX
▪ NEXT INDEX
▪ END
```

```
Ok. run
? 5
? 40
? 60
 40
 45
 50
 55
 60
Ok.
```

Expressions can also be used on the right side of the FOR statement. A statement like

```
FOR TAB = A^2 TO B/C STEP .5
```

works perfectly well if it has meaning for your programming problem. You cannot, however, use an expression on the left side of the FOR statement to replace the control variable. As with the LET statement, this variable denotes a storage location. It houses the values that control the loop process.

Nested FOR loops

The program of Figure 7–22 uses two FOR loops to print two lists. One loop keeps track of how many lists are printed. The other keeps track of the names to be read

Figure 7–22. Nested FOR loops

```
FOR COUNT = 1 TO 2
    PRINT "This is list number";COUNT
    PRINT
    PRINT "Beautiful Parks in the USA"
    PRINT
    FOR NAMES = 1 TO 4
        READ PARK$
        PRINT PARK$
    NEXT NAMES
    PRINT
NEXT COUNT
DATA Yosemite, Crater Lake, Grand Canyon
DATA Sequoia, Yellowstone, Grand Teton
DATA Death Valley, Glacier
END
```

```
Ok. run
This is list number 1

Beautiful Parks in the USA

Yosemite
Crater Lake
Grand Canyon
Sequoia

This is list number 2

Beautiful Parks in the USA

Yellowstone
Grand Teton
Death Valley
Glacier

Ok.
```

and printed. As with DO LOOPS, nested FOR loops have the requirement that the inner loop be completely nested within the outer loop. That is, the inner loop must run to completion during a single iteration of the outer loop. In Figure 7–22, an entire list of national parks is read and printed by the NAMES loop before the COUNT loop control variable is incremented and the COUNT loop makes another iteration.

The EXIT FOR statement

```
EXIT
FOR
```

The EXIT FOR statement is used only within a FOR loop to interrupt the normal execution of the loop. Use it as in Figure 7–23 to send control out of the loop to the line following the NEXT statement.

As with EXIT DO, EXIT FOR is really a GO TO statement. Using it may be contrary to the concept that each module in a well-constructed program has only one entry point and one exit. Exits in this program segment can occur in two places: in the IF statement within the FOR loop and at the end of the FOR loop. Although it works perfectly well, you still have to examine this module closely to follow its logic.

Figure 7–23. Use of EXIT FOR

```
LET RESULT$ = "Valid Data"
FOR INDEX = 1 TO 10
    READ WAGE
    IF WAGE < 0 THEN
        LET RESULT$ = "Invalid Data"
        EXIT FOR
    ELSE
    END IF
NEXT INDEX
DATA 15.4,55.6,-66,32.4,12.8,45.7,32.9,10.1,64.7,5.5
PRINT RESULT$
END
```

```
Ok. run
Data Invalid
Ok.
```

Figure 7–24 shows how the program of Figure 7–23 could be rewritten without EXIT FOR. The latter program has the advantage that the logic of the routine is clear. It reads through all of the data checking to see if any is invalid. When the routine ends, the results are available in RESULT$. It has the disadvantage that the reading continues even after the IF statement proves some data are invalid. However, this disadvantage is minor in comparison to the advantage of good programming style. When the choice is between clarity and efficiency in programming, clarity always wins.

Figure 7–24. Without using EXIT FOR

```
LET RESULT$ = "Data Valid"
FOR INDEX = 1 TO 10
    READ WAGE
    IF WAGE < 0 THEN
        LET RESULT$ = "Data Invalid"
    ELSE
    END IF
NEXT INDEX
DATA
    15.45,55.67,-66,32.45,12.80,45.78,32.90,10.15,64.75,5.50
PRINT RESULT$
END
```

```
Ok. run
Data Invalid
Ok.
```

Combining FOR and DO loops

You can combine FOR and DO loops when it suits your project. Once again, you must be sure that the inner loop is completed before the outer loop makes another iteration. The program of Figure 7–25 creates the same quiz of Canadian capitals as in Figure 7–14, page 94. The difference is that this example takes advantage of the FOR loop to control reading exactly seven questions.

Figure 7–25. A DO loop within a FOR loop

```
FOR ASK = 1 TO 7
    LET COUNT = 0
    READ QUESTION$,ANSWER$
    PRINT "What is the capital of ";QUESTION$
    DO
        INPUT GUESS$
        LET COUNT = COUNT +1
    LOOP WHILE GUESS$ <> ANSWER$
    PRINT "You got that one in ";COUNT;" guesses."
    PRINT
NEXT ASK
DATA "British Columbia", Victoria
DATA Alberta, Edmonton
DATA Saskatchewan, Regina
DATA Manitoba, Winnipeg
DATA Ontario, Toronto
DATA Quebec, Quebec
DATA Newfoundland, St.John's
END
```

(continued on p. 102.)

Figure 7 – 25. *(continued)*

```
Ok. run
What is the capital of British Columbia
? Winnipeg
? Victoria
You got that one in  2  guesses.

What is the capital of Alberta
? Winnipeg
? Calgary
? Edmonton
You got that one in  3  guessess

What is the capital of Saskatchewan
?
```

Summary

If computers did nothing more than repeat tasks efficiently and tirelessly, which is what they do when they are under the control of a program loop, they would still be a revolutionary way to process information. The capability to automatically carry on with a job is one of the fundamental contributions computers have made to the problem of coping with enormous amounts of information and data.

Programming skills

The DO and LOOP statements

DO WHILE and DO UNTIL
LOOP WHILE and LOOP UNTIL
The EXIT DO statement

The FOR and NEXT statements

The STEP modifier
The EXIT FOR statement

Computer concepts

Leading decision loop control structure
Trailing decision loop control structure
Nested loops

Review questions

1. *Corrections.* Determine whether each of the following True BASIC statements is correct. If it is, write "correct" on your answer sheet. If not, rewrite it correctly.

Consider each statement separately. These statements are *not* part of the same program.

a. ∎ DO WHILE NAM$ <> JAMES

b. ∎ LOOP UNTIL COUNT = X

c. ∎ FOR ABLE = BAKER TO CHARLIE STEP JIM

d. ∎ NEXT 40

e. ∎ FOR DAY = 1 TO 7 STEP -1

f. ∎ FOR 4*B TO C STEP -5

g. ∎ FOR P$ = 100 TO 1 STEP -2

h. ∎ IF A*B + C > 45 THEN EXIT DO

i. ∎ DO WHILE MORE INFO.

j. ∎ LOOP FOR X = 1 TO 10

2. *Programs to Read.* What will be printed when each of the following programs is run? If input from the keyboard is needed, show some sample input that would fit with the program.

a.
```
∎ Let H = 0
∎ DO
∎      PRINT H^H
∎      LET H = H + 2
∎      IF H > 16 THEN EXIT DO
∎ LOOP
∎ END
```

b.
```
∎ DO WHILE NUM <> X
∎      FOR NUM = 1 TO 500
∎          LET X = X * NUM
∎      NEXT NUM
∎ LOOP
∎ END
```

c.
```
∎ LET NUM1 = 5
∎ LET NUM2 = 78
∎ LET NUM3 = 45
∎ FOR T = 100 TO 1 STEP -1
∎      IF T = NUM1 THEN PRINT T,
∎      IF T = NUM2 THEN PRINT T,
∎      IF T = NUM3 THEN PRINT T,
∎ NEXT T
∎ END
```

d.
```
∎ FOR L = 1 TO 5
∎      FOR S = 1 TO L
∎          PRINT "1 ";
∎      NEXT S
∎ PRINT
∎ NEXT L
∎ END
```

e.
```
∎ FOR X = 3 TO 19 STEP 4
∎      PRINT X - 2
∎      PRINT X + 2
∎ NEXT X
∎ END
```

3. Have the computer ask a person's age. Then print out YOU ARE A SUPERSTAR once for every year of the person's life.

4. Use a DO loop to control a quiz that reads DATA about some states and their capitals. Quiz the user about the capital of each state and indicate whether the answer is right or wrong. End the program when all of the questions have been asked.

5. Write a computer program that stores the current registration figures for the adult education classes in a DATA statement. Ask a potential student the number of the course he wants to take and tell him if there is any room left. Each course is limited to an enrollment of 20.

6. Use a DO loop to control a routine that prints random numbers in the range of 1 to 10. Have the program end when the same number is generated two times in a row.

Print out the count of how many random numbers were produced before the matching numbers appeared.

7. Write a program that quizzes the user on the times table for the number 9. When the quiz is finished tell her how many she got correct.

8. Use a DO loop to determine how many words are in a sentence entered at the keyboard. The sentence must end with a period.

9. Use a FOR loop to answer the Fibonacci question about the number of bunnies produced in any number of months the user wishes to see. (Each month, the number produced is equal to the sum of bunnies produced in the preceding two months). Have the computer calculate and print each number in the sequence.

10. Use a DO loop to keep track of the supply of chocolate chip, watermelon, and strawberry ice cream for the Tutti Frutti Ice Cream Parlor. When a cone is sold, subtract 4 ounces. When the supply of one flavor runs out, tell the customer to try another. When all of the ice cream is gone, tell the customer to come again another day.

11. Write a program that acts like an adding machine. Every time a number is entered it is added to the previous numbers. When all of the numbers have been entered, the sum is printed.

12. Use a DO loop to compute numbers in the Fibonacci sequence until the user presses any key. Then have the computer display the last Fibonacci number computed, and indicated which number in the sequence it is.

13. Each Tuesday the participants in Wait Watchers line up in their usual order and weigh in. Write a program that keeps track of all 15 dieters' last week's weight. As they enter this week's poundage, have the computer print CONGRATULATIONS! if they have lost weight. Otherwise tell them how much they gained.

14. A *palindrome* is a word or number that reads the same backwards or forwards. The word "Otto" is a palindrome. Program the computer to see if a line of input is a palindrome. Have it accept the input, test it, and then print out: THAT IS A PALINDROME or THAT IS NOT A PALINDROME.

## Chapter 8

Subscripts and matrices

If you take a week-long Hawaiian holiday you can use the computer to list stops along your tour. If the stops are numerous enough, you can take advantage of the READ and DATA statements, as shown in Figure 8-1. If you travel for longer, however, the list of places to visit will grow and the READ and PRINT combination of statements will become unwieldy. There will be too many variables and too many PRINT statements to type.

You are faced with the question of how to efficiently store and retrieve lists of related information. Known as *list processing* (or *array handling* or *matrix manipulation*), this need is so common that True BASIC, like other programming lan-

Figure 8-1. An ordinary list

```
PRINT "The beautiful places to see are:"
PRINT
READ FIRST$,SECOND$,THIRD$,FOURTH$,FIFTH$
PRINT "Monday",FIRST$
PRINT "Tuesday",SECOND$
PRINT "Wednesday",THIRD$
PRINT "Thursday",FOURTH$
PRINT "Friday",FIFTH$
DATA Oahu,Kauai,Maui,Lanai,Molokai
END
```

```
Ok. run
The beautiful places to see are:
Monday          Oahu
Tuesday         Kauai
Wednesday       Maui
Thursday        Lanai
Friday          Molokai
Ok.
```

guages, has statements to make the job easy. This chapter explains the use of subscripted variables and the DIM and MAT statements you will need to manage lists of related data.

The DIM statement

```
DIM
```

The DIM (dimension) statement in True BASIC informs the computer of the name and the length of a list. Figure 8–2 shows how to use the DIM statement. The DIM statement prepares the computer for setting aside five consecutive memory locations for the elements of the list, PLACE$. A subscript written as a number in parentheses denotes the position of each list element and distinguishes one from the other. Thus, PLACE$(1) is the first list element, PLACE$(2) follows, and PLACE$(5) is the fifth, or last, in the list. Once you dimension a list with a DIM statement, the variables associated with the list are known to the computer and you can use them like any other variables in your program. In the travel example, the READ statement assigns data to the variables in the list, and the PRINT statements reference the subscripted variables in order to print the list.

The program of Figure 8–2 is no more efficient than that of Figure 8–1. The true power of subscripted variables emerges when you use the subscript itself as a variable. Figure 8–3 shows that by using FOR and NEXT, you can work with a list of 500 places as easily as with a list of 5. The same short READ and PRINT statements

Figure 8–2. A DIMensioned list

```
■ DIM PLACE$(5)
■ PRINT "The beautiful places to see are:"
■ PRINT
■ READ PLACE$(1),PLACE$(2),PLACE$(3),PLACE$(4),PLACE$(5)
■ PRINT "Monday",PLACE$(1)
■ PRINT "Tuesday",PLACE$(2)
■ PRINT "Wednesday",PLACE$(3)
■ PRINT "Thursday",PLACE$(4)
■ PRINT "Friday",PLACE$(5)
■ DATA Oahu,Kauai,Maui,Lanai,Molokai
■ END
```

```
Ok. run
The beautiful places to see are:

Monday          Oahu
Tuesday         Kauai
Wednesday       Maui
Thursday        Lanai
Friday          Molokai
Ok.
```

Figure 8-3. Using variables as subscripts

```
■ DIM PLACE$(500)
■ PRINT "The beautiful places to see are:"
■ PRINT
■ FOR COUNT = 1 TO 500
■     READ PLACE$(COUNT)
■     PRINT "Day";COUNT,PLACE$(COUNT)
■ NEXT COUNT
■ DATA Kauai,Molokai,Maui,Lanai,Molokai
■ DATA Zamboanga,Mindanao,Leyte,Iloilo,Luzon
■ DATA Osumi,Kyushu,Shikoku,Honshu,Hokkaido
■ !DATA ............        485        .................
■ !DATA ............        More       .................
■ !DATA ............        Islands    .................
■ !DATA ...................................Nantucket
■ END
```

```
Ok. run
The beautiful places to see are:

Day 1          Kauai
Day 2          Molokai
Day 3          Maui
Day 4          Lanai
Day 5          Molokai
Day 6          Zamboanga
Day 7          Mindanao
Day 8          Leyte
Day 9          Iloilo
Day 10         Luzon
Day 11         Osumi
Day 12         Kyushu
Day 13         Shikoku
Day 14         Honshu
Day 15         Hokkaido
   .              .
   .              .
   .              .
Ok.
```

(a)

```
■ DIM PLACE$(5)
■ PRINT "The beautiful places to see are:"
■ PRINT
■ FOR COUNT = 1 TO 5
■     READ PLACE$(COUNT)
■     PRINT "Day";COUNT,PLACE$(COUNT)
■ NEXT COUNT
■ DATA Oahu,Kauai,Maui,Lanai,Molokai
■ END
```

(continued)

Figure 8-3. *Continued*

```
Ok. run
The beautiful places to see are:

Day 1          Oahu
Day 2          Kauai
Day 3          Maui
Day 4          Lanai
Day 5          Molokai
Ok.
```

(b)

retrieve all of the data in both program examples of Figure 8-3. This is because the statements are embedded in FOR loops and use the control variable as a subscript. As COUNT progresses from 1 to 5 (or to 500), so do the PLACE$ subscripts in the READ and PRINT statements.

Related lists

Using the same subscript in several lists with related data makes it possible to retrieve from all the lists information concerning one individual. For instance, if the computer stores the names of students and their hometown addresses in separate lists, the same subscript can find the information for any one student, as in Figure 8-4.

Figure 8-4. Related lists

```
■ DIM NAME$(5),CITY$(5)
■ FOR COUNT = 1 TO 5
■     READ NAME$(COUNT),CITY$(COUNT)
■ NEXT COUNT
■ PRINT "Enter the student number"
■ INPUT CHOICE
■ PRINT
■ PRINT "Student:  ";NAME$(CHOICE)
■ PRINT "City: ";CITY$(CHOICE)
■ DATA A. Herman,Boulder
■ DATA M. Chaucer,Topeka
■ DATA F. Romero,Harrisburg
■ DATA P. Bunyan,Louisville
■ DATA C. Griffin,Fresno
■ END
```

```
Ok. run
Enter the student number
? 4

Student: P. Bunyan
City: Louisville
Ok.
```

The key to a successful search is that information in both lists is stored in the same order. The name for student 4 and the city for student 4 have position 4 in their respective lists. Thus, the same subscript works for both lists. In this example, the computer accesses all information about one person by using the variable CHOICE as the subscript in both lists.

Notice the DIM statement in Figure 8–4. You must dimension each list that you intend to use, but you can do them all in one DIM statement.

Sorting lists

The opposite technique—using different subscripts to retrieve data in the same list—makes it possible to sort information in ascending or descending order. The different subscripts allow you to compare two items in the same list and decide whether the data they hold are in the proper, sorted relationship. If not, you need to rearrange them.

Bubble sort.   Much has been written on the topic of computer sorting. The sorting method you use greatly affects the speed at which the computer works. The program of Figure 8–5 sorts a list of names by means of the *bubble sort*. Although this method is relatively slow (it is useful for a list of about 100 items), it clearly shows how subscripts play a key role in a sorting routine. The bubble sort compares the items in each position in the list with every item farther down in the list. When the comparison reveals two items that are out of order, the computer exchanges their places in the list. Eventually, every item "bubbles up" to its proper position in the list. The nested FOR lists in the example provide the two subscripts that make it possible to compare an item with the next one in the list. The IF statement compares the two items and exchanges them, if necessary. Finally, a FOR loop prints the sorted list.

Using subscripts

The innermost loop in the program of Figure 8–5 shows that subscripts can be expressions as well as constants and variables. NAME\$(POSITION + 1) represents the name that is one position farther down the list than the name in the spot represented by POSITION. When POSITION = 1, NAME\$(POSITION + 1) is the second name in the list. The computer calculates the value of the expression (POSITION + 1) and then retrieves data from that list position.

True BASIC allows you to use integer subscripts in the range of $-1E9$ to $+1E9$. You cannot, however, use exponential notation in the subscript, and if you use other noninteger subscripts, True BASIC rounds the subscript up to the next highest integer.

By default, when you define an array in a DIM statement, the computer

Figure 8–5. A bubble sort

```
DIM NAME$(5)
PRINT "The Handy Dandy Alphabetizer"
PRINT
REM read names into the list
FOR POSITION = 1 TO 5
    READ NAME$(POSITION)
NEXT POSITION
FOR POSITION = 1 TO 5                            !The position being sorted
    FOR NEXTONE = (POSITION + 1) TO 5        !The next item in the list
        IF NAME$(POSITION) >= NAME$(NEXTONE) THEN    !If these two names
            LET TEMP$ = NAME$(POSITION)              !are not in alphabetical
            LET NAME$(POSITION) = NAME$(NEXTONE)     !order, switch their
            LET NAME$(NEXTONE) = TEMP$               !list positions
        ELSE
        END IF
    NEXT NEXTONE
NEXT POSITION
REM print the results
PRINT "The Sorted list:"
PRINT
FOR POSITION = 1 TO 5
    PRINT NAME$(POSITION)
NEXT POSITION
DATA Herman,Chaucer,Romero,Bunyan,Griffith
END
```

```
Ok. run
The Handy Dandy Alphabetizer

The Sorted list:

Bunyan
Chaucer
Griffith
Herman
Romero
Ok.
```

assumes your first subscript is 1. However, you can set whatever beginning and ending bounds you need. For instance, the statement

```
DIM PROFITS(-100 to 100)
```

establishes a numeric array, PROFITS, with subscripts ranging from -100 to $+100$. Likewise, the statement

```
DIM YEAR$(1944 to 1984)
```

establishes a string array beginning with YEAR$(1944) and ending with

YEAR$(1984). Setting lower and upper bounds that are meaningful to the problem at hand is good programming practice. It makes the logic of your processing easier to program and understand.

Double subscripts

Often it is not helpful to relate information by a position in a list. How hard it would be to find a seat in the stadium if your ticket were stamped with a single number telling which of the many seats it represents! Tickets with two notations do a good job. They tell you where to sit by pinpointing first your row and then your seat.

The mapmakers of the world use this convention. Paris, Athens, Oslo, and Rome are located, not as 1, 2, or 300, but in terms of degrees of latitude and longitude — two numbers that tell how far north or south of the equator and how far east or west of the prime meridian they lie.

True BASIC allows you to organize information this way. As you plan your program you can conceive of a rectangular honeycomb or matrix in which to store your data. You can put each item in a "cell" and retrieve any one by referring to its row and column address. The DIM statement establishes the name and the dimension of the matrix:

```
10 DIM A(2,3)
```

This tells the computer to reserve two rows and three columns in memory for the numeric information that will be placed in matrix A. As Figure 8–6 shows, the first number gives the row address and the second gives the column address.

Once you define the matrix, use the variables for these memory locations just like any other variable. If these cells represent safe deposit boxes, Figure 8–7 reports on the value of the jewels locked in any one.

The READ statements assign the numeric amounts in DATA to the variables in the matrix. The dollars in DATA and the variables in the READ are all carefully arranged to correspond with the value of the jewels in the actual arrangement of safe deposit boxes at the bank. Matrix A matches the vault shown in Figure 8–8.

When you enter row R and column C, these variables become subscripts which PRINT uses to locate and retrieve the amounts stored in the variable that represents cell R, C of the matrix.

Figure 8–6. Matrix A in memory

	Column 1	Column 2	Column 3
Row 1	1,1	1,2	1,3
Row 2	2,1	2,2	2,3

Figure 8–7. Using double subscripts for rows and columns

```
■ DIM A(2,3)
■ READ A(1,1), A(1,2), A(1,3)
■ READ A(2,1), A(2,2), A(2,3)
■ PRINT "ENTER THE ADDRESS OF YOUR SAFE DEPOSIT BOX"
■ INPUT PROMPT "ROW?":R
■ INPUT PROMPT "COLUMN?":C
■ PRINT "THE CONTENTS OF THE BOX IN ROW";R;"AND COLUMN" ;C;"ARE WORTH"
■ PRINT A(R,C);"DOLLARS"
■ DATA 200, 500000, 0,
■ DATA 999.99, 1000000, 45
■ END
```

```
OK.run

ENTER THE ADDRESS OF YOUR SAFE DEPOSIT BOX
ROW? 2
COLUMN? 1
THE CONTENTS OF THE BOX IN ROW 2 COLUMN 1 ARE WORTH
999.99 DOLLARS
```

Effective use of double subscripts

As with single subscripts, double subscripts can be variables or expressions. Once again, this makes it practical to store and search through large amounts of data since you can use the counting variable of a FOR . . . NEXT loop as a subscript. Use two loops because there are two subscripts.

Figure 8–9 makes room reservations at a large resort hotel with 10 floors, each of which has 15 rooms. Notice the style of this program. Even though it contains only a few lines, it is written in a modular fashion. There are three definite sections: one for initialization, one for reservations, and one for output.

Section 1 assigns blanks to every element of the HOTEL$(,) matrix that represents the hotel in the computer's memory. As reservations are made, they will be replaced by the initials of the hotel guest. Nested FOR . . . NEXT loops make it easy to manipulate the entire matrix. They are set up so that the inner loop, the J loop, represents the rooms on each floor. This loop runs completely for each of the 10 floors. The outer loop, the I loop, represents the 10 floors and RUNs to completion just once.

Section 2 accepts reservations and uses the INPUT variables as subscripts for the HOTEL$(,) matrix variables to discover if the room is occupied. The IF . . .

Figure 8–8. Central Bank vault

	Column 1	Column 2	Column 3
Row 1	$200	$500,000	0
Row 2	$999.99	$1,000,000	$45

Figure 8-9. Using double subscripts to represent the floors and rooms of a hotel

```
DIM HOTEL$(10,15)
REM Section 1:Initialization
LET C = 0
For I = 1 TO 10
    FOR J = 1 TO 15
        LET HOTEL$ (I, J) = ""
    NEXT J
NEXT I
REM Section 2:Reservations
PRINT"WELCOME to the Troutebrooke Hotel"
PRINT
DO UNTIL C = 150                      ! until all rooms are filled
    PRINT"Which room do you want?"
    INPUT PROMPT "Floor ": F
    INPUT PROMPT "Room ": R
    IF HOTEL$(F,R) <> "" THEN
        PRINT "That room is reserved. Try Again"
    ELSE
        PRINT "You may have that room."
        INPUT PROMPT "Enter your initials ": HOTEL$(F,R)
        LET C = C+1
    END IF
LOOP
REM Section 3: Output
PRINT "The hotel is full."
PRINT "Here is the reservation list."
PRINT
FOR I = 1 to 10
    FOR J = 1 to 15
        PRINT HOTEL$(I,J);" ";
    NEXT J
    PRINT
NEXT I
END
```

THEN check determines whether the matrix variable still stores a blank. If so, the room is available. It is reserved when a guest's initials are entered.

The DO UNTIL check sets the final section in motion. When C, the counter that goes up by 1 each time a reservation is made, reaches 150, all of the rooms are occupied. Control goes to Section 3 and then to the nested FOR . . . NEXT loops. They print the matrix as 10 rows each with 15 sets of initials.

Taking some time to enter Figure 8-9 into the computer will clarify the use of double-subscripted variables. Use dummy names and watch it run. You should see something like Figure 8-10 on your screen.

Multiple subscripts

True BASIC allows at least ten dimensions, but depending on your computer type, even more may be available to you (255 on the IBM PC, for example). The statement

```
DIM WORD$(500,100,50,20,8)
```

Figure 8–10. Running the program in Figure 8–9 to reserve hotel rooms

```
Ok. run
WELCOME to the Troutebrooke Hotel

Which room do you want?
Floor 3
Room 5
You may have that room.
Enter your initials GRT
Which room do you want?
Floor 3
Room 4
You may have that room.
Enter your initials HFD
Which room do you want?
Floor 3
Room 5
That room is reserved. Try Again
Which room do you want?
Floor 6
Room 2
You may have that room.
Enter your initials DDB
Which room do you want?
Floor
          .
          .
          .
        (eventually)
THE HOTEL IS FULL
HERE IS THE RESERVATION LIST

FDR JFK RFR LBJ GWK AWO ASW JMM HHM HBH KBH PLK SOC
PDP TRS

IGR LPA TTY MFR HPL APL MSW BFG KNN NBM TGW ORD CCR
MXM APP
          .
          .
          .
        (and so on, with initials for 10 floors)
          .
          .
          .
```

sets up a string array, WORD$, with five dimensions. Each dimension has a range of values that begins with 1 (the default beginning value) and goes up to the value given in the DIM statement. The range of the first dimension is 1–500, the second is 1–100, the third is 1–50, and so on.

You can't draw a picture of a 5-dimensional array as you can of a 1-dimensional list, with each element following the other in a line. However, you can visualize such an array if you realize that each dimension represents a particular attribute of each list item. The five dimensions of the WORD$ array might, for example, help you locate each of a series of words by specifying the following:

Dimension	Attribute
First (subscript 500)	Which library shelf holds the book containing a particular word. Shelves are numbered from 1 to 500.
Second (subscript 100)	Which shelf position holds the book. Shelf positions are numbered from 1 to 100.
Third (subscript 50)	Which book page contains the word. Pages are numbered from 1 to 50.
Fourth (subscript 20)	Which line on the page contains the word. Lines are numbered from 1 to 20.
Fifth (subscript 8)	Which word on the line is the one you want. Words are numbered from 1 to 8.

The variable WORD$(350,75,49,19,2) contains the particular word that is located in the book on shelf 350, in shelf position 75, on page 49, line 19 in the book, the second word on the line.

Subscripts can represent any attributes that make sense for your problem, such as your date of birth, salary, or ZIP code.

You can specify the lower and upper bounds of each dimension in the DIM statement. The statement

```
DIM (40, 1900 to 1999)
```

tells the computer that the values of the subscripts in the first dimension range from 1 (the default value) to 40. The subscripts in the second dimension range from 1900 to 1999.

Subscript functions

True BASIC provides functions that return the current values for the dimensions of an array. These subscript functions are listed in Figure 8–11. You can use these functions as you would numeric and other functions, wherever expressions are allowed. To display the upper bound of the 5th dimension of the WORD$ array, for instance, write:

```
PRINT UBOUND(WORD$,5)
```

The computer will print *8*.

The MAT PRINT statement

MAT
PRINT

In the computer world the term *matrix* is a synonym for the term *array*. Usually, *matrix* refers to arrays with more than one dimension. True BASIC includes powerful statements — known as MAT, or matrix manipulation, statements — that allow you to set initial values, read, print, or do arithmetic with entire matrices as easily as with single variables.

Figure 8–11. Array dimension functions

Function name	*Value specified*
SIZE(ITEMS)	The number of elements in the 1-dimensional array ITEMS
SIZE(ITEMS,5)	The number of elements in the fifth dimension of the multidimensional array ITEMS
LBOUND(ITEM)	The lower bound of the only dimension in the 1-dimensional array ITEM
LBOUND(ITEM,3)	The lower bound of the third dimension in the multidimensional array ITEM
UBOUND(ITEM)	The upper bound of the only dimension in the 1-dimensional array ITEM
UBOUND(ITEM,9)	The upper bound of the ninth dimension in the multidimensional array ITEM

MAT PRINT prints the data in a matrix. Figure 8–12 shows that you need specify only the matrix name and the computer will print the entire matrix. The single MAT PRINT statement has the effect of the following two PRINT statements:

```
PRINT TABLE(1,1),TABLE(1,2),TABLE(1,3),TABLE(1,4)
PRINT TABLE(2,1),TABLE(2,2),TABLE(2,3),TABLE(2,4)
```

With **MAT PRINT** the computer prints the elements of each dimension across a line with one element in each print zone. As it processes an array, the computer selects elements from the matrix so that the last subscript is varied completely before the next one starts to vary. Each printed row in the example represents a complete pass through the elements of one dimension.

Figure 8–12. Use of the MAT PRINT statement

```
▮ DIM TABLE(2,4)
▮ FOR ROW = 1 TO 2
▮     FOR COL = 1 TO 4
▮         READ TABLE (ROW,COL)
▮     NEXT COL
▮ NEXT ROW
▮ PRINT
▮ MAT PRINT TABLE
▮ DATA 4.75,5.7,0.95,9.99,3.25,6.5,7.75,8.5
▮ END
```

```
Ok. run

    4.75            5.7             0.95            9.99
    3.25            6.5             7.75            8.5

Ok.
```

Compressed printing

If the matrix has more elements in a dimension than can be printed in the print zones of the line, you can use semicolons to compress the printing. Semicolons work with MAT PRINT just as they do with a PRINT statement. The program of Figure 8–13 prints the TABLE matrix using a trailing semicolon on the MAT PRINT statement.

The numbers in the matrix are printed as numbers usually are with leading and trailing spaces. Using semicolons with string items, however, causes them to be printed with no spaces surrounding them.

Figure 8–13. MAT PRINT with semicolons: compressed printing

```
DIM TABLE(2,4)
FOR ROW = 1 TO 2
    FOR COL = 1 TO 4
        READ TABLE (ROW,COL)
    NEXT COL
NEXT ROW
PRINT
MAT PRINT TABLE;
DATA 4.75,5.7,0.95,9.99,3.25,6.5,7.75,8.5
END
```

```
Ok. run

 4.75   5.7   0.95   9.99
 3.25   6.5   7.75   8.5

Ok.
```

Printing multiple matrices

You can use a single MAT PRINT statement to print several matrices if you wish. Each matrix name is separated from any that follow by a semicolon or a comma to tell the computer whether to print in the compressed or zone-width fashion. For example, the statement

```
MAT PRINT TABLE; CHART,PLAN
```

prints the TABLE matrix in semicolon format, CHART in comma format, and PLAN (because there is no trailing punctuation mark) in the default comma format.

The MAT READ statement

MAT
READ

The MAT READ statement reads entire matrices at a time. The program of Figure 8–14 uses MAT READ to read the TABLE matrix. MAT READ, like MAT PRINT, saves typing and makes your program very clear. No matter how many dimensions

Figure 8-14. Use of the MAT READ statement

```
■ DIM TABLE (2,4)
■ MAT READ TABLE
■ PRINT
■ MAT PRINT TABLE
■ DATA 4.75,5.7,.95,9.99,3.25,6.5,7.75,8.5
■ END
```

```
Ok. run

  4.75            5.7              .95              9.99
  3.25            6.5             7.75              8.5

Ok.
```

the matrix has, with MAT READ you do not need nested loops to read matrix items from a DATA statement. You can use MAT READ for matrices with either numeric or string data.

Like MAT PRINT, MAT READ accepts the elements in the array so that the last subscript is varied completely before the next one starts to vary. The MAT READ statement in Figure 8-9 is the equivalent of the following two statements:

```
READ TABLE(1,1),TABLE(1,2),TABLE(1,3),TABLE(1,4)
READ TABLE(2,1),TABLE(2,2),TABLE(2,3),TABLE(2,4)
```

Reading multiple matrices

One MAT READ statement can read several matrices at once. By separating the matrix names in the MAT READ statement with commas, you cause the computer to assign the data items to the first matrix named, then the second, and so on. The

Figure 8-15. The MAT READ statement for multiple matrices

```
■ DIM NAMES$(4),DATES$(4)
■ MAT READ NAMES$,DATES$
■ PRINT
■ MAT PRINT NAMES$,DATES$
■ DATA Huey,Louie,Duey,Buggsy
■ DATA Dec. 25, Apr. 1, Jul. 4, Oct. 12
■ END
```

```
Ok. run

Huey  Louie  Duey  Buggsy

Dec. 25          Apr. 1          Jul. 4          Oct. 12

Ok.
```

program of Figure 8–15 reads all the elements of the NAME$ matrix before beginning to read the DATE$ matrix.

Figure 8–16 shows how statements like MAT READ and MAT PRINT can make your programming life easier. It presents the bubble sort program discussed earlier (see Figure 8–5, page 110), but rewritten to take advantage of these statements. The FOR loops for reading and printing the array have been replaced by MAT READ and MAT PRINT. The result is the same, but the program is shorter and easier to understand.

Figure 8–16. Using MAT statements for a bubble sort

```
DIM NAME$(5)
PRINT "The Handy Dandy Alphabetizer"
PRINT
REM read names into the list
MAT READ NAME$
FOR POSITION = 1 TO 5                      !The position being sorted
    FOR NEXTONE = (POSITION + 1) TO 5      !The next item in the list
        IF NAME$(POSITION) >= NAME$(NEXTONE) THEN   !If these two names
            LET TEMP$ = NAME$(POSITION)             !are not in alphabetical
            LET NAME$(POSITION) = NAME$(NEXTONE)    !order, switch their
            LET NAME$(NEXTONE) = TEMP$              !list positions
        ELSE
        END IF
    NEXT NEXTONE
NEXT POSITION
REM print the results
PRINT "The Sorted list:"
PRINT
MAT PRINT NAME$
DATA Herman,Chaucer,Romero,Bunyan,Griffith
END
```

```
Ok. run
The Handy Dandy Alphabetizer

The Sorted list:

Bunyan          Chaucer         Griffith        Herman          Romero

Ok.
```

The MAT INPUT statement

| MAT INPUT |

The MAT INPUT statement allows data entered at the keyboard to be accepted into a matrix. It accepts the information element by element, with the last subscript of the matrix being varied completely before the next one starts to vary. The program of Figure 8–17 accepts the rates charged for the three suites on both floors of the Weekman Arms Hotel. It reprints the matrix to illustrate the order in which MAT INPUT has stored the rates.

Figure 8-17. Using the MAT INPUT statement

```
■ DIM RATE(2,3)
■ PRINT "Enter the current rates."
■ MAT INPUT RATE
■ PRINT
■ PRINT "Weekman Arms Luxury Rates"
■ PRINT
■ PRINT RATE(1,1),RATE(1,2),RATE(1,3)
■ PRINT RATE(2,1),RATE(2,2),RATE(2,3)
■ END
```

```
Ok. run
Enter the current rates.
? 120,130,115,235,250,300

Weekman Arms Luxury Rates

   120              130              115
   235              250              300
Ok.
```

The rules for the type and amount of data entered in response to the MAT INPUT statement are the same as for the INPUT statement. There must be enough, not too much, data, and any data series that continues onto another line must be marked by a comma at the end of the first line.

Inputting multiple matrices

MAT INPUT can accept data for more than one matrix at a time. The matrix names must be separated by commas in the MAT INPUT statement. For instance, the statement

```
MAT INPUT BOXES,BOTTLES,CANS
```

will cause a question mark prompt to be printed for each element of all three matrices. The first data entered will be stored in BOXES until that matrix is filled. The next sequence of data will be stored in BOTTLES. And the last data entered will be stored in CANS. The data must be entered one item at a time, separated by commas.

The MAT LINE INPUT statement

```
MAT
LINE
INPUT
```

The MAT LINE INPUT statement is the matrix counterpart of the LINE INPUT statement. The matrix must be a string matrix. Each matrix element contains everything entered between the input prompt and the press of the *enter* key. The computer can accept several matrices with one MAT LINE INPUT if the names of the arrays are separated by commas. For instance, the statement

```
MAT LINE INPUT QUESTION$, ANSWER$
```

accepts the series of line-long questions into the QUESTION$ matrix, followed by a series of line-long answers into the ANSWER$ matrix.

The MAT LINE INPUT PROMPT statement

```
MAT LINE
INPUT
PROMPT
```
The MAT LINE INPUT PROMPT statement prints a phrase before displaying an input prompt question mark for each response. As Figure 8–18 shows, the computer prints the phrase once and then prints a question mark for each element of the matrix.

Figure 8–18. Using the MAT LINE INPUT PROMPT statement

```
■ DIM CREW$(4)
■ MAT LINE INPUT PROMPT "Who rows in your boat? ":CREW$
■ PRINT
■ PRINT "Crew for the Club Regatta"
■ PRINT
■ MAT PRINT CREW$
■ END
```

```
Ok. run
Who rows in your boat? John Forrest, Lakeland, Connecticut
? Tom Mark, Harrisburg, Pennsylvania
? Ed Glass, Boston, Masschusetts
? Will MacMillan, Chicago, Illinois

Crew for the Club Regatta

John Forrest, Lakeland, Connecticut
Tom Mark, Harrisburg, Pennsylvania
Ed Glass, Boston, Massachusetts
Will MacMillan, Chicago, Illinois

Ok.
```

Redimensioning

Redimensioning is the term used to describe True BASIC's ability to change the number of elements or the upper or lower bound of a dimension. You change these attributes of a dimensioned array by means of the MAT INPUT, MAT LINE INPUT, and MAT READ statements.

MAT INPUT redimensions matrices in two ways. It allows you to specify a new bound or size for an array. For 1-dimensional arrays, it also lets you change the upper bound to conform with the actual amount of entered data.

For example, if the dimensions of the matrix named YEARS had been established with the statement

```
DIM YEARS(2,1900 TO 1954)
```

then the statement

```
MAT INPUT YEARS(2,1951 TO 1954)
```

tells the computer to redimension YEARS as a matrix with two rows and four columns (subscripts ranging from 1951 to 1954).

The question mark in the statement

```
MAT INPUT CHILD$(?)
```

tells the computer to change the upper bound of the CHILD$ array to match the number of replies actually entered. The program of Figure 8–19, for instance, prints the names of the children in the respondent's family. Notice that there is no need for the programmer to know in advance how many names will be entered. The computer accepts all data up to the press of the *enter* key. The question mark subscript in the array name indicates that the array will be redimensioned by the number of elements actually entered. After the MAT INPUT statement executes, the SIZE function recognizes the new dimension. An array redimensioned in this fashion changes its upper bound only; the lower bound remains as originally dimensioned.

Figure 8–19. The MAT INPUT statement and redimensioning

```
▪ DIM CHILD$(25)
▪ PRINT "Enter the names of your children."
▪ MAT INPUT CHILD$(?)
▪ PRINT
▪ PRINT SIZE(CHILD$);
▪ PRINT " kids make a nice family!"
▪ END
```

```
Ok. run
Enter the names of your children.
? Maggie,Fredie,Polly,Suzie

 4 kids make a nice family!
Ok.
```

Matrix arithmetic

True BASIC allows the following arithmetic operations with matrices:

Operation	Example
Addition	MAT TOTAL = TAX + PRICE
Subtraction	MAT PROFIT = INCOME − COST
Multiplication	MAT PRODUCT = B * C

The names TOTAL, TAX, PRICE, PROFIT, INCOME, COST, PRODUCT, B, and C all represent matrices that have been previously dimensioned. The True BASIC matrix arithmetic operations follow the same rules as normal matrix arithmetic.

Matrix addition and subtraction

For addition and subtraction you can have as many dimensions as you wish, but all matrices involved must have the same number of dimensions and the same size in each dimension. For example, if matrix A is (4,2) and matrix B is (2,3) you cannot add them. The matrices would have to both be (4,2) or both be (2,3). The target matrix that holds the resulting sum or difference would be changed to the same size and shape as the operand matrices. Changing the target matrix in this way is known as *implicit redimensioning*. Figure 8–20 illustrates matrix addition.

Figure 8–20. Matrix addition

```
DIM SUM(10,10), A(4,2), B(4,2)
PRINT "The first dimension of SUM is ";
PRINT UBOUND(SUM,1);"BY";UBOUND(SUM,2)
PRINT
MAT READ A
MAT READ B
MAT SUM = A + B          !SUM matches A and B
PRINT "The new dimension of SUM IS ";
PRINT UBOUND(SUM,1);"BY";UBOUND(SUM,2)
PRINT
PRINT "After addition, SUM looks like:"
MAT PRINT SUM
DATA 1, 2, 3, 4, 5, 6, 7, 8, 10, 20, 30, 40, 50, 60, 70, 80
END
```

```
Ok. run
The first dimension of SUM is 10 BY 10

The new dimension of SUM is 4 BY 2

After addition, SUM looks like:
 11             22
 33             44
 55             66
 77             88

Ok.
```

Matrix multiplication

For multiplication the arrays must be either 1-dimensional or 2-dimensional. To create a matrix product, the number of columns in one matrix in the expression must equal the number of rows in the other. For 2-dimensional arrays, if you wish to multiply matrix A by matrix B, and matrix A has N rows and M columns, then matrix B must have M rows and K columns. The result is matrix AB that has N rows and K columns.

Figure 8–21 portrays matrix multiplication where matrix A is shaped (2,2) and matrix B is shaped (2,3). The program in Figure 8–22 multiplies these two matrices and shows the resulting matrix, PRODUCT, which is a 2 by 3 matrix. You *must* be careful to write the expression in the matrix multiplication statement in a particular order. In this example, you must say

```
MAT PRODUCT = A * B
```

and not

```
MAT PRODUCT = B * A
```

The computer compares the number of columns in the first matrix with the number of rows in the second before beginning to multiply. If they match, the multiplication proceeds; otherwise the "mismatched array size" error message appears.

If either matrix in the expression has only a single dimension, then the product matrix PRODUCT will become a 1-dimensional array. The product AB is a 1-dimensional array with K elements if matrix A is a 1-dimensional array of M elements and B is a 2-dimensional array of M rows and K columns. If B is a 4-element array and C is a (4,5)-dimensional array, then the product BC becomes a 5-element 1-dimensional array.

The order of multiplication matters here also. You can multiply B and C with a statement like

```
MAT RESULT = B * C
```

The computer considers B a 4-column matrix and is satisfied that the columns of B match the rows of C.

As these matrix arithmetic examples show, MAT arithmetic operations redimension the target array. Notice also, you *must* dimension the target array as well as the expression arrays *before* your arithmetic is performed. Once the arithmetic operation is complete, the number of dimensions in the target array remains

Figure 8–21. Multiplying matrices

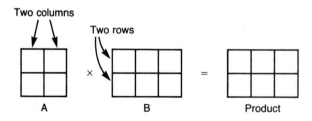

Figure 8–22. Matrix multiplication

```
DIM PRODUCT(4,5),A(2,2),B(2,3)
PRINT "The starting dimension of PRODUCT is ";
PRINT UBOUND(PRODUCT,1);"by";UBOUND(PRODUCT,2)
PRINT
MAT READ A
MAT READ B
MAT PRODUCT = A*B
PRINT "The new dimension of PRODUCT is ";
PRINT UBOUND(PRODUCT,1);"BY";UBOUND(PRODUCT,2)
PRINT
PRINT "After multiplication, PRODUCT looks like:"
MAT PRINT PRODUCT
DATA 2,1,3,2,1,2,-1,1,1,1
END
```

```
Ok. run
The starting dimension of PRODUCT is 4 by 5

The new dimension of PRODUCT is 2 BY 3

After multiplication, PRODUCT looks like:
 3               5               -1
 5               8               -1
Ok.
```

the same, but the number of elements in each dimension and the upper bound of each dimension depend upon the result of the arithmetic operation.

You can multiply an array by a scalar number represented as a constant or a variable. When you do, each element of the array is multiplied by the scalar value. You write the multiplication statement by giving first the scalar number and then the array name. The statement

```
MAT GROWTH = .12 * BASE
```

tells the computer to multiply every element in the BASE matrix by the scalar number .12. The result is stored in the GROWTH matrix which has the same shape as BASE.

Built-in matrices

True BASIC provides standard, built-in matrices that are used only for initializing other matrices. You can use them, for example, to initialize an array with every element set to zero or to the null string, "". The built-in matrices appear only in MAT statements to the right of the equals sign. They stand alone or as part of a scalar multiplication expression and produce, to the left of the equals sign, a target array to be used in other matrix operations. As always, you must dimension the target array, but you do not need to dimension the built-in arrays.

Figure 8–23 illustrates the use of the built-in *identity matrix* (every element on the diagonal is a 1; all other elements are 0) to create a matrix named FOUR with every diagonal element set to 4. The identity matrix is multiplied by 4 and the result is assigned to the target matrix FOUR.

If you wish to redimension FOUR at the same time you are initializing it to the diagonals 4, add arguments to the built-in matrix that give the new dimensions. The target matrix changes to conform to these arguments. If you write

```
MAT FOUR = 4 * IDN(5,5)
```

then matrix FOUR will become a 5 by 5 square matrix with 4s along the diagonal.

You can use matrices derived from the standard matrices in any matrix arithmetic operations as long as you follow the rules of matrix arithmetic. Figure 8–24 lists the True BASIC built-in matrices.

Figure 8–23. Using the identity matrix

```
▮ DIM FOUR(3,3), IDEN(3,3)
▮ MAT IDEN=idn
▮ PRINT "The identity matrix looks like:"
▮ MAT PRINT IDEN
▮ MAT FOUR = 4 * IDN
▮ PRINT"FOUR looks like:"
▮ MAT PRINT FOUR
▮ END
```

```
OK. run
The identity matrix looks like:
 1               0               0
 0               1               0
 0               0               1

FOUR looks like:
 4               0               0
 0               4               0
 0               0               4

Ok.
```

Figure 8–24. True BASIC built-in matrices

Matrix name	Matrix specified
CON	An array with every element set to 1; same size as the target array
CON(A,B, . . . n)	An array with every element set to 1; same dimension and size as the arguments A,B; can be up to 10 arguments
IDN	An identity matrix in which the diagonal elements are 1 and the rest are 0; must be square and the same size as target array
IDN(A) or IDN(A,A)	A square identity matrix with A elements in each direction; target array takes the same size and shape
NUL$	A string array with each element set to the null string, " "; same size and shape as target array
NUL$(A,B . . . n)	An array with each element set to the null string, " "; target array takes size and shape of the arguments A,B; can be up to 10 arguments
ZER	A string array with each element set to 0; same size and shape as target array
ZER(A,B . . . n)	An array with each element set to 0; target array takes the size and shape of arguments A,B; can be up to 10 arguments

Built-in matrix manipulation functions

True BASIC also includes built-in functions that provide tools for matrix manipulation. You can use these functions, which are listed in Figure 8–25, in the same situations you would use other True BASIC functions — that is, anyplace where expressions are allowed.

Figure 8–25. True BASIC matrix manipulation functions

Function name	Value returned
INV(SQUMAT)	The inverse of the nonsingular, square matrix SQUMAT
TRN(MTR)	The transpose of the 1-dimensional or 2-dimensional matrix MTR
DET	The determinant of the last matrix inverted by the INV function. If no matrix has been inverted or the inverted matrix was singular, the DET returns 0
DET(SQUMAT)	The determinant of the square matrix SQUMAT. If SQUMAT is singular, the determinant is zero
DOT(A,B)	The dot, or inner, product of the two 1-dimensional arrays or vectors A and B

Summary

Subscripted variables efficiently manipulate lists of information. The power of subscripted variables emerges when the subscript itself is a variable.

Programming skills

The DIM statement
Double subscripts
Subscript functions
The MAT PRINT statement
The MAT READ statement
The MAT INPUT statement
Built-in matrices
Matrix manipulation functions

Computer concepts

Related lists
Sorted lists
Redimensioning matrices
Matrix arithmetic

Review questions

1. If the digits 1 through 9 were input in ascending order to the following program, what would be the output?

```
DIM  A(3,3)
LET  T = 0
FOR  A =  1  TO  3
     FOR  S =  1  TO  3
          INPUT  N(A,S)
          LET  T = T+N(A,S)
     NEXT  S
NEXT  A
PRINT  T,  N(2,3)
END
```

2. Make use of a single subscript variable to simplify the program that prints out the Fibonacci sequence for as many intervals as the user wishes to see.

3. A name and integer score is typed in at the terminal for each of the 50 golfers in a tournament. Make the computer print out a table showing each golfer's name, score, and how many scored higher.

4. A 1-dimensional array named ARRAY contains 10 elements. Place the largest of these in the variable GREATEST and the element number of GREATEST in POSITION. Print out which element was the largest and exactly how large it was.

5. Use the computer to keep track of the use of computer facilities at the office computer center. There are 35 terminals available for staff members. Keep a program running during one day that allows you to enter the number of users at each hour from 8:00 AM to 5:00 PM. At the end of the day, have the computer print out a report giving the time (such as 8 AM, 12 NOON, and 3 PM) and the number of terminals in use at that hour.

6. The Best Bakery is so busy that it must receive deliveries of its 10 most needed ingredients each day: sugar, salt, pepper, butter, chocolate, flour, milk, vanilla, baking powder, and baking soda. Write a program that runs all day and accepts the inventory number of the items that are delivered. At the end of the deliveries, have the computer print out the list of goods not delivered so that the errand boy can do some emergency shopping.

7. The fourth-graders are reluctant to dress differently from their classmates. Use the computer to help pick out three colors that all will wear today. Select them at random from a list of 10 possible colors.

8. The Flower Farm wants to spur its five packing employees to greater productivity. At the end of the week the number of boxes packed by each person on each day will be entered on the computer. The computer will then calculate and print the information below. Write a program that accomplishes this.
   a. The average of boxes packed in one day
   b. The highest number packed by one person
   c. The employee number and the day that the top packer achieved such success

9. The Wrestling League gives awards to individual wrestlers as well as to the championship team. Write a program that the league chairman can use to enter the season's points for each wrestler in the league (each team has five wrestlers). Have it print out the top five wrestlers and their team name. Assume this league has only two teams: North High and South High.

10. Write a program that keeps track of reservations on the Speedy Piper Cub Airways' only plane. It has four rows of three seats each. Whenever a seat is reserved, store the initials of the passenger for that seat. When the plane is full, print out the following seating chart:

```
BJK   HHM   JMM
TTY   KBL   JAM
MMM   VAA   ACM
RAM   ROM   IBM
```

## Chapter 9

Subroutines and functions

Subroutines and functions are programming modules dedicated to performing specific tasks. They are the building blocks upon which a complete program is built. Program modules make it possible to use the computer to support even the most complex projects. The spaceflights that sent astronauts to the moon, for example, relied upon over a million lines of computer program code. It was only because this code was organized into modules that the project was manageable and the results reliable.

True BASIC includes statements that enable you to create subroutines and functions. This chapter begins with an overview of how to write a program using these modules, including a definition of terms regarding modules. Then it explains how to use the CALL, SUB, DECLARE, and DEF statements, which allow you to create and manage subroutines and functions.

Overview of programming with subroutines

The primary module of any program is the *driver,* or main routine. This driver module controls processing by calling subroutines in the order they are needed. It includes the prologue, line comments and key statements that make it clear what the program does. Aside from the prologue, which may be quite long, driver modules usually occupy less than one typewritten page. Figure 9–1 gives sample pseudocode for a driver module. Notice that it includes the statements that open and close all files used in the program, the END statement, and the statements that call upon the other program subroutines.

Calling a subroutine

When a main routine calls a subroutine, the computer transfers control to the subroutine. When the last statement of the subroutine has been executed, control returns to the calling routine. If the calling routine is a typical main routine, it

Figure 9-1. A sample driver

```
■ REM+***********************************
■ REM Title
■ REM Programmer: H. Morrill              *
■ REM Date of last Update: 8/8/88         *
■ REM Environment: IBM PC  256K           *
■ REM Language: True BASIC Version 1.0    *
■ REM Purpose: Illustrate a Driver Module *
■ REM ************************************
■ OPEN DATA FILE ! Driver opens all files
■ CALL READ       ! Read the file records
■ CALL SORT       ! Sort the file records
■ CALL UPDATE     ! Write out newly organized file records
■ CLOSE FILE      ! Driver closes all files
■ END             ! Driver ends program
```

usually calls another subroutine and then another until the job of the program is done. Figure 9-2 illustrates the relationship between a subroutine and the main routine that calls it. Notice that when control returns to the main routine, it returns to the statement following the call to the subroutine.

Figure 9-2. Transfer of control between a main routine and a subroutine

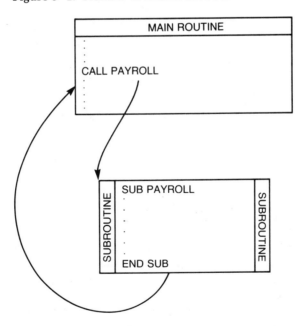

External subroutines

External subroutines may appear as separate programs in the computer's directory of programs and data files or they may be appended to another program module. They begin with a prologue and end with an END SUB statement. They are considered external because they are completely outside of the END statement of the routine that calls them or of any other module, and when they execute no other program modules are active.

Because the variables that these subroutines use are in external program modules, they are local variables not recognized by any other modules. Thus, the external subroutine and the caller can use the same variable name without conflict. When they do use the same variable name, the values the variable takes as the subroutine runs do not affect the variable of the same name used when the calling module runs. Figure 9–3 illustrates the separation of variables between an external subroutine and its caller. It shows that the variables in each module represent different memory locations. While the computer executes one routine there is no effect on the variables and instructions in the other routine.

Figure 9–3. Local variables

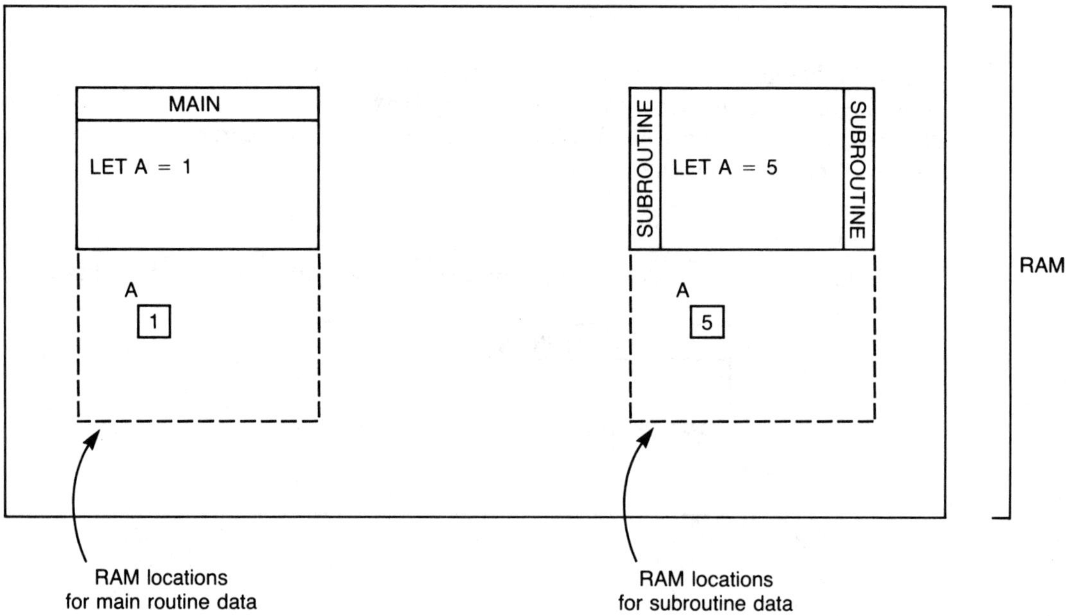

RAM locations
for main routine data

RAM locations
for subroutine data

Arguments and parameters

In spite of the separation between modules, subroutines often use values that have been defined by the calling modules and passed to the subroutine. When a driver calls upon a file reading routine, for example, it gives that subroutine the name and format of the file it has opened for reading.

Argument is the term applied to information that is passed to the subroutine by its caller. The argument or argument list is actually a list of variables that have taken values in the calling routine. The arguments are appended to the CALL statement that activates the subroutine.

When the subroutine is written it includes a *parameter* list, with one variable to match each variable in the argument list. These parameters will receive the arguments when the subroutine is actually called. Thus, even though the actual values to be passed are not known, the programmer must know the number and type of data that will arrive. The variables in the argument and the parameter lists need

Figure 9–4. Sample arguments and parameters

Caller: `CALL PAY(hours,wage,tax,NAME$)`   ←arguments
              ↕   ↕   ↕   ↕

Subroutine: `SUB PAY(time,money,IRS,EMPLOYEE$)` ←parameters

not have the same name (usually they don't), but the lists must match in number, type, and sequence of variables.

Figure 9–4 gives an example of a CALL statement with arguments and a SUB statement with matching parameters. The double-headed arrows indicate corresponding arguments and parameters. PAY is the subroutine name. The variables in parentheses make up the argument and the parameter lists. The author of the calling routine and of the subroutine have agreed that there will be four variables passed and that they will appear in the following order: time spent, hourly wage, tax deduction, and a string containing the employee's name. The lists reflect this agreement. The variables agree in number, type, and placement.

Passing values by means of argument and parameter lists works because the matching variables in these lists represent the same memory locations. Figure 9–5 shows a subroutine and a caller sharing variables in RAM.

Subroutines do not always have parameter lists. When there are no parameters, you do not need parentheses in the SUB or CALL statements.

Figure 9–5. Shared variables

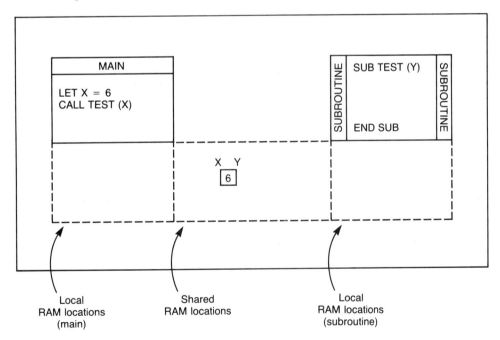

Local
RAM locations
(main)

Shared
RAM locations

Local
RAM locations
(subroutine)

Returning values from a subroutine

Although many subroutines perform tasks during their processing that do not directly affect their caller, such as printing a letter or creating a screen display, many subroutines do return values to their callers. The arguments and parameters are also the vehicles for returning values from subroutines to their callers. As subroutine processing occurs, the variables in the parameter list change value. When these variables change, so do the corresponding variables in the argument list. When control returns to the caller from an external subroutine, the argument list variables can have new values as a result of the work done in the subroutine.

Characteristics of subroutines

As different as subroutines may be, they all share similar characteristics that make it possible for them to fit within the structure of a larger program. These characteristics are listed in Figure 9–6.

Figure 9–6. Characteristics of subroutines

1. Subroutines begin with a prologue, which gives not only the usual identification and environment information, but also the number and type of parameters expected and the name of the calling routine.
2. Subroutines have only one entry point and one exit. The entry point is the first statement in the subroutine. The exit is the last statement in the subroutine. The computer transfers control to a subroutine when the CALL statement is executed in the calling routine. It returns control to the caller when the END SUB (the last line of the subroutine) is executed.
3. Subroutines receive values by means of the parameter list.
4. Subroutines return values to the calling routine by assigning values to variables in the parameter list.

The SUB and END SUB statements

SUB

The SUB statement appears first in a subroutine. It provides the subroutine name and the list of parameters. The END SUB statement is the last line of the subroutine. When it is executed, control returns to the caller.

Figure 9–7. Using an external subroutine

```
REM*******************************
REM       External Subroutine     *
REM*******************************
SUB ANNOUNCE(CLAS$,DAY$,TEACH$)
PRINT CLAS$
PRINT DAY$
PRINT TEACH$
PRINT
PRINT "COLLEGE OF NEW IDEAS"
PRINT "ROCKY MOUNTAIN ROAD"
PRINT "HIGHLAND, COLORADO"
END SUB
```

```
True BASIC here.
Ok.
```

■ END
■ SUB

Figure 9-7 shows a subroutine that prints college course announcements. The subroutine name — ANNOUNCE in this example — must be any legal variable name not appended with a $. The subroutine parameters here are the three strings CLAS$, DAY$, and TEACH$.

This subroutine's job is to use the information passed by the caller to print new course details as well as the usual college identification. When the job is done, control reaches the END SUB statement and returns to the calling routine. Figure 9-8 shows the subroutine in action.

Figure 9-8. Using an external subroutine

```
■ REM*****************************
■ REM         Main Routine        *
■ REM*****************************
■ DO WHILE MORE DATA
■     READ COURSE$,HOUR$,PROF$
■     CALL ANNOUNCE(COURSE$,HOUR$,PROF$)
■ LOOP
■ DATA "English Poetry","M-W-F", "Keats"
■ DATA "Archeology", "TU-THR", "Mead"
■ END
■ REM*****************************
■ REM      External Subroutine    *
■ REM*****************************
■ SUB ANNOUNCE (CLAS$,DAY$,TEACH$)
■     PRINT CLAS$
■     PRINT DAY$
■     PRINT TEACH$
■     PRINT
■     PRINT "COLLEGE OF NEW IDEAS"
■     PRINT "ROCKY MOUNTAIN ROAD"
■     PRINT "HIGHLAND, COLORADO"
■     PRINT
■ END SUB
```

```
Ok. run
English Poetry
M-W-F
Keats

COLLEGE OF NEW IDEAS
ROCKY MOUNTAIN ROAD
HIGHLAND, COLORADO

Archeology
TU-THR
Mead

COLLEGE OF NEW IDEAS
ROCKY MOUNTAIN ROAD
HIGHLAND, COLORADO

Ok.
```

The lines between the REM statements and the END statement in Figure 9–8 form the main routine. The CALL statement in the main routine tells the computer that ANNOUNCE is a subroutine that expects three string parameters. When CALL executes, it passes the arguments to ANNOUNCE, and the subroutine uses them to print an announcement. At exit from ANNOUNCE, control returns to the line following the CALL statement. In this example, control returns to the LOOP statement that creates another iteration of the DO WHILE loop. The subroutine is called each time there is an iteration.

Parameters in the SUB statement are always variables. They hold a place for the data that are to come. Arguments in the CALL statement can be string or numeric variables, constants, or expressions. If the argument is a variable, the matching parameter may change its value during subroutine processing. When this occurs, the argument variable in the calling routine changes also. Figure 9–9 shows a subroutine that passes values back to its caller by changing parameter values.

The author of the subroutine of Figure 9–9 is aware that Professor Keats is no longer on the payroll. The subroutine changes any occurrences of Keats's name passed as arguments to the name of his replacement, Simpson. When the change is made to the parameter variable TEACH$, an equivalent change is made to the argument variable PROF$. The main routine informs Simpson, not Keats, that the course has been announced. Only arguments passed as variables can be changed this way. Arguments that are passed as constants, expressions, or substrings cannot be changed by the subroutine.

```
EXIT
SUB
```

True BASIC allows you to use an EXIT SUB statement to bypass statements and return control to the main routine from the middle of the subroutine. Using EXIT SUB is actually a way to jump to the END SUB statement and then back to the caller.

True BASIC also allows you to open disk data files within a subroutine. But in structured programming it is preferable to open and close all files in the main routine of the program.

Overview of programming with user-defined functions

True BASIC provides a means for defining your own functions that work for you in the same way that the built-in functions like SQR(X) work for you. Such a user-defined (programmer-defined) function is actually a program module that performs a task and returns a single value to the calling routine. If it is stored as a separate program in the computer's directory, program modules can call upon it whenever they need its services. User-defined functions are invoked in the same manner as the functions internal to True BASIC. Their names, and any necessary arguments, are given in a PRINT, LET, or other statement that allows expressions. When this statement executes control passes to the function.

Sometime during its processing, the function assigns a value, or function result, to the function name. Once the function definition ends, control returns to the statement invoking the function and the newly found function result replaces the expression that activated the function definition. Figure 9–10 illustrates the relationship between a user-defined function definition and the statement that invokes it. Notice that the function replaces its name in the statement that invokes it.

Figure 9–9. Passing a value from an external subroutine

```
REM*****************************
REM          Main Routine        *
REM*****************************
DO WHILE MORE DATA
    READ COURSE$,HOUR$,PROF$
    CALL ANNOUNCE(COURSE$,HOUR$,PROF$)
    PRINT "Professor ";Prof$;", I have announced your course."
    PRINT
LOOP
DATA "English Poetry","M-W-F", "Keats"
DATA "Archeology", "TU-THR", "Mead"
END
REM*****************************
REM      External Subroutine     *
REM*****************************
SUB ANNOUNCE (CLAS$,DAY$,TEACH$)
IF TEACH$ = "Keats" THEN          !Professor Keats is
    LET TEACH$ = "Simpson"        !no longer on the faculty.
ELSE
END IF
    PRINT CLAS$
    PRINT DAY$
    PRINT TEACH$
    PRINT
    PRINT "COLLEGE OF NEW IDEAS"
    PRINT "ROCKY MOUNTAIN ROAD"
    PRINT "HIGHLAND, COLORADO"
    PRINT
END SUB
```

```
Ok. run
English Poetry
M-W-F
Simpson

COLLEGE OF NEW IDEAS
ROCKY MOUNTAIN ROAD
HIGHLAND, COLORADO

Professor Simpson, I have announced your course.

Archeology
TU-THR
Mead

COLLEGE OF NEW IDEAS
ROCKY MOUNTAIN ROAD
HIGHLAND, COLORADO

Professor Mead, I have announced your course.

Ok.
```

Figure 9–10. Transfer of control between a driver and a function definition

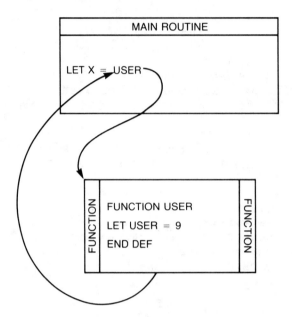

Arguments and parameters

All the variables in the function definition are local variables, including those in the function parameter list. Just as with subroutines, functions receive values by means of parameters that must correspond in number and type of variables to the arguments in the statement that invokes the function. For function definitions, however, the argument list and the parameter list do not share memory locations. Thus, changes made to the variables in the parameter list as the function definition progresses do not affect the arguments in the routine that invoked the function.

Returning values from a function

Function values are returned to the caller by means of a LET statement that invokes the function name. Figure 9–11 shows a statement in one routine that invokes a function, and a statement within the function definition that returns the function result.

Figure 9–11. Invoking a function and returning a value

Calling module
```
PRINT USERDEF(A,B,C)  ←  Invoking a user-defined function
```

Function definition
```
      LET USERDEF = 75  ←  Returning a value from a function
```

Characteristics of user-defined functions

Defining your own functions can make your programming life a lot easier. This is because user-defined functions make it possible to create a useful routine once and use it over and over again. And as unique as any user-defined function may be, all user-defined functions share certain characteristics that make them generally as useful as those built into True BASIC. Figure 9–12 lists the characteristics of user-defined functions.

Figure 9–12. Characteristics of user-defined functions

1. Function definitions begin with a prologue that details not only the usual identification and environment information, but also the number and type of parameters required.
2. Function definitions have only one entry point and one exit. The entry point is the first statement in the function definition. The exit statement is the END DEF statement, the last line of the function.
3. The computer transfers control to a function definition when the function name is invoked in a PRINT, LET, or other statement that allows expressions. The computer returns control to the caller when the END DEF statement is executed. A value must have been assigned to the function name before END DEF.
3. Function definitions receive values by means of a parameter list.
4. Function definitions return only one value to the calling routine — the value assigned to the function name.

The FUNCTION and END DEF statements

FUNCTION

END DEF

The FUNCTION statement, as the first statement in a function definition, tells the computer a function definition follows and provides the function name, the function's data type, and the parameter list, if any. END DEF is the last statement in a function definition. It marks the end of the function program code and returns control to the calling routine.

Figure 9–13 shows a function definition that incorporates a routine to select the highest of three numbers. This FUNCTION statement establishes that the function's name is HIGH, that its data type is numeric (because HIGH is a numeric variable name), and that it needs three arguments. The lines between the FUNCTION statement and the END DEF statement work out the logic of the function definition. The logic of the function must lead to execution of one of the LET statements before the END DEF statement is reached. LET assigns the function result to the function name and is the means by which the result is returned to the caller. Control actually returns to the caller when the END DEF statement executes.

Figure 9–13. An external function

```
REM*****************************
REM       External Function     *
REM*****************************
FUNCTION HIGH(A,B,C)
    IF A>B THEN
        IF A>C THEN
            LET HIGH = A
        ELSE
            LET HIGH = C
        END IF
    ELSE IF C>B THEN
        LET HIGH = C
    ELSE
        LET HIGH = B
    END IF
END DEF
```

Ok.

The DECLARE DEF statement

DECLARE
DEF

Figure 9–14 shows the function HIGH in use by another program. Since it is an external function, the module for HIGH is shown appended to the calling program after the END statement.

The DECLARE DEF statement must appear in any routine that calls an external function. Here it tells the computer that HIGH represents a function and is not to be considered an ordinary variable name. You must write the DECLARE DEF statement in the calling routine before you invoke the function. In this example, the main routine begins by accepting three numbers. Later, it calls the function by means of the statement

```
PRINT HIGH(X,Y,Z)
```

which passes the three numbers, X, Y, and Z, as arguments. Because the parameter list for the function HIGH matches the argument list, HIGH uses the same three numbers in the same order as the calling program. It selects the highest of the three numbers for the main routine, and, in a flash, this number appears on the screen.

Functions may have as many parameters as necessary or no parameters at all. If there are no parameters, there is no need for parentheses in the FUNCTION statement or in the statement that calls the function.

String functions

Functions can do string manipulations as well as numeric operations. When they do, the function name must be a string variable, the argument must be a string, and the result, not surprisingly, is a string value. Figure 9–15 shows a function that creates

Figure 9–14. An external function in action

```
REM*****************************
REM          Main Routine        *
REM*****************************

DECLARE DEF HIGH
INPUT PROMPT "What are your three numbers?":X,Y,Z
PRINT "The highest number is ";
PRINT HIGH (X,Y,Z)
END
REM*****************************
REM       External Function      *
REM*****************************
FUNCTION HIGH(A,B,C)
    IF A>B THEN
        IF A>C THEN
            LET HIGH = A
        ELSE
            LET HIGH = C
        END IF
    ELSE IF C>B THEN
        LET HIGH = C
    ELSE
        LET HIGH = B
    END IF
END DEF
```

```
Ok. run
What are your three numbers? 12,89,56
The highest number is 89
Ok.
```

Figure 9–15. An external function that manipulates strings

```
REM***********************
REM         Main Routine       *
REM***********************
DECLARE DEF ADVERB$
INPUT PROMPT "What is your adjective? ": ADJECTIVE$
PRINT "The adverb you want is ";ADVERB$(ADJECTIVE$)
END
REM***********************
REM      External Function   *
REM***********************
FUNCTION ADVERB$(WORD$)
    LET ADVERB$ = WORD$&"ly"
END DEF
```

```
Ok. run
What is your adjective? swift
The adverb you want is swiftly
Ok.
```

adverbs out of adjectives. It takes advantage of the ampersand operator (&), which is the True BASIC string operator that concatenates two strings.

True BASIC lets you open files within a function definition, and automatically closes them when control returns to the caller. But opening and closing files in a routine other than the main one makes it difficult to keep track of program input and output and is, therefore, contrary to good programming style.

True BASIC also provides an EXIT DEF statement to return control to the caller. You can only use EXIT DEF within the function definition *after* the LET statement that defines the function has been executed.

Internal subroutines and user-defined functions

True BASIC allows you to incorporate subroutines and function definitions into another program module. Usually these internal definitions appear *after* the main program code and *before* the END statement. Figure 9–16 schematically depicts a program made up of a main routine, an internal subroutine, and an internal function. Even though these internal modules are located at the end of the program module, the main routine can call upon them as freely as it calls external subroutines and functions.

Creating internal subroutines is another freedom allowed by True BASIC that it is better to ignore. Internal subroutines and functions lack many of the advantages of external program modules. Variables in these internal subroutines and functions are not local. Therefore, these modules cannot be written independent of the program modules that contain them. They might use variables that affect the encompassing routine in ways not anticipated. In addition, functions and subroutines that are embedded within larger modules cannot be called by other, independent modules. The time, effort, and genius represented by the internal modules have

Figure 9–16. Internal subroutines and functions

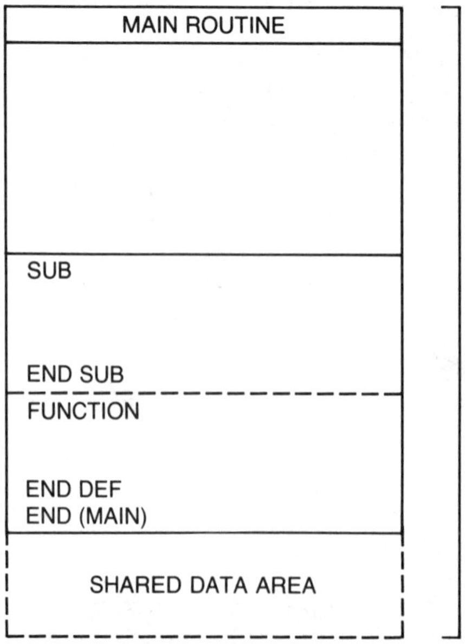

only limited usefulness. Finally, large program modules that include subroutines and function definitions are harder to maintain and understand.

You can do anything with an external subroutine or function that can be done with an internal one. Make a habit of using external functions and subroutines as you develop your programs.

One-line functions

There is one exception to the rule against using internal functions, however—that is, using a one-line function definition within a module. True BASIC lets you give a function name, give any parameters, define the function process, assign a value to the function name, and return control to the calling expression, all in one program statement. Using these types of user-defined functions within a module saves programming effort without detracting from good programming style. Figure 9–17 presents the adverb-maker function discussed earlier as a one-line internal function.

For one-line function definitions the FUNCTION statement does the work of several statements. On the left of the equals sign it defines the function name, data type, and arguments, if any. On the right of the equals sign it defines the logic of the function. The FUNCTION statement also eliminates the need for a DECLARE DEF statement.

```
FUNCTION
(ONE LINE)
```

Figure 9–17. An internal one-line function

```
▌ REM*********************************
▌ REM   Main Routine with an Internal, *
▌ REM     One-Line Function Definition *
▌ REM*********************************
▌
▌ FUNCTION ADVERB$(WORD$)= WORD$&"ly"
▌ INPUT PROMPT "What is your adjective? ":ADJECTIVE$
▌ PRINT "The adverb you want is "; ADVERB$(ADJECTIVE$)
▌ END
```

```
Ok. run
What is your adjective? swift
The adverb you want is swiftly
Ok.
```

The EXTERNAL statement

```
EXTERNAL
```

External subroutines and functions need not be appended to the program modules that use them. In fact, they are most useful when saved in a disk library file, thereby making them accessible to any module.

The EXTERNAL statement is the first line of the disk library file, and it is followed by one or a series of subroutines and function definitions. Although the

Figure 9–18. Creating a library of external functions

```
■ EXTERNAL
■ REM******************************
■ REM       External Function       *
■ REM******************************
■ FUNCTION HIGH(A,B,C)
■     IF A>B THEN
■         IF A>C THEN
■             LET HIGH = A
■         ELSE
■             LET HIGH = C
■         END IF
■     ELSE IF C>B THEN
■         LET HIGH = C
■     ELSE
■         LET HIGH = B
■     END IF
■ END DEF
■ REM******************************
■ REM       External Function       *
■ REM******************************
■ FUNCTION ADVERB$(WORD$)
■     LET ADVERB$ = WORD$&"ly"
■ END DEF
```

```
Ok. save func.lib
```

library file looks like the usual programming code, it is never actually run as a program. The library file resides on the disk and is referenced by other modules needing the services of the program modules it contains.

Figure 9–18 shows a library file of external routines, and shows the *save* command, which writes the library file to the disk. Notice that the *save* command includes the library file name *func.lib*. Using an extension like *.lib* is optional but useful. It reminds you that this is a library file and not a data file or True BASIC program. Remember, however, that the True BASIC *files* command only shows you programs having the *.tru* extension. You need to use the operating system directory command (DIR on the IBM PC) to list all the files, including libraries stored on your disk.

The LIBRARY statement

LIBRARY

The LIBRARY statement occurs within a program that uses a function or subroutine from a disk library. It tells the computer that subroutines and functions needed by this program are to be found in a disk library file and specifies the name of the library file. Once this statement executes, your program can use any of the routines in the library. Figure 9–19 shows a main routine that uses the ADVERB$ function in the library saved under the name *func.lib* in Figure 9–18. The main routine is a short

Figure 9-19. Using a library of external functions

```
■ LIBRARY "func.lib"
■ DECLARE DEF ADVERB$
■ INPUT PROMPT "What is your adjective? ":ADJECTIVE$
■ PRINT "The adverb you want is ":ADVERB$(ADJECTIVE$)
■ END
```

```
Ok. run
What is your adjective? swift
The adverb you want is swiftly
Ok.
```

one, and there is no need to append the subroutines and functions that the program uses. The programmer only needs to know in what library they can be found.

Using library files for external subroutines and functions exemplifies good programming style. It also ensures that modules will be written and tested separately and, thus, become reliable blocks upon which to build a larger program.

Summary

The primary module of any program is the driver, or main routine. This module controls processing by calling subroutines in the order they are needed. A user-defined function is a program module that performs a task and returns a single value to the calling routine.

Programming skills

The CALL statement
The SUB and END SUB statements
The FUNCTION and END DEF statements
The DECLARE DEF statement
One-line function definitions
The EXTERNAL statement
The LIBRARY statement

Computer concepts

Driver
Arguments
Parameters
Local variables
Shared variables
External subroutines and functions
Internal subroutines and functions
Program library

Review questions

1. *Corrections.* Determine whether each of the following True BASIC statements is correct. If it is, write "correct" on your answer sheet. If not, rewrite it correctly. Consider each statement separately. These statements are *not* part of the same program.

   a. ∎ SUB
   b. ∎ DEF ADVERB$
   c. ∎ DECLARE FUNCTION ACOUNT(MONEY)
   d. ∎ END DEF
   e. ∎ EXIT DEF
   f. ∎ FUNCTION HIGH(A,B,C)
   g. ∎ FUNCTION = ANS
   h. ∎ EXTERNAL SUB
   i. ∎ DEF LIMIT = X/2 - 2 * X + 1
   j. ∎ CALL SUB SCORES

2. *Corrections.* Determine whether each of the following True BASIC statements is correct. If it is, write "correct" on your answer sheet. If not, rewrite it correctly. Consider each statement separately. These statements are *not* part of the same program.

   a. ∎ DEF HIGH(ANS) = X * 4
   b. ∎ CALL SUB PRINTER
   c. ∎ DECLARE FUNCTION ACOUNT(MONEY)
   d. ∎ SUB END
   e. ∎ SUB EXIT
   f. ∎ SUB CLASS(COUNT,NAME$,AVE)
   g. ∎ CALL AVERAGES
   h. ∎ EXIT FUNCTION
   i. ∎ LET SUB RESULT = (A + B + C) / Z
   j. ∎ FUNCTION(WAGES,HOURS)

3. What will be printed when the following program runs?

```
∎ REM ********************************
∎ REM *                              *
∎ REM *            Main Routine       *
∎ REM *                              *
∎ REM *                              *
∎ REM ********************************
∎ FOR I = 1 TO 3
∎    FOR J = 1 TO 4
∎       PRINT "GL";
∎       CALL ILETTER(I)
∎       CALL JLETTER(J)
∎    NEXT J
∎    PRINT
∎ NEXT I
∎ END
∎ REM ********************************
∎ REM *                              *
∎ REM *       External Subroutines    *
∎ REM *                              *
∎ REM *                              *
∎ REM ********************************
∎ SUB ILETTER(I)
∎    SELECT CASE I
∎    CASE IS = 1
∎       PRINT "A";
∎    CASE IS = 2
∎       PRINT "E";
∎    CASE IS = 3
∎       PRINT "I";
```

```
    END SELECT
END SUB
SUB JLETTER(J)
    SELECT CASE J
    CASE IS = 1
        PRINT "S",
    CASE IS = 2
        PRINT "P",
    CASE IS = 3
        PRINT "T",
    CASE IS = 4
        PRINT "R",
    END SELECT
END SUB
```

4. What will be printed when the following program runs?

```
REM *********************************
REM *                               *
REM *        One-Line Function       *
REM *                               *
REM *                               *
REM *********************************
FUNCTION TRANSFORM(A) = A^2 - 2*A - 1
    PRINT "X", "TRANSFORM (X)"
    FOR X = 1 TO 5
        PRINT X, TRANSFORM(X)
    NEXT X
END
```

5. Use the computer to give advice to tennis players. Ask users 10 questions that will show their knowledge of the game. If they answer zero questions correctly, have the computer question their ability to read; if they get fewer than 3 correct, print out TRY ANOTHER SPORT; if they get 4–6 correct, print out the basic rules of the game; if they get 7–9 correct, print out tips to improve their game; and if they get all 10 correct, give them a list of important tennis tournaments to play in.

6. Once a person knows how to operate a particular program, it is boring to see the instructions each time it runs. Write a routine that might be included in other programs (such as that of Problem 8) and that asks the user if she wishes to see instructions. If she does, send control to a subroutine that prints them out.

7. Write a computer program that gives a quiz on all of the multiplication tables from 1 to 12. Use a subroutine to print out responses to each user's answer. If the answer is correct, give a cheery response. If the answer is wrong, be negative. In order to make the quiz more interesting, store several cheery answers and several negative ones and randomly pick which one will be used. Keep a count on the number of correct answers, and report the final score.

8. Write a computer quiz with 10 questions on any topic you choose. Make the computer seem more "human" by varying its response to the user's answers. Each time an answer is correct, have the computer pick a cheery reply from several choices in a DATA statement. Each time an answer is incorrect, randomly pick a negative response from DATA.

9. Standby flight reservations are made on a first-come, first-served basis. Use the computer to tell a standby passenger at flight time whether he will be able to board. Use a multiple-line string function to search through the passenger list in DATA for the passenger's name.

10. All employee numbers are 6 digits long. Write a program that uses a subroutine to verify that the number entered has no more nor less than the expected number of digits.

## Chapter 10

Trapping errors

From a programmer's point of view, there are three types of errors that may occur in the life of a program: logical errors, compile-time errors, and run-time errors.

Logical errors in the design of your program or in the data it uses can never be caught by the computer. The phrase *garbage in, garbage out* (GIGO) refers to the fact that the only way to discover logical errors is by observing erroneous results during the run of a program. The best protection against logical errors is rigorous testing. Before sending a program out into the world as a finished product, test it in the most unlikely situations. Depending upon the program, try using very large and very small numbers, or very unlikely — but possible — combinations of character data.

Compile-time errors are those errors that appear once you give the RUN command. As True BASIC tries to compile your program, it points out any language-related error by moving the blinking cursor to the error in the edit window and printing an explanatory message in the command window. Once you correct the error and switch control to the command window, the computer tells you the next sequential error in the program.

The compiler error messages protect you from programming errors such as missing quotation marks but not from *run-time errors,* that is, problems that can only arise during a program run, such as input/output errors or user mistakes. When a run-time error occurs, True BASIC stops the program run and prints a message describing the error. Sometimes you can correct such an error and rerun the program successfully.

Frequently, your program can anticipate some of the potential run-time errors. True BASIC includes *exception-handler statements,* which recognize a run-time error and enable action intended to prevent the computer from bringing the program to a halt. This chapter explains how to create and use exception handlers.

The WHEN EXCEPTION IN, USE, and END WHEN statements

WHEN EXCEPTION IN

Exception handlers get control whenever a run-time error occurs in the program code they are protecting. If the error is one you have specified, your error processing routine receives control. If the error is not one you have specified, True BASIC

USE

END
WHEN

handles the error in the usual way; it stops the program and prints an error message.

Figure 10-1 shows an exception handler that catches division by zero and prints a scolding message to the user. The figure also shows that other errors are handled in the usual manner. The WHEN EXCEPTION IN statement precedes the lines of program code protected by the exception handler. If the error of attempting to divide by zero occurs during the execution of any of these protected lines, control falls to the error-processing portion of the exception-handling routine.

Figure 10-1. Using an exception handler

```
WHEN EXCEPTION IN
     INPUT PROMPT "Enter a denominator. ":DENOM    !PROTECTED CODE
     LET RESULT = 64/DENOM                         !possible error
     PRINT "The answer is ":RESULT                 !if no error
USE
     IF EXTYPE = 3001 THEN                          !ERROR-PROCESSING:
        PRINT "I can't divide by zero!!"            !code = 3001 is
        PRINT "Sorry you're out of luck."           !divide-by-zero
     ELSE                                           !error
        EXIT HANDLER                                !let True BASIC
     END IF                                         !handle error
END WHEN
PRINT "That's enough math for now."                 !UNPROTECTED CODE
END
```

```
Ok. run
Enter a denominator. 0
I can't divide by zero!!
Sorry you're out of luck.
That's enough math for now.
Ok. run
Enter a denominator. a denominator
String given instead of number. Please retry from bad item.
?
```

The USE statement in Figure 10-1 marks the beginning of the program's error-processing statements. True BASIC EXTYPE is a True BASIC function that returns the code number of the most recent run-time error. The IF statement checks EXTYPE to see if the error that sent control to the routine is number 3001, which is the code number for the error that interests the programmer: division by zero. If EXTYPE returns the code for the sought-after error, the error-processing portion of the exception handler takes control. In this example, the message coded by the programmer appears, and control then falls to the line following the END WHEN statement.

If the error is not the one of interest, control falls to the ELSE clause of the exception-handling routine. Here, the EXIT HANDLER statement sends control out of the program to True BASIC. The normal run-time error processing occurs; the appropriate True BASIC error message is printed and program execution stops.

True BASIC error codes and messages

Figure 10-2 is a list of the True BASIC error codes. Notice there is a message associated with each one. The message associated with the most recent error is stored in the True BASIC variable EXTEXT$. You can use it in any way you see fit. Often, exception handlers display the usual True BASIC by PRINTing EXTEXT$ message but then let program execution continue.

Figure 10-2. True BASIC error codes and messages

Code	Message	Code	Message
0	No error has occurred.	6001	Mismatched array sizes.
		6002	DET needs a square matrix.
1-999	Available for programmer use.	6003	INV needs a square matrix.
		6004	IDN must make a square matrix.
1000	Overflow.		
1051	String too long.	7001	Channel # must be 1 to 1000.
2001	Subscript out of bounds.	7002	Can't use number 0 here.
		7003	Channel is already open.
3001	Division by zero.	7004	Channel isn't open.
3002	Negative number to nonintegral power.	7101	Unknown OPEN option.
		7102	Too many channels open.
3003	Zero to negative power.	7103	File's record size doesn't match OPEN RECSIZE.
3004	LOG of number <= 0.		
3005	SQR of a negative number.	7104	Wrong type of file.
3006	MOD and REMAINDER can't have 0 as 2nd argument.	7202	Must be record or byte file for SET RECORD.
3008	Can't use ANGLE(0,0).	7250	Can't SET RECSIZE on nonempty record file.
3009	Can't invert singular matrix.	7251	Must be BYTE file or empty for SET RECSIZE.
4001	VAL string isn't a proper number.	7252	File pointer out of bounds.
4003	Improper ORD string.	7301	Can't erase file not opened as OUTIN.
4004	SIZE index out of range.	7302	Can't output to INPUT file.
4005	TAB column not between 1 and margin.	7303	Can't input from OUTPUT file.
4006	Margin less than ZONEWIDTH.	7350	Can't PRINT to middle of text file.
4007	ZONEWIDTH out of range.		
4008	LBOUND out of range.	7351	Must be byte file for READ BYTES.
4009	UBOUND out of range.		
4010	REPEAT$ count < 0.		
4020	Improper NUM string.	8001	Reading past end of data.
4501	Error in PLAY string.	8002	Too few input items.
		8003	Too many input items.
5000	Out of memory.	8011	Reading past end of file.

Figure 10-2. *Continued*

Code	Message	Code	Message
8101	Data item isn't a number.	9005	Diskette removed or wrong diskette.
8103	String given instead of number.	9006	Disk full.
8104	Data item isn't a string.	9666	Program stopped.
8105	Badly formed input line.		
8201	Badly formed USING string.	10001	ON index out of range, no ELSE given.
8202	No USING item for output.	10002	RETURN without GOSUB.
8301	Output item bigger than RECSIZE.	10004	No CASE selected, but no CASE ELSE.
8302	Input item bigger than RECSIZE.	10005	CHAIN statement error message.
8304	Must SET RECSIZE before WRITE.		
8501	Must be text file.	11000	Can't do graphics on this computer.
8502	Must be record or byte file.	11001	Window minimum = maximum.
8601	Cursor set out of bounds.		
8700	No GET MOUSE on this computer.	11002	Screen minimum >= maximum.
		11003	Screen bounds must be 0 to 1.
9001	File is read or write protected.	11004	Can't SET WINDOW in picture.
9002	Trouble using disk or printer.	11005	Channel isn't a window.
9003	No such file.	11008	No such color.
9004	File already exists.		

Correcting a run-time error

Frequently, the goal of the exception-handling routine is to send control back to the line where the error occurred in order to re-execute the line. This is particularly useful when the error results from incorrect input. One way to accomplish this goal is to use a programming technique known as *setting a flag*. Figure 10-3 illustrates how this works.

The DO LOOP in the example is a trailing decision loop governed by the FLAG$ variable. FLAG$ is set to "problem" by the exception handler when division by zero is attempted. FLAG$ is set to "none" when the protected code is executed successfully. As a result, the program does not fail when a user enters a zero denominator. Rather, it loops back to again ask for input. When input is not a zero, FLAG$ is set to "none," processing proceeds in the normal fashion, and there is no need to loop back for more input.

If any other run-time error occurs during execution of the protected code, the EXIT HANDLER statement receives control and turns it over to True BASIC. Errors that occur outside of the protected code are also handled by True BASIC in the usual manner.

Figure 10-3. Correcting a run-time error

```
■ DO
■     WHEN EXCEPTION IN
■         INPUT PROMPT "Enter a denominator. ": DENOM   !PROTECTED code
■         LET RESULT = 64/DENOM                         !possible error
■         LET FLAG$ = "none"                            !set flag no
■     USE
■         IF EXTYPE = 3001 THEN                         !ERROR CHECK
■         PRINT "I can't divide by zero! Try again."    !error response
■             LET FLAG$ = "problem"                     !set flag yes
■         ELSE                                          !
■             EXIT HANDLER                              !control to
■         END IF                                        !True BASIC
■     END WHEN
■ LOOP WHILE FLAG$ = "problem"                          !trailing decision
■ PRINT "The result is ";RESULT                         !MAIN ROUTINE
■ END
```

```
Ok. run
Enter a denominator. 0
I can't divide by zero! Try again.
Enter a denominator. 4
The result is 16
Ok.
```

Nesting exception handlers

Figure 10-4 depicts nested exception handlers. It shows that you can nest an exception handler within the protected code of another exception handler. That is, the protected lines of code within an exception handler statement can contain the WHEN EXCEPTION IN, USE, and END WHEN statements. The error-processing portion of the exception handler, however, cannot have nested protected lines.

Neither the protected lines nor the error-processing code within an exception handler can contain subroutine, function, or picture definitions. However, the protected code can CALL such program modules.

Percolation

If an EXIT HANDLER statement is being executed in an exception handler that is nested within another exception handler, control is not sent to True BASIC but to the higher-level (outer) exception handler. If this exception handler has also been nested and also executes an EXIT HANDLER statement, control bubbles up to the next higher exception handler. This process, known as *percolation*, continues until there is no higher exception handler to take control. At that point, True BASIC handles the error.

Figure 10-4. Nested exception handlers

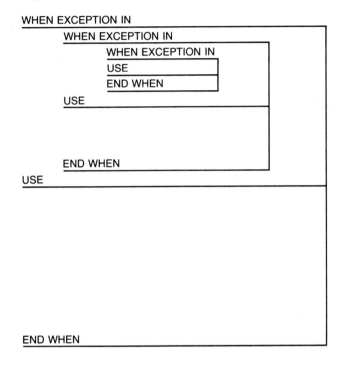

Figure 10-5 presents a program involving percolation. The higher-level exception handler checks EXTYPE for number 7004, the code for an unopen channel; the nested exception handler checks EXTYPE for number 8101, the code for non-numeric data. This example purposely includes an error. The statement

```
INPUT #1: WAGE, OVER
```

will work only if a file has been opened. But no file has been opened in this program, so when it runs, this error brings the exception handlers into play.

First the inner exception handler that checks for error number 8101 takes control. Since the problem is not one of invalid data, the inner exception handler gives control to its EXIT HANDLER statement. But, because the inner exception handler is nested, the EXIT HANDLER sends control to the higher exception handler rather than to True BASIC. The higher exception handler recognizes error number 7004 and informs the user that the necessary file has not been opened.

Percolation also occurs between calling modules and subroutines or functions. The protected code of a WHEN EXCEPTION IN-END WHEN statement can call a subroutine, picture, or function that itself has a WHEN EXCEPTION IN-END WHEN statement. When an error occurs in protected code in a subroutine, for example, the exception handler of the subroutine takes control. If the error is one that the exception handler is looking for, the exception handler takes care of it and execution continues through the subroutine. If the exception handler cannot recognize the error and executes an EXIT HANDLER statement, control percolates to the protected code in the program that called the subroutine.

When an error occurs outside of protected code in a subroutine, picture, or function, no percolation occurs. Control returns to True BASIC for normal run-time error processing.

Figure 10–5. Percolation

```
WHEN ERROR IN
        WHEN ERROR IN
              PRINT "Reading regular and overtime hours."
              READ R,O
              DATA 40, 3.5
              INPUT #1: WAGE, OVER
              LET TOTAL = WAGE * REG + OVER * XTRA
        USE
              IF EXTYPE = 8101 THEN        ! data item isn't a number
                 PRINT "This data is not numeric."
              ELSE
                 EXIT HANDLER
              END IF
        END WHEN
USE
     IF EXTYPE = 7004 THEN                 ! channel isn't open
        PRINT "Salary file not yet available."
     ELSE
        EXIT HANDLER
     END IF
END WHEN
PRINT "We might as well stop."
END
```

```
Ok. run
Reading regular and overtime hours.
Salary file not yet available.
We might as well stop.
Ok.
```

The CAUSE EXCEPTION statement

CAUSE
EXCEPTION

You can set up your own error codes (with numbers below 999) and test for these values in your exception-handling routine as well as for True BASIC codes. The CAUSE EXCEPTION statement makes this possible.

When a CAUSE EXCEPTION statement is being executed, the computer functions as though a real error had occurred. For example, the statement

```
CAUSE EXCEPTION 2001
```

assigns 2001 to the EXTYPE variable and makes the computer respond as though a "subscript out of bounds" error had occurred. If your program has an exception handler, control passes to it; otherwise True BASIC prints the message "Subscript out of bounds" and stops the program.

If you give an error number lower than 999, the EXTYPE variable takes that value. If you also give a message, the EXTEXT$ variable takes that value. Thus, the statement

```
CAUSE EXCEPTION 100, "Too Many Tries"
```

sets EXTYPE to 100 and EXTEXT\$ to "Too Many Tries". Figure 10–6 shows that you can write your exception handler to check for and recognize this code. If no exception handler exists when a code lower than 999 occurs, True BASIC receives control and prints a message saying that error number xxx was CAUSED.

Figure 10–6. CAUSE EXCEPTION

```
WHEN ERROR IN
     DO
          INPUT PROMPT "How many miles to the moon? ";FAR
          IF FAR = 238857 THEN
             PRINT "GOOD FOR YOU!!"
          ELSE
             IF ABS(FAR - 238857) > 100000 THEN
                CAUSE EXCEPTION 100, "You're way off!"
             ELSE
                PRINT "You're close. Try again."
             END IF
          END IF
     LOOP WHILE FAR <> 238857
USE
     IF EXTYPE = 100 THEN
          PRINT EXTEXT$
     ELSE
          EXIT HANDLER
     END IF
END WHEN
PRINT "Thanks for playing."
END
```

```
Ok. run
How many miles to the moon? 50000
You're way off!
Thanks for playing.
Ok. run
How many miles to the moon? 325000
You're close. Try again.
How many miles to the moon? 238857
GOOD FOR YOU!!
Thanks for playing.
Ok.
```

The exception handler prevents the game from continuing if a player gives a wild guess. If the guess is 100,000 miles too high or 100,000 miles too low, the CAUSE EXCEPTION statement in the protected lines of code executes, and control passes to the exception handler. The computer prints the message stored in EXTEXT\$, informing the player that the guess was unrealistic, and then gracefully ends the game.

Summary

From a programmer's point of view, there are three types of errors that can occur in the life of a program: logical errors, compile-time errors, and run-time errors. Exception-handler routines get control in place of the default True BASIC error handler whenever a run-time error occurs in the code they are protecting.

Programming skills

The WHEN EXCEPTION IN, USE, and END WHEN statements
The EXIT HANDLER statement
The EXTYPE function
The EXTEXT$ function
The CAUSE EXCEPTION statement

Computer concepts

Logical errors
Compile-time errors
Run-time errors
Percolation

Review questions

1. List and define the three types of program errors.
2. Define *percolation*.
3. Determine whether each of the following True BASIC statements is correct. If it is, write "correct" on your answer sheet. If not, rewrite it correctly. Consider each statement separately. These statements are *not* part of the same program.
   a. ■ USE
   b. ■ END EXCEPTION
   c. ■ CAUSE EXCEPTION
   d. ■ EXIT EXCEPTION
   e. ■ WHEN EXCEPTION
   f. ■ CAUSE EXCEPTION
   g. ■ WHEN
   h. ■ USE EXTYPE
   i. ■ END WHEN
   j. ■ WHEN EXCEPTION IN
4. Write a program that traps the READING PAST END OF DATA error and informs the user that the information being sought after is not in the computer's memory.
5. Write a program that traps the SUBSCRIPT OUT OF BOUNDS error and informs the user that because of this the program cannot continue.
6. Write a program that traps the SUBSCRIPT OUT OF BOUNDS error and informs the user the program will continue assuming that the highest list item set by a DIM statement is what the user really wanted.
7. Write a program that traps the DIVISION BY ZERO error and asks the user to enter a valid denominator or a −1 to indicate the program should end.

8. Write a program that uses your own error code. Ask for a user's age. If it is less than 16 give the message YOU'RE TOO YOUNG TO DRIVE A CAR and print the number of years until the user is 16 and old enough to drive. Repeat the routine for 10 potential drivers.

9. Write a program that illustrates percolation with two errors: READING PAST END OF DATA and DATA ITEM ISN'T A NUMBER. Use a loop to read numbers. First, check to see if the error is READING PAST END OF DATA. Then check to see if DATA ITEM ISN'T A NUMBER.

## Chapter 11

Fine-tuning printed output and string input

The print and screen designs that you provide for the users of the program you write are ambassadors for the genius and usefulness of your work. Frequently they determine how often your program will be used, or if, in fact, it will be used at all. Where people have a choice, they will certainly prefer a program that is clear but does less to one that is more powerful but cryptic.

True BASIC includes statements that make it easy to write clear, user-oriented input and output routines. This chapter explains the PRINT USING, PRINT TAB, and True BASIC string functions, which are some of the True BASIC programming tools that make such effective and friendly programs possible.

Formatted printing

If you have not yet done so, you will soon discover that the PRINT statement has many limitations. For example, it prints or displays decimals to six digits of precision left-justified without aligning the decimal points. Using PRINT to create a report of utility costs, for instance, could produce something like the output of Figure 11–1. The numbers are really unsuitable for dollar amounts and are hard to read if you

Figure 11–1. PRINT statement formatting

```
True BASIC here
Ok. run

UTILITY COSTS
Water           45.176
Electricity     125
Telephone       9.56
Heat            1800
```

wish to compare categories. You need to line up the decimal points, round off the decimal positions, append zeros to the right, and, possibly, include dollar signs. The enhanced versions of the PRINT statement can do these things; some are more powerful than others. PRINT TAB allows you to control horizontal spacing. PRINT USING reformats numbers and character strings.

The PRINT TAB statement

PRINT
TAB

The PRINT TAB statement is actually a combination of the PRINT statement and the TAB function. Together, they control spacing across the print line. You can specify as the argument of the TAB function the character position where you want the next data item printed. For example, the statement

```
PRINT TAB(20);"MARATHON"
```

prints MARATHON beginning in position 20 of the print line.

In one PRINT statement you can specify as many tab positions as you find useful, except that you cannot ask the computer to reverse direction on a line and print to the left of a position already printed. If you do specify a tab position that has been passed, the cursor moves to the next line and begins printing in the tab position. Thus, the statement

```
PRINT TAB(10);"COW";TAB(30);"JUMPED";TAB(5);"THE"
```

places COW and JUMPED at positions 10 and 30 on the first print line and THE in position 5 on the second print line.

Placing a comma right after the TAB function argument, as in

```
PRINT TAB(20),"COW"
```

moves the cursor, before printing begins, to the next print zone after the tab position. In this example, if the default print zones that begin in tab positions 1, 17, 33, and 49 are in effect, COW is printed in position 33, the first position of the third zone, because TAB(20) first places the cursor four characters into the second print zone.

Placing a punctuation mark after the entire TAB function specification controls the cursor *after* printing is completed. A *trailing semicolon* leaves the cursor at the last character printed. A *comma* moves the cursor to the next print zone. *No punctuation* moves the cursor to the start of the next line. Thus, the statement

```
PRINT TAB(20);"COW",
```

prints COW at position 20 and then moves the cursor to the start of the next print zone.

You can use variables and expressions as arguments in the TAB function. Figure 11–2 uses the TAB function to print the graph of $Y = 2X$ as X varies from 1 to 5. The expression in the TAB function calculates the placement of the asterisk on the print line. It allows for an indent of at least six character positions, and three

Figure 11-2. Variables and expressions in the TAB function

```
FOR X = 5 TO 1 STEP -1
    PRINT TAB (6 + (3*X)); " * "
    FOR Y_AXIS = 1 TO (2*X) - (2*(X - 1) - 1)
        PRINT
    NEXT Y_AXIS
NEXT X
PRINT "X VALUES";
FOR X_AXIS = 1 TO 5
    PRINT X_AXIS;
NEXT X_AXIS
END
```

```
Ok.
                                    *


                        *


                    *


                *



            *



        X VALUES  1  2  3  4  5
        Ok.
```

print positions for each mark (space, asterisk, space). The nested Y-AXIS loop determines the slope of the graph by calculating the number of print lines between the asterisk just printed and the next one to be printed. To do this it finds the current function value, (2*X), and subtracts the next value, (2*(X − 1)). Finally, it reduces the result by 1 to take into account the print line of the mark itself. The X-AXIS loop prints the bottom line of the graph. This last PRINT statement ends with a semicolon to keep the output of the loop all on one line.

The PRINT USING statement

PRINT
USING

The PRINT USING statement prints string or numerical data according to a line format of your own design. PRINT USING requires two pieces of information: which print format specification to use and which information to display using that format.

The format specification is a string composed of literal characters and format fields that describe how and where each item of data should appear on the print line. The format fields themselves are composed of special format descriptor characters. Figure 11–3 lists the complete set of True BASIC format descriptors.

Figure 11–3. Summary of USING descriptors

Descriptor	Meaning	Example	
*	Print leading zeros as asterisks.	Constant: Format: Result:	56.75 ****** *****57
%	Print leading zeros as zeros.	Constant: Format: Result:	23 %%%%% 000023
#	Print leading zeros as spaces.	Constant: Format: Result:	123 ##### 123
+	Print a number with a leading plus sign or minus sign, as appropriate.	Constant: Format: Result:	-56 +## -56
—	Print a number with a leading space or minus sign.	Constant: Format: Result:	56 -## 56
$	Print a number with a leading dollar sign.	Constant: Format: Result:	56.00 $##### $ 56
, (comma)	Place comma in this spot.	Constant: Format: Result:	45678234 ##,###,### 45,678,234
. (decimal point)	Place decimal point in this spot.	Constant: Format: Result:	7.88 ##.# 7.9
^	Print the exponent field.	Constant: Format: Result:	12.34 ####^^^^ 1234e-02

(continued)

Figure 11–3. *Continued*

Descriptor	*Meaning*	*Example*	
<	Left-justify a data item.	Constant:	`"me"`
		Format:	`<###`
		Result:	`me`
>	Right-justify an item.	Constant:	`"me"`
		Format:	`###>`
		Result:	`me`

In the PRINT USING statement the format specification and the data are separated by a colon. Figure 11–4 shows how they work together to format the

Figure 11–4. The PRINT USING statement

```
■ PRINT USING "$##.##":5.5812
■ END
```

```
Ok. run
$ 5.58
Ok.
```

printing of a number. In this example the format specification contains one format field, which uses the dollar sign, pound sign (#), and the decimal point descriptors to tell the computer to display up to four digits, to precede them with a dollar sign, and to print two decimal digits after the decimal point.

You can use either a constant or a variable to denote the format specification, and you can use constants or variables to represent the data. Generally speaking, you should provide one item of data for each format field in the format specification. If you provide more data than format fields, the computer reuses the format fields for the extra data. If you provide fewer data items than format fields, the extra format fields will be ignored.

Figure 11–5 uses variables for the format specification and for the data in a

Figure 11–5. Variables in the PRINT USING statement

```
■ LET T = 4.1315
■ LET F = 5.5
■ LET FORMAT$ = "##.##    ##.###"
■ PRINT USING FORMAT$:F,T
■ END
```

```
Ok. run
 5.50  4.131
Ok.
```

PRINT USING statement that prints two numbers. It also represents an example of printing a number (5.5) that has fewer decimal places than indicated by the format field. The computer appends a right-hand zero to make the number conform to the format. It prints "5.50."

PRINT USING for numbers

To format the printing of a number you must tell the computer four things:

> The number of digits to appear in the number
> What precedes the number
> What is embedded in the number
> What follows the number

Number of digits. The maximum number of digits to print is specified by the number of digit descriptors in the format field. Numbers with fewer digits will be right-justified in the format field. There are three digit descriptors available. The one you use depends upon what you wish the computer to do if the number has fewer digits than descriptors. The choices are:

Digit descriptor	Action to be taken when the number has fewer digits than specified by the format field
#	Print leading zeros as blanks.
*	Print leading zeros as asterisks.
%	Print leading zeros as zeros.

If the number to be printed has more integers than digit descriptors in the format field, the entire field is printed with asterisks, to indicate a format field overflow.

What precedes the number. The symbol descriptors that can precede digit descriptors in the format field and the symbols they produce are:

Symbol descriptor	Symbol produced
+	A leading plus sign or minus sign
$	A leading dollar sign
–	A leading minus sign or blank space

Using more than one of these preceding descriptors causes the symbol to always appear next to the number. Each additional symbol descriptor holds a place for a digit as though it were a digit descriptor.

The symbol descriptors that can be embedded in a format field and the symbols they produce are:

Symbol descriptor	Symbol produced
, (comma)	A comma in the same position as the descriptor
. (decimal point)	A decimal in the same position as the descriptor

What is embedded in the number. The placement of the comma in the format field specifies the placement of the comma in the printed number. If the number has fewer digits than indicated by the format field, the unused commas are not printed. The placement of the decimal point in the format field specifies the placement of the decimal in the output. If the number to be printed according to this format has fewer decimal digits specified, the computer appends zeros on the right. If the number has more decimal digits than indicated in the format field, the computer rounds up the extra digits.

What follows the number. The symbol descriptors that can follow the digit descriptors in the format field, and the symbols they produce, are:

Symbol descriptor	*Symbol produced*
^^^^	The four characters of exponential notation

PRINT USING for character strings

You can tell the computer how you want character data to be printed by designing format fields made up of character descriptors. The placement of the string format field in the overall format specification indicates where on the output line you want the characters printed.

To format a character string print field you must tell the computer two things: the number of characters to print, and — if there are fewer characters than allowed for by the field — whether the characters are to be left-justified or right-justified in the format field.

Number of characters. To show how many characters are to be printed you can use any True BASIC format descriptor as a place holder. For example, an asterisk tells the computer to print one character. Three pound signs (###) tell the computer to print three characters, one for each descriptor.

Right- or left-justification. If there are fewer characters in the string than descriptors in the format field, the computer centers the characters in the field unless your format field also includes the descriptors that specify right-justification (>) or left-justification (<).

All descriptors in a string format field count for one character position. Thus, if you wish to print up to five characters, while left-justifying strings that are shorter, your format field should look like:

```
PRINT USING "<####"
```

The < counts for one character position; the four #s count for the other four positions.

Literal characters in format specifications

You can include the following literal characters in your format specification:

letters
digits
= ' : ! ( ) ? / -
embedded blanks

These are not part of the True BASIC format descriptor set. The computer prints them exactly as you have written them, regardless of whether the format descriptors and data are all used. Figure 11–6 includes the literal phrase

```
"The interest and amount are:"
```

as part of the PRINT USING output.

Figure 11–6. Literals in the PRINT USING statement

```
▌ LET A = 4500.56
▌ LET I = 12.73
▌ LET F$ = "Interest and amount: $##.##     $##,###.##"
▌ PRINT USING F$: I, A
▌ END
```

```
Ok. run
Interest and amount: $12.73     $ 4,500.56
Ok.
```

Figure 11–7 shows how PRINT USING provides the solution to the problem posed in Figure 11-1, that is, how to print a table of utility costs. The format

Figure 11–7. Formatting a report

```
▌ PRINT TAB (7); "Utility Costs"
▌ PRINT
▌ LET FORMAT$ = "<##########     $#,###.##"
▌ DO WHILE MORE DATA
▌    READ UTIL$, COST
▌    PRINT USING FORMAT$: UTIL$,COST
▌ LOOP
▌ DATA "water", 45.176
▌ DATA "electricity", 125
▌ DATA "telephone", 9.56
▌ DATA "heat", 1800
▌ END
```

```
Ok. run
       Utility Costs

water           $    45.18
electricity     $   125.00
telephone       $     9.56
heat            $ 1,800.00
Ok.
```

specification FORMAT$ contains two format fields: a string field and a number field. Each time the PRINT USING statement executes, the computer takes the data items in sequence and fits them into the plan of the format specification. Notice that the data items UTIL$ and COST match the format fields. They represent two data items to be printed on each line: a string and a number.

The program of Figure 11–7 produces a report with the decimal points lined up and the numerical amounts presented as dollars and cents. It is the type of report that computer users will find helpful.

String functions

String-handling functions are among the most powerful True BASIC formatting tools. They add flexibility and effectiveness to both input and output by bridging the gap between the variety of human responses and the rigid numerical codes of the computer.

Figure 11–8 shows how string functions simplify the swimming coach's task of entering race results for all swimmers in all events for every team in the league. The coach needs only to enter an unbroken string that gives the event, the time, and the name for each swimmer. She doesn't need to worry about spacing, capitalization, or punctuation. The string-handling functions separate the input string into the substrings and numbers that the program needs.

Figure 11–8. String functions

```
■ PRINT "Enter results in the order of Event, Time, Name."
■ PRINT
■ LET DASH$ = REPEAT$("-",5) !for later use
■ FOR SWIMMER = 1 TO 20
■     LET EVENT$= " "
■     PRINT "Enter results for swimmer #:"; SWIMMER
■     INPUT RESULT$                    !the results for one swimmer
■     LET R$ = TRIM$(RESULT$)          !eliminate the unwanted blanks
■     LET CHAR = 1                     !stating position for string search
■     DO WHILE ORD(R$(CHAR:CHAR)) => 65
■        LET EVENT$ = EVENT$ & R$(CHAR:CHAR)
■        LET CHAR = CHAR + 1
■     LOOP
■     LET CLOCK = VAL(R$(CHAR:CHAR + 2))
■     LET NAME$ = R$(CHAR + 3:MAXNUM)
■     PRINT
■     PRINT "The name is ";UCASE$(NAME$)
■     PRINT "The event is ";LCASE$(EVENT$)
■     PRINT "The time is ";DASH$;CLOCK;DASH$
■     PRINT
■     PRINT "By the way, the name has";
■     PRINT LEN(NAME$);"characters."
■     PRINT
■ NEXT SWIMMER
■ END
```

Figure 11-8. *Continued*

```
True BASIC here
Ok. run
ENTER RESULTS IN THE ORDER OF EVENT, TIME, NAME

Enter the results for swimmer #: 1?FreeStyle128belden

The name is BELDEN
The event is freestyle
The time is -----128-----

By the way, the name has 6 characters

Enter the results for swimmer #: 2?
program stopped
```

The DASH$ variable holds the result of the REPEAT$ function that produces as many copies as you specify of any character you specify. In the example DASH$ becomes a string of five dashes used later on in the program to enhance the output.

Before the DO loop, the computer examines R$. If there are any leading or trailing blanks around the input string, the TRIM$ function eliminates them. Once it is entered, the DO loop concatenates the first characters of R$ to produce the word that spells the swimmer's event. With each iteration the ampersand operator (&) in the statement

```
LET EVENT$ = EVENT$ & R$(CHAR:CHAR)
```

appends the current character to the ones previously stored in EVENT$.

To govern the DO loop, the ORD function retrieves the ASCII value of each character read and compares it to 65, the lowest ASCII value for an alphabetic character. As long as the ASCII value is equal to or greater than 65, the program assumes the character is a letter belonging to the name of the swimmer's event. Once the ASCII value drops below 65, the program assumes it has found the digit portion of the input string, and control falls out of the loop.

The value of CHAR goes up by 1 with each pass through the loop and represents the character position of the last character read. When the loop ends, it represents the starting position of the substring made up of the time digits. It is used in the statement

```
LET CLOCK = VAL(R$(CHAR:CHAR+2))
```

and in the statement

```
LET NAME$ = R$(CHAR + 3:MAXNUM)
```

to create the substrings CLOCK and NAME$.

For formatting the output of the program, the UCASE$ and LCASE$ functions provide uppercase or lowercase. The string of dashes produced by DASH$ highlights the swimmer's time, CLOCK. Finally, just to show off the string functions, the programmer uses the LEN function to print the number of characters in the swimmers name, NAME$.

The string functions have greatly improved computer–human relations. The coach can concentrate on the statistics with which she is working and enter them quickly. The computer can find the information it needs to tally the results, perhaps store them, and print a useful report. There is no need to worry about such human inconsistencies as inadvertent leading blanks or names of varying lengths. The same character-manipulating strings can evaluate the results for any number of swimmers.

REPEAT$, TRIM$, ORD, UCASE$, LCASE$, VAL, and LEN are all examples of string function names. As Figure 11–8 shows, the arguments can be expressions, constants, or variables. String function results such as -------, 6, freestyle, BELDEN, and 128 can be character strings or numbers. String functions, like other built-in functions, appear in PRINT, LET, and other statements where expressions occur. Figure 11–9 lists the True BASIC string functions and gives examples of how to use them.

Figure 11–9. True BASIC string functions

Function	Result	Example	
CHR$(X)	Character that has the ASCII value X	Format: Result	CHR$(65) "A"
DATE	Current year and day as a number in the form *yyddd*	Format: Result:	DATE 94252
DATE$	Current date as a string in the format *yyyymmdd*	Format: Result:	DATE$ "19941125"
LEN(X$)	Number of characters in X$	Format: Result:	LEN("longword") 8
LCASE$(X$)	X$ rewritten as all lowercase letters	Format: Result:	LCASE$("JunGle") jungle
LTRIM$(X$)	X$ without leading blanks	Format: Result:	LTRIM$(" FIG") "FIG"
NUM(X$)	The numeric string X$ (previously created by the NUM$() function) converted to a number	Format: Result:	NUM(Num$(345)) 345
NUM$(X)	The number X converted to a character string in the IEEE format useful in True BASIC record files	Format: Result:	NUM$(345) IEEE format for internal use
ORD(X$)	ASCII value of the single character X$	Format: Result:	ORD("A") 65
POS(X$,Y$)	The position of the first occurrence of Y$ in X$	Format: Result:	POS("AUTUMN","M") 5
POS(X$,Y$,n)	The position of the first occurrence of Y$ in X$ after position n	Format: Result:	POS("AUTUMN HARVEST MOON","M",6) 16
REPEAT$(X$,n)	A string made up of n occurrences of X$	Format: Result:	REPEAT$("HO",6) HOHOHOHOHOHO

Figure 11 – 9. *Continued*

Function	Result		Example
RTRIM$(X$)	X$ without trailing blanks	Format: Result:	RTRIM$("FIG ") "FIG"
STR$(X)	The number X converted to a string and formatted as it would be by the PRINT statement except for leading and trailing blanks	Format: Result:	STR$(.34512e3) "345.12"
TIME	A number that is the time since midnight, in seconds	Format: Result:	TIME 2003
TIME$	A string that is the time, in the format *hh: mm: ss*	Format: Result:	TIME$ 11:34:28
TRIM$(X$)	X$ without trailing or leading blanks	Format: Result:	TRIM$(" FIG ") "FIG"
UCASE(X$)	X$ rewritten with all uppercase letters	Format: Result:	UCASE("JuNglE") JUNGLE
USING(X$,N$,N)	Formats string or number items (N$,N) according to the PRINT USING format field X$	Format: Result:	USING$(">#####","BIG", 8.6) BIG 9
VAL(X$)	The numeric characters in X$ translated to a number. The digits need not have been previously converted to a string by NUM$	Format: Result:	VAL("345") 345

Summary

The print and screen designs that you provide for the users of the program you write are ambassadors for the genius and usefulness of your work. The enhanced versions of the PRINT statement, along with string functions, give you control over your program output.

Programming skills

The PRINT TAB statement
The PRINT USING statement
String functions

Computer concepts

Format specification

Format descriptors
Literal characters

Review questions

1. *Corrections.* Determine whether each of the following True BASIC statements is correct. If it is, write "correct" on your answer sheet. If not, rewrite it correctly. Consider each statement separately. These statements are not part of the same program.

   a. ■ `PRINT TAB(X):X`
   b. ■ `PRINT TAB(45);"Juniors","Seniors"`
   c. ■ `LET VAL(M$) = V$`
   d. ■ `LEN(CLASS$) = 500`
   e. ■ `IF LEN(A$,2) = 16 THEN PRINT "This is O.K."`
   f. ■ `PRINT CHR$(56)`
   g. ■ `PRINT LTRIM( R$)`
   h. ■ `PRINT REPEAT$(8,X$)`
   i. ■ `PRINT UCASE(X$)`
   j. ■ `PRINT TAB(34);  "MEN";TAB(40);"WOMEN";TAB(30);"CHILDREN"`

2. *Programs to Read.* What will be printed when each of the following programs is run? If input is required, give an example that would make sense to the program.

   a. ■ `LET HO$ = "35"`
      ■ `LET VALUE = val(ho$)`
      ■ `print 3*value`
      ■ `end`

   b. ■ `LET R$ = "R"`
      ■ `LET T = ord(R$)`
      ■ `LET G = T^2 + T*5`
      ■ `PRINT G *len(R$)`
      ■ `END`

   c. ■ `LET R$ = "Rumpelstiltskins"`
      ■ `LET P$ = "s"`
      ■ `LET X = pos(R$,P$,4)`
      ■ `print X^2`
      ■ `END`

   d. ■ `LET V$ = "<########    $###.##"`
      ■ `PRINT "REPORT ON WAGES"`
      ■ `PRINT`
      ■ `FOR X = 1 TO 3`
      ■ `READ N$,W$`
      ■ `PRINT USING V$:N$,W$`
      ■ `NEXT X`
      ■ `DATA Herpin,4.25,Bartram,4.75, Driscoll,3.85`
      ■ `END`

3. Write a computer program that prints out the mailing labels for the Department Store catalog. Use the customers' name, street, city, and ZIP code stored in DATA statements.

4. Write a program that produces a table with the title:
   `THE ASCII CODE FOR CAPITAL LETTERS`
   Include in the table both the decimal ASCII value and the capital letters it represents.

5. Often a program gives a user a choice as to whether he or she wants the program to run again or stop. Write a routine that might be added to any program, but that gives users the freedom to answer the query "Do you wish to play again?" with "Yes" or "Yeah" or "Yep" or any word beginning with Y. If they do answer so, send control back to the beginning of the program; otherwise, stop the run.

6. Computers are used to flash the special messages up high in Times Square. Write the New Year's Eve program that counts down the last 60 seconds of the old year and then prints out:
   `HAPPY`
   ` NEW`
   `YEAR`

7. Nutritionists have discovered that kittens need 1½ ounces of Katty Food each day in order to grow at a healthy rate. Each ounce of this food contains the following amounts

of essential nutrients: protein, 2 mg; vitamin A, 10 mg; vitamin C, 15 mg: and iron, 9 mg. Use PRINT USING to produce a report, like the one below, that tells how much of each nutrient 1½ ounces of Katty Food provides.

```
OUNCES REQUIRED TO GROW
PROTEIN        3.0
VIT. A        15.0
VIT. C        22.5
IRON          13.5
```

8. Write a program that accepts for the National Weather Bureau the weekly weather transmission from northern New England. The transmission gives the temperature and the percent cloud cover for each day of the week. The data arrive in the following format: Monday22cp50 (day, temperature — in degrees Celsius, cp = cloud percent = 50%). Your program should accept the data and then print it out in a readable chart.

Chapter 12

Colors, cursors, keys, sounds, and songs

As helpful as variations on the PRINT statement may be, True BASIC includes many more powerful output statements. This chapter explains the SET COLOR, SET CURSOR, GET KEY, and KEY INPUT statements that allow you to create colorful displays and to control interaction with program users. Subsequent chapters explain how to provide animated, multiscreen displays.

Using color

True BASIC makes it possible to create colorful displays, if your computer system includes the necessary hardware components. Since color capabilities vary widely among computer types, be sure to consult the *True BASIC User's Guide* for your computer. It will give you tips on fine-tuning the True BASIC color capabilities described here.

Run the program in Figure 12–1 to see the True BASIC colors available to you. Their names are listed in the DATA statements.

Figure 12–1. Displaying True BASIC colors on the IBM PC

```
SET MODE "GRAPHICS"
PRINT TAB(4);"THESE ARE THE TRUE BASIC COLORS:"
PRINT "Push return when the rectangle disappears"
FOR C = 1 TO 9
    READ C$
    SET COLOR C$
    PLOT AREA: .2,.2;.8,.2;.8,.8;.2,.8
NEXT C
DATA red,green,magenta,yellow,blue
DATA cyan,brown,white,black
END
```

Notice that two programming steps are needed to make colors appear:

1. Invoke a color with the SET COLOR statement.
2. Create a screen display with a statement like PLOT AREA.

You can, if you wish, follow this example and print text using the PRINT statement. But most likely, when you use color you will prefer to create your display by using SET CURSOR and the graphics statements that make it easy to draw lines and place text anywhere on the screen. (The True BASIC graphics statements are explained in the next chapter.) The PLOT AREA statement in the example is a graphics statement that outlines a rectangle and then paints it in the current foreground color.

Color choices

Even though True BASIC includes nine colors, the colors your True BASIC programs actually display depend upon the components of your computer system. Both the computer and the display must be capable of creating color if your program is to work as intended.

Fortunately, you can program for color even if there is a possibility that your program will be used on systems that do not have equivalent color capabilities. True BASIC makes black and white or color substitutions for you. If your computer system has more colors than True BASIC, the SET COLOR statement allows you to bypass True BASIC in order to use all of them. Even then, True BASIC still makes color substitutions when your program ends up on a system that has fewer colors.

Generally speaking, if you limit your color use to True BASIC's list, your program will run as you intend on a wider variety of computer systems. Keep in mind that portability and predictability are as important as creativity when producing truly useful programs.

The SET COLOR and SET BACKGROUND COLOR statements

```
SET
COLOR
```

```
SET
BACKGROUND
COLOR
```

The SET COLOR statement selects colors for the foreground alone or for both the foreground and the background. SET BACKGROUND COLOR selects background colors only. Both statements require a string or numeric argument indicating the color you wish. The argument can be either a constant or a variable.

If you are selecting True BASIC colors, you must choose from the colors listed in Figure 12–2. The list includes nine colors and the current background color. Black is the default background color, but you may change it to any one of the others.

Figure 12–2. SET COLOR choices

Red	Cyan
Magenta	Brown
Yellow	White
Green	Black
Blue	BACKGROUND

You can change the foreground color to red by using either the statement

```
SET COLOR "RED"
```

or a combination like

```
LET C$ = "RED"
SET COLOR C$
```

Subsequent display output will be red on whatever background color has been set. You can change the foreground color to blue and the background color to green by using either the statement

```
SET COLOR "BLUE/GREEN"
```

or the combination

```
SET COLOR "BLUE"
SET BACKGROUND COLOR "GREEN"
```

When you are bypassing True BASIC and using colors unique to your computer system, give numeric arguments for these statements. The *True BASIC User's Guide* that documents the computer you are using lists the colors and their associated numbers for your computer. The statements

```
SET COLOR 1
```

and

```
SET BACKGROUND COLOR 4
```

change the foreground color to color number 1 and the background color to color number 4 for the computer running your program. On the IBM PC, for example, these statements prepare for a green display on a cyan background.

The ASK MAX COLOR function

You can find out if your system has more foreground colors than True BASIC by running the program in Figure 12–3, which asks the computer how many foreground colors it can display at one time, and then displays each one in turn. For the IBM PC, this program displays green, red, and yellow, the three colors on the default palette.

Figure 12–3. Displaying your computer system colors

```
▪ SET MODE "GRAPHICS"
▪ ASK MAX COLOR X
▪ FOR C = 1 TO X
▪     SET COLOR C
▪     PLOT AREA: .2,.2;.8,.2;.8,.8;.2,.8
▪ NEXT C
▪ END
```

Once the ASK MAX COLOR statement executes, the variable X contains the count of how many foreground colors are simultaneously available on your computer. Because each color is associated with a number between 1 and the maximum number of colors, using X as the limit of the FOR-NEXT loop produces all these colors. With each iteration the SET COLOR statement using X invokes a different color.

The CLEAR statement

```
CLEAR
```

The CLEAR statement erases the screen and leaves the cursor in the top left corner. Use it at the beginning of each new display you wish to create. Simply write:

```
CLEAR
```

Controlling the cursor

Once you've decided upon the color of your display, you can think about the organization of the screen. Menus, or panels of information, provide a visual organization that enhances the effectiveness of your program. By moving the cursor to appropriate screen locations and executing INPUT and PRINT statements you can improve the interaction between your program and the outside world.

The SET CURSOR function

You can position the cursor on the text screen by giving the line and column positions in the SET CURSOR statement. The number of lines and columns available depends upon your computer type. On the IBM PC, for example, the text screen has 24 lines numbered from 1 at the top to 24 at the bottom. It has 80 horizontal "column" positions, ranging from 1 on the left to 80 on the right. The statement

```
SET CURSOR 10,40
```

moves the cursor to the middle of the text screen, down 10 lines from the top and over 40 columns from the left margin.

Figure 12–4 uses these screen control features to set up a data entry screen that automatically positions the cursor for each entry. Notice that the SET CURSOR statement positions the INPUT statement prompt (?) as well as the PRINT statement values.

When this sample program runs, the computer prints the entry headings and then positions the cursor for the first INPUT request on line 6 column 20. After each INPUT response the cursor moves to the next INPUT position. When all INPUT is complete, instructions on how to proceed appear and the computer waits until the word *next* is entered for the variable GO$.

Figure 12–4. Using SET CURSOR to format a display

```
■ CLEAR

■ REM Display Format

■ SET CURSOR 4,25
■ PRINT "Sample Form"
■ SET CURSOR 6,20
■ PRINT "First Name";
■ SET CURSOR 7,20
■ PRINT "Last Name";
■ SET CURSOR 8,20
■ PRINT "Street Address";
■ SET CURSOR 9,20
■ PRINT "City Address";
■ SET CURSOR 10,20
■ PRINT "State Address";

■ REM Accept Replies

■ SET CURSOR 6,35
■ INPUT FIRST$
■ SET CURSOR 7,35
■ INPUT LAST$
■ SET CURSOR 8,35
■ INPUT STREET$
■ SET CURSOR 9,35
■ INPUT CITY$
■ SET CURSOR 10,35
■ INPUT STATE$
■ SET CURSOR 12,10
■ PRINT "Type 'next' to proceed to the next form."
■ INPUT GO$
■ END
```

```
Ok. run
                      Sample Form

             First Name      ? Jim
             Last Name       ? Martin
             Street Address ? 112 Rt. 41
             City Address    ? Lakeville
             State Address   ? Connecticut

         Type 'next' to proceed to the next form.
? next
```

The INPUT statements in this program keep the display on the screen. Once the END statement executes, True BASIC clears the screen and returns to the usual edit and history windows. The GET KEY statement described below is an alternate means of prolonging text screen displays. It is useful when you do not need elaborate input and do not want to display the (?) prompt.

The ASK CURSOR function

As a counterpart to SET CURSOR, True BASIC provides an ASK CURSOR function that tells your program where the cursor is currently located. For instance, the statement

```
ASK CURSOR L,C
```

puts the current line position of the cursor in variable L and the current column position in variable C.

True BASIC also provides a SET CURSOR "ON" and a SET CURSOR "OFF" function to control whether or not the cursor is visible. You can substitute variables set to the word "ON" or "OFF" for the actual character strings. The counterpart for this is the ASK CURSOR function with a string variable.

```
ASK CURSOR S$
```

sets the variable S$ to the state of the cursor. It is either visible, and therefore "ON", or invisible, and therefore "OFF".

True BASIC includes the function

```
ASK MAX CURSOR L,C
```

which tells you in the variable L the total number of lines on the display screen you are using and in the variable C how many columns your display screen has.

Key codes and the GET KEY statement

```
GET
KEY
```

The GET KEY statement lets the computer receive a single keystroke from the keyboard without waiting for the press of the enter key or displaying the INPUT statement question mark prompt. When the statement

```
GET KEY A
```

executes, the computer pauses until a key — any key — is pressed. As soon as this occurs, the variable A takes the character code value for the character represented by the pressed key, and program execution carries on. If you wish, you can check for this key value and, depending on the results, select a path through your program.

As you read further in this book you will discover several ways to incorporate the GET KEY function in your programs and evaluate the results. Figure 12–5 gives an example of the GET KEY statement being used to decide which way to move a character on the screen. The program gives the user the illusion that pressing the correct key moves the "*" up the screen.

Notice that the program uses the key code value to determine whether the key of interest has been pressed. The statement

```
IF move = 328 THEN
```

checks to see if the key with code number 328 has been pressed. (On the IBM PC this is the up-arrow key.)

Figure 12-5. One use of the GET KEY statement

```
■ CLEAR
■ SET CURSOR 10,35
■ PRINT "*"
■ SET CURSOR 5,10
■ PRINT "Hit the right key (the 'mystery key!') to move the star."
■ GET KEY MOVE
■ If MOVE = 328 THEN
■    SET CURSOR 10,35
■    PRINT " "                  !erase the first "*"
■    SET CURSOR 9,35
■    PRINT "*"                  !display a new "*" up one line
■ ELSE
■    SET CURSOR 19,10
■    PRINT "There's no place to go but up!"
■ END IF
■ GET KEY KEEP                  !keep the display on the screen
■ END
```

Ok. run

Hit the right key (the 'mystery key!') to move the star.

                                  *

There's no place to go but up!

When a key, such as an alphabetic one, has an ASCII code number associated with it, True BASIC uses this as the key code returned by the GET KEY statement. For keys with no ASCII equivalent the code number used by True BASIC depends upon the computer type. The *True BASIC User's Guide* for your computer contains a map of the keyboard that gives the code number for each key.

When the program of Figure 12-5 runs, the screen clears and an asterisk appears. The computer waits, with no prompts or messages, until any key is pressed. If the key pressed has the key code value 328, the MOVE variable is set to 328. The program proceeds to clear the screen of the original asterisk and produce another one higher up the screen.

The final statement,

```
GET KEY KEEP
```

is one way to keep the text display on the screen. The screen display remains until any key is pressed, thereby giving a value to the KEEP variable. Then, the END statement executes and control returns to the True BASIC edit and history windows.

The KEY INPUT statement

```
KEY
INPUT
```

The KEY INPUT statement is similar to the GET KEY statement, for both statements recognize when any key has been pressed and neither statement gives a prompting message. They differ in that GET KEY stops the program while awaiting key input, whereas KEY INPUT permits program execution and program output to continue.

KEY INPUT is actually a logical expression:

KEY INPUT = FALSE   when no key has been pressed since the last INPUT, GET KEY, KEY INPUT or any statement has received keyboard input

KEY INPUT = TRUE   when a key has been pressed since a statement has received keyboard input

Figure 12–6 uses KEY INPUT to stop a continuous display of the current time being used to reserve the computer while the programmer takes a coffee break.

Figure 12–6. Using KEY INPUT

```
■ DO UNTIL KEY INPUT
■     CLEAR
■     SET CURSOR 10,30
■     PRINT TIME$
■ LOOP
■ END
```

The DO UNTIL KEY INPUT statement tells the computer to reiterate the loop until KEY INPUT becomes true. That is, it tells the computer to repeat the loop until any key is pressed. The statement

```
PRINT TIME$
```

is actually a PRINT statement that displays the value of the True BASIC TIME$ variable. If you set the computer's clock at the start of your computing session, this variable displays the correct time. When a key is pressed in this example, control falls to the line following the LOOP statement. This is the END statement that executes and returns control to the True BASIC edit and history windows.

The SOUND statement

SOUND

The SOUND statement produces sound at the frequency (in Hertz) and for the duration (in seconds) that you specify. Normally a SOUND statement waits for the preceding SOUND statement to finish before making its own sound. However, a SOUND statement with a duration of zero interrupts any preceding SOUND statement by turning it off, even if it has not yet run for the duration specified. The *True BASIC User's Guide* will tell you whether you can use the True BASIC SOUND statement on your computer. If you can, run the program of Figure 12–7 to see how the SOUND statement works.

Figure 12–7. SOUND effects

```
FOR X = 3 TO 3000 STEP 100    !FREQUENCY OF X
    SOUND X,1                  !DURATION OF 1 SECOND
NEXT X
END
```

The PLAY statement

PLAY

The PLAY statement makes it possible to compose musical phrases and play them in various combinations as your program runs. PLAY has its own set of commands that enable you to set the tempo, the octave, and many other musical attributes of a tune. To create a tune, you combine these commands into string constants and assign them to a string variable. When you wish a particular command to be heard, you refer to that variable in the PLAY statement. Figure 12–8 is a program that uses the PLAY statement to recreate the "Happy Birthday" tune. The first few lines define its phrases; the remaining PLAY statements execute them.

Figure 12–8. PLAYING "Happy Birthday"

```
LET STYLE$ = "MF"                          !music foreground
LET FIRST$ = "L8 MS 03 GG L4 AG 04 C 03 L2 B"
LET SECOND$= "L8 MS 03 GG L4 AG 04 D L2 C"
LET THIRD$ = "L8 MS 03 GG L4 04 GE L8 CC 03 L4 B A"
LET FOURTH$= "04 L8 FF L4 ECD L1 C"
PLAY STYLE$
PLAY FIRST$
PLAY SECOND$
PLAY THIRD$
PLAY FOURTH$
END
```

All of the PLAY statement commands are listed in Figure 12–9. As you use them you will see that they allow you a great deal of flexibility in creating melodies. Reflect a minute on the ingenuity of the computer scientists who have found yet another way to use the binary code!

Figure 12-9. The PLAY statement commands

Command	Meaning
Command	*Meaning*
A to G	Play the note indicated by the letter.
A to G, followed by #, +, or —	Play the note indicated by the letter and the sign: # or + means sharp; — means flat.
Ln	Play the notes that follow for an interval of 1/n each. L1 is a whole note, L2 is half note.
On	Set the octave to octave n. There are 8 octaves (0 to 7). Octave 4 is the default octave. Octave 5 starts at middle C; each octave runs from C to B.
Rn or Pn	Rest or pause for a length of 1/n.
Tn	Set the tempo (number of quarter notes per minute). The default tempo is 120 quarter notes per minute.
> and <	Move up (>) or down (<) an octave.
ML	Music legato. Each note plays the full interval specified by the L command.
MN	Music normal. Each note plays ⅞ of the time specified by the L command.
MS	Music staccato. Each note plays ¾ of the time specified by the L command.
MF	Music foreground. Each note waits until the previous note is finished. Program execution halts until playing has finished. MF is the default condition.
MB	Music background. Subsequent notes are stored and played while the rest of the program runs, repeating until stopped by a PAUSE statement or an MF command.

Background music

Some say that background music is an effective way to enhance computer results or to calm an impatient customer who must wait (while the dating program, for example, progresses). The program of Figure 12-10 uses foreground printing and background music to make the birthday greeting of Figure 12-8 more personal. The MB command has replaced the MF in the STYLE$ variable, and all of the phrases are concatenated to form a new string, SONG$. As a result, the program does not wait

Figure 12-10. PLAYing background music

```
■ LET STYLE$   = "MB"                    !music background
■ LET FIRST$   = "L8 MS 03 GG L4 AG 04 C 03 L2 B"
■ LET SECOND$  = "L8 MS 03 GG L4 AG 04 D L2 C"
■ LET THIRD$   = "L8 MS 03 GG L4 04 GE L8 CC 03 L4 B A"
■ LET FOURTH$  = "04 L8 FF L4 ECD L1 C"
■ LET SONG$    = STYLE$ & FIRST$ & SECOND$ & THIRD$ & FOURTH$
■ PLAY SONG$
■ FOR X = 1 TO 175
■     PRINT "Arthur MacKenzie"
■ NEXT X
■ END
```

for the music to complete to display the name of the birthday fellow. Rather, the music plays while the FOR loop proceeds. Arthur's name appears while his birthday song plays in the background.

Summary

Color and cursor control add further vitality to your program input and output.

Programming skills

The SET COLOR and SET BACKGROUND COLOR statements
The ASK MAX COLOR function
The CLEAR statement
The SET CURSOR and ASK CURSOR functions
The GET KEY statement
The KEY INPUT statement
The SOUND statement
The PLAY statement

Computer concepts

Color facilities on your computer: See the *True BASIC User's Guide*
Cursor control and screen design
Key codes

Review questions

1. Given the following information:

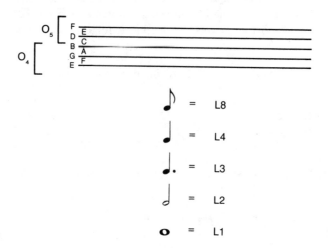

Make the computer sing the following tunes (identify them for extra credit):

2. Create a program that shows all of the True BASIC colors one at a time, each appearing in a different part of the screen. To make the result more pleasurable, have one of the tunes shown in Problem One play softly in the background.
3. Draw a box at the bottom of the screen. Enter (by INPUT) a range of frequencies and a length of time at each frequency. Have the computer sing out at each range, and have the box grow taller as the frequency increases. Have the box shrink as the frequency decreases.
4. Have the computer draw a falling box that changes color each time it falls a specified amount.
5. Make the computer draw your name at a random point on the screen each time a key is pressed. Have the computer sing at a random frequency each time your name appears.

Chapter 13

Graphics: Lines, boxes, windows, and pictures

True BASIC does a great deal to take the "computer" out of "computer graphics." That is, the True BASIC graphics statements minimize the necessity to think about the hardware you are working with and allow you to concentrate on the concepts you are illustrating. When you begin working in graphics, for example, there is no need to invoke the graphics mode; True BASIC recognizes the graphics statements and invokes the graphics mode for your graphics routine.

True BASIC views the display screen as a grid of points and includes statements that allow you to create screen displays by lighting these points in the colors and patterns you wish. As you work you can think of the display screen grid in the way mathematicians and engineers normally do; the X axis is horizontal, the Y axis is vertical, and points are described by first giving the X coordinate and then the Y coordinate (X, Y). Since True BASIC lets you choose the starting and ending values for the points across and down the screen, there is no need to translate the X and Y coordinates of your graph into preset X and Y coordinates of the computer system.

True BASIC graphics statements are useful for far more than line graphs alone. They make it possible for you to create and combine colorful shapes, and to store and display them simultaneously. You can divide the screen into windows, and then program each one separately. And, most important, you can do these things without getting lost in the complexity of your computer system. This chapter begins by explaining the statements that plot points and lines. It then describes how to create areas and shapes. Finally, it explains how to store and recall your pictures whenever you wish.

The SET WINDOW statement

<table>
<tr><td>SET
WINDOW</td><td>When you display points and draw lines, you must refer to screen locations by giving their horizontal and vertical addresses. At start-up time, True BASIC sees display screen points as running from point 0 on the left to point 1 on the right, and from 0 on</td></tr>
</table>

Figure 13–1. Location (.5, .66)

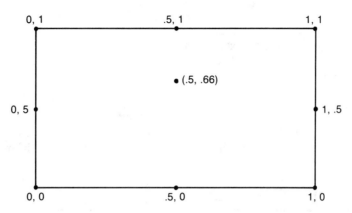

the bottom to 1 on the top. As Figure 13–1 illustrates, the points in between have decimal values. Point (.5,.66), for instance, is halfway across and about two-thirds the way toward the top edge.

The SET WINDOW statement lets you redefine the display screen window. That is, it lets you define the horizontal (X) range and vertical (Y) range of display screen points. When you write the SET WINDOW statement, give your starting and ending X values first and then give your Y values. For example, the statement

```
SET WINDOW -5,8,-10,15
```

tells the computer that X values range from −5 on the left edge of the display to 8 on the right edge. The Y value at the bottom of the screen is −10; the Y value at the top edge is 15.

As long as your program refers to X and Y points within these set ranges, the points will be displayed in their proper place on the screen. If a statement should refer to X or Y values outside of these set ranges, the values will be ignored and points having those coordinates will not be displayed. You can also change the display screen coordinates as your program runs by executing new SET WINDOW statements.

Setting your own coordinates makes drawing graphs a straightforward process. Figure 13–2 and Figure 13–3 contrast an early version of BASIC and a True BASIC routine, each drawing the graph of Y = 3*X as X ranges from 1 to 5. Notice how much more complex the earlier version is than the True BASIC version. The arithmetic expressions in Figure 13–2 translate each value for 3*X to vertical and horizontal screen locations. With the True BASIC routine of Figure 13–3, the SET WINDOW statement defines the coordinates of the display screen to match the problem. (They range from 0 to 5 on the X axis and from 0 to 15 on the Y axis, with

Figure 13–2. Early BASIC graph of Y = 3*X

```
FOR X = 5 TO 1 STEP -1
    PRINT TAB(6+(3*X));" * "
    FOR Y = 1 TO (3*X) - (3*(X-1)-1)
        PRINT
    NEXT Y
NEXT X
END
```

Figure 13–3. True BASIC graph of Y = 3*X

```
■ SET MODE "GRAPHICS"          (on the IBM PC only)
■ SET WINDOW 0,5,0,15
■ FOR X = 1 TO 5
■     PLOT POINTS: X,3*X
■ NEXT X
■ END
```

the origin (0,0) in the lower left corner of the screen.) Then, the PLOT POINTS: statement lights the correct display screen points without translation.

The PLOT POINTS: statement

PLOT
POINTS

The PLOT POINTS: statement displays a point on the screen that lies within the default True BASIC display screen ranges or within the ranges you establish with a preceding SET WINDOW statement. To use PLOT POINTS: you must specify the point's horizontal (X) location first, and then the vertical (Y) location. The statement

```
PLOT POINTS: 3,5
```

lights the point three spaces to the right and 5 spaces up from point (0,0).

You can light several points in one statement by separating the coordinates for each point with semicolons. For instance, the statement

```
PLOT POINTS: .2,.5;  .5,.5;  .8,.5
```

lights three points across the middle of the start-up screen, using the default window coordinates. Since you can use any combination of constants, variables, or arithmetic expressions to denote each coordinate, you can also display the points across the middle of the display by using the statements

```
LET X = .2
LET Y = .5
PLOT POINTS: X,Y;  X +.3,Y;  X +.5,Y
```

Type in and run the program of Figure 13–3 to see how the SET WINDOW and PLOT POINTS: statements draw the graph of Y = 3*X. Experiment with the range of values for each screen dimension and the coordinates for the points you display. For instance, try the changes to the SET WINDOW or the FOR statement shown in Figure 13–4. This program has a wider range in each dimension and displays more points.

Figure 13–4. New values for the graph of Y = 3*X

```
■ SET MODE "GRAPHICS"              (on the IBM PC only)
■ SET WINDOW -100,100,-350,350
■ FOR X = -100 TO 100 STEP 2
■     PLOT POINTS: X, 3*X
■ NEXT X
■ END
```

The PLOT LINES: statement

```
PLOT
LINES
```

The PLOT LINES: statement draws lines from the first point you specify to the next point you specify, right through to the last point you name. As usual, you refer to each point by its horizontal and vertical screen coordinates according to the current screen window values. If the default window is in effect, the statement

```
PLOT LINES:  0,0;  .5,0;  .5,.5;  0,.5;  0,0
```

draws a line from the lower left corner to the middle of the bottom row, up to the center of the screen, back to the left edge, and down to the lower left corner again, creating the rectangle shown in Figure 13–5.

Figure 13–5. PLOT LINES: 0,0; .5,0; .5,.5; 0,.5; 0,0

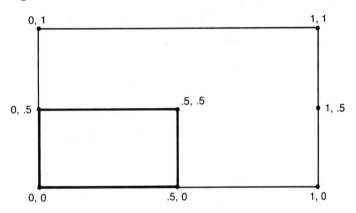

Notice that you must specify the last point even if it is the same as the first. With PLOT LINES: the computer does not complete a rectangle, or any shape, unless you specifically tell it to do so. Notice also that the coordinates for each point are separated by a semicolon.

The PLOT AREA: statement

```
PLOT
AREA
```

The PLOT AREA: statement draws a shape and then colors it in. PLOT AREA: always closes the shape by drawing a line from the last point you specify back to the first one. The statement

```
PLOT AREA:  0,0;  .5,0;  .5,.5;  0,.5
```

draws and colors in the same rectangle created in Figure 13–5.

The PLOT TEXT, AT X,Y: statement

> ```
> PLOT
> TEXT
> ```

Use PLOT TEXT to label your graphics designs. PLOT TEXT, like the PRINT statement, places text on the display screen. Unlike PRINT, however, PLOT TEXT allows you to specify, by means of coordinates in the current window, where to place the text. For instance, the statements

```
SET WINDOW 1,10,1,10
PLOT TEXT, AT 1,9:"True BASIC here!"
```

display a message in the upper left corner of the screen. The horizontal and vertical coordinates you specify in the PLOT TEXT statement indicate where to begin display of the lower left corner of the first character of your text. A text string or a string variable represents the message itself. Each PLOT TEXT statement displays only one text message at a time.

As you work with PLOT TEXT, remember that graphics-mode screen lines usually accommodate 40 characters that are twice as wide as normal text characters. You must allow for this as you plan your display labels.

In Figure 13–6 the phrase RIGHT EDGE is properly right-justified. The word CENTER is centered, and LEFT EDGE begins at the left edge. Once you set

Figure 13–6. Placing text on the graphics screen

```
■ SET WINDOW 1,40,1,40
■ PLOT TEXT, AT 1,1:"LEFT EDGE"
■ PLOT TEXT, AT 18,20:"CENTER"
■ PLOT TEXT, AT 30,39:"RIGHT EDGE"
■ END
```

the window to a range of 1 to 40 on the X axis in order to match the 40 print positions, it is easy to calculate the X coordinate that determines where each phrase will begin. The X coordinate becomes the horizontal tab position.

If you wish to display numeric data on the graphics screen you must either use PLOT TEXT with the USING functions or incorporate the STR$() function in the PLOT TEXT statement. For example, the statements

```
SET WINDOW 1,10,1,10
PLOT TEXT, AT 5,5: STR$(42^2)
```

calculate the square of 42, translate the result to the numeric string "1764", and print the characters at window position (5,5).

When labeling is done, you can set your window to new coordinates and continue drawing shapes or plotting lines according to coordinates that fit your work. Your labels will remain in place.

The GET POINT: statement

> ```
> GET
> POINT:
> ```

True BASIC includes statements that accept input from light pen and mouse devices. For example, the statement

```
GET POINT: X,Y
```

places a graphics cursor (crosshairs, an arrow, or whatever your computer uses) at window coordinates X (across) and Y (up from the bottom). Once the cursor appears, you can move it with a light pen, mouse, or cursor key and then press the *enter* key or button. Then, X and Y take the values of the new cursor coordinates. The only restriction is that you must keep the cursor in the current window. Your computer may be capable of even more specific mouse-device controls. You can find out about these in the *True BASIC User's Guide* for your computer.

Animating displays with the BOX statements

True BASIC makes animation possible by means of statements that read or write areas of the screen very rapidly. The process of rapidly drawing, erasing, and re-drawing a shape in a new screen location makes the shape appear to move.

The BOX LINES, BOX AREA, BOX CIRCLE, BOX ELLIPSE, and BOX CLEAR statements draw and erase rectangular areas of the screen. When you write one of the BOX statements, give coordinates in the same way you give coordinates for the SET WINDOW statement. List the starting and ending values for the X coordinates and then the starting and ending values for the Y coordinates. For example, a BOX LINES statement that outlines the rectangle in Figure 13–7 would be written as

```
SET WINDOW 1,10,1,10
BOX LINES 2,10,6,9
```

because the sides of the box range from point 2 to point 10 on the horizontal (X) axis and from point 6 to point 9 in the vertical (Y) direction.

Figure 13–7. Using coordinates in BOX statements

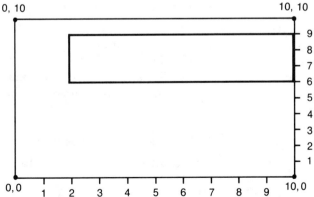

The BOX LINES statement

> BOX
> LINES

The program of Figure 13–8 draws the following rectangle:

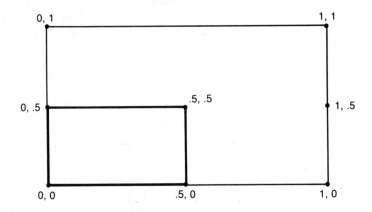

It is the same as the rectangle in Figure 13–5 (page 187), except BOX LINES draws it more rapidly.

Figure 13–8. The BOX LINES statement

```
▮ SET MODE "GRAPHICS"        (on the IBM PC only)
▮ SET COLOR "RED/BLUE"
▮ BOX LINES 0,.5,0,.5
▮ END
```

The arguments in this BOX LINES statement represent, first, the starting and ending horizontal points and, then, the starting and ending vertical points. They are X and Y values that fall within the default window that runs from 0 to 1 on the X axis and from 0 to 1 on the Y axis.

The BOX AREA statement

> BOX
> AREA

BOX AREA draws a rectangle and fills it in with the current foreground color. Figure 13–9 changes the BOX LINES statement of the previous figure to a BOX AREA statement. The numbers given also represent the starting and ending horizontal points followed by the starting and ending vertical ones. Run this new program and see how quickly BOX AREA not only outlines but also paints in the rectangle.

Figure 13–9. The BOX AREA statement

```
▮ SET MODE "GRAPHICS"        (on the IBM PC only)
▮ SET COLOR "RED/BLUE"
▮ BOX AREA 0,.5,0,.5
▮ END
```

The BOX CLEAR statement

| BOX |
| CLEAR |

The BOX CLEAR statement erases a box leaving the screen in the background color. Figure 13–10 combines the BOX CLEAR statement with the BOX LINES statement to make rectangles appear to move around the screen.

Figure 13–10. An animated box

```
■ SET MODE "GRAPHICS"        (on the IBM PC only)
■ SET COLOR "RED/BLUE"
■ SET WINDOW 1,100,1,100
■ FOR SIDES = 2 TO 100 STEP 2
■     BOX LINES SIDES,SIDES+2,SIDES,SIDES+2
■     BOX CLEAR SIDES, SIDES+2,SIDES,SIDES+2
■ NEXT SIDES
■ END
```

The BOX CIRCLE and BOX ELLIPSE statements

| BOX |
| CIRCLE |

The BOX CIRCLE statement draws a circle within the imaginary box defined by the left, right, bottom, and top coordinates you give. The more square your box, the more likely the result will be a perfect circle. If the box is a rectangle, the circle becomes an ellipse. Figure 13–11 outlines a red circle in the default window, its width ranging from .2 to .8 across the screen, and its height stretching from .1 up to .9.

Figure 13–11. The BOX CIRCLE statement

```
■ SET MODE "GRAPHICS"        (on the IBM PC only)
■ SET COLOR "RED/BLUE"
■ BOX CIRCLE .2,.8,.1,.9
■ END
```

| BOX |
| ELLIPSE |

Since this circle is actually an ellipse, it is better programming style to replace the BOX CIRCLE statement with the BOX ELLIPSE statement. Both statements work the same way, but using the one that matches your design provides better documentation of what your program does.

The FLOOD statement

| FLOOD |

On some computers, like the IBM PC, you can use True BASIC's FLOOD statement to repaint large areas of the screen. In the default window the statement

```
FLOOD .5,.5
```

tells the computer to repaint all points neighboring the center one (.5,.5) that have the same color as it does. The new color is the most recently set foreground color. It also says to paint the neighbors of these points as well. Neighbors with original colors different from the color of the point given in the FLOOD statement do not change color.

Figure 13–12 paints the circle in the previous example green. The FLOOD statement works because the starting point given is within the circle and its color matches that of all its neighbors and their neighbors until the red outline points are reached. Check the *True BASIC User's Guide* to see if your computer supports the FLOOD statement. If it does, enter this sample program into your computer and watch what happens.

Figure **13–12.** The FLOOD statement

```
■ SET MODE "GRAPHICS"        (on the IBM PC only)
■ SET COLOR "RED/BLUE"
■ BOX CIRCLE .2,.8,.1,.9
■ SET COLOR "GREEN"
■ FLOOD .5,.5
■ END
```

Working with many screens

True BASIC makes it possible to define different areas of the display screen as independent mini-screens, or programming windows. Once you have opened a channel to a programming window, you can work within its coordinates to create a display without affecting other display screen areas. As your program runs, you can transfer control from one mini-screen to another to produce several separate, simultaneous displays. You can, for example, display statistical data in one mini-screen, and the line graph it produces in another. Or you can have fun with many animated displays and lots of color.

Figure 13–13 draws a house with two windows and a front door. Then it turns on a light in an upstairs window. The display is actually made up of four screens: the default, full screen, which is always open on channel 0, and three smaller screens opened on channels #1, #2, and #3.

The OPEN #n: SCREEN statement

```
┌─────────┐
│  OPEN   │
│ SCREEN  │
└─────────┘
```

Each time a screen is opened, control is transferred to the area defined by the coordinates in the OPEN #n: SCREEN statement. The coordinates are always given in the following order: the left-most and right-most X values and then the lowest and highest Y values of the new screen. As soon as the new screen is opened, it becomes the current programming window, and the INPUT, PRINT, DRAW, SET, and PLOT statements that follow the OPEN #n: SCREEN statement take effect for the new screen only.

Figure 13–13 begins by using the full screen and drawing the house according to the default coordinates of 0 to 1 for the X axis and 0 to 1 for the Y axis. Since screen #0 is the default and is always opened, there is no need for an OPEN #0:

Figure 13-13. Using many screens

```
▪ SET MODE "GRAPHICS"        (on IBM PC only)
▪ SET COLOR "RED/GREEN"                        !red foreground, green background
▪ PLOT LINES:0,0;1,0;1,.8;.5,1;0,.8;0,0   !draw house in whole screen
▪ REM
▪ REM open the first mini-screen (the front door)
▪ OPEN #1: SCREEN .4,.6,.01,.49           !coordinates within whole screen
▪ SET WINDOW 0,10,0,10                     !coordinates for screen #1
▪ PLOT LINES: 0,0;10,0;10,10;0,0           !coordinates within screen #1
▪ PLOT TEXT, AT 1,7:"WELCOME"              !coordinates within screen #1
▪ REM
▪ REM open the second mini-screen (left side, upstairs)
▪ OPEN #2: SCREEN .1,.3,.5,.75             !coordinates within whole screen
▪ SET WINDOW 0,10,0,10                     !coordinates for screen #2
▪ PLOT LINES: 0,0;10,0;10,10;0,10          !coordinates within screen #2
▪ PLOT LINES: 5,0;5,10                     !coordinates within screen #2
▪ PLOT LINES: 0,5;10,5                     !coordinates within screen #2
▪ REM
▪ REM open the third mini-screen (right side, upstairs)
▪ OPEN #3: SCREEN .7,.9,.5,.75             !coordinates within whole screen
▪ SET WINDOW 0,10,0,10                     !coordinates for screen #3
▪ PLOT LINES: 0,0;10,0;10,10;0,10          !coordinates within screen #3
▪ PLOT LINES: 5,0;5,10                     !coordinates within screen #3
▪ PLOT LINES: 0,5;10,5                     !coordinates within screen #3
▪ WINDOW #2                                !transfer control to screen #2
▪ REM
▪ REM turn on the light
▪ SET COLOR "YELLOW"                       !light up screen #2 only
▪ BOX AREA 0,10,0,10                       !coordinates within screen #2
▪ CLOSE #1
▪ CLOSE #2
▪ CLOSE #3
▪ END
```

SCREEN statement, and all of the PLOT and SET statements at the outset of the program refer to the whole display screen.

When another screen, screen #1, is opened by the statement

```
OPEN #1: SCREEN .4,.6,.01,.49
```

control is transferred to the smaller area, which ranges from .4 to .6 on the X axis and from .01 to .49 on the Y axis. This becomes the current programming window, and the SET and PLOT statements following it refer to this mini-screen.

The WINDOW #n statement

```
WINDOW
```

The WINDOW #n statement provides a means of transferring control to screens that have been previously opened. In Figure 13-13, the statement

```
WINDOW #2
```

returns control to screen #2, the second mini-screen created. The statements that follow,

```
SET COLOR "YELLOW"
BOX AREA: 0,10,0,10
```

simulate turning on the light by shading all of screen #2 a bright yellow.

You can experiment with the WINDOW #n statement by typing in the house-drawing program of Figure 13–13. If you think the door needs painting, switch control to that screen area with the statement

```
WINDOW #1
```

Paint the door yellow with the statements

```
SET COLOR "YELLOW"
BOX AREA 0,10,0,10
```

Add a chimney on the roof by switching control to the larger, default screen with the statement

```
WINDOW #0
```

The CLOSE #n statement

CLOSE

You can prevent further activity without erasing a mini-screen by closing the channel to it. The statement

```
CLOSE #1
```

permanently breaks the relationship between channel #1 and the mini-screen you have been working with. Once closed, channel #1 can be used for other purposes if you wish.

If you do not execute a CLOSE #n statement, True BASIC will, by default, close all channels except channel #0 when your program ends. But using CLOSE exemplifies good programming style, since, even though you may not need it, the statement documents that you expect no more activity on a particular screen.

Using graphics subroutines

Usually you want to use shapes that are more complex than rectangles when you create animated displays. Graphics subroutines not only make it possible to maintain a modular program when using graphics, but also make it worthwhile to spend time creating interesting visual effects. You can store your creations in a PICTURE subroutine and use them over and over again.

The DRAW statement

```
DRAW
```

As the graphics equivalent of the CALL statement, the DRAW statement is used in your main routine to activate graphics subroutines. Like the CALL statement, DRAW includes an optional argument list for passing numeric or string information to the graphics subroutines. The subroutine begins with the PICTURE statement containing a parameter list that matches the argument list. Graphics subroutines can return values to the caller by transforming the values of some or all of the arguments. Usually, however, graphics subroutines do not change the values passed to them. They use the values in creating screen displays.

Unlike the CALL statement, the DRAW statement also includes transformations that give directions on how to modify the basic drawing in the subroutine. The DRAW statement in Figure 13–14, for example, tells the computer to turn the drawing upon its head by rotating it 180 degrees. Before doing so, the main routine executes the OPTION ANGLE DEGREES statement that informs the computer that references to angles in this program will be in degrees rather than radians. It also gives the name of the "AUTOS" library file where the CAR subroutine is stored.

Figure 13–14. A DRAW statement that rotates a picture

```
■ LIBRARY "AUTOS"
■ OPTION ANGLE DEGREES
■ SET MODE "GRAPHICS"        (on the IBM PC only)
■ SET WINDOW - 10 , 10 , - 10 , 10
■ DRAW CAR( "RED" ) WITH ROTATE( 180 )
■ END
```

The DRAW statement passes the argument "RED" to subroutine CAR. It uses the ROTATE transformation to tell the computer to draw the car at an angle 180 degrees counterclockwise to the way it is drawn in the subroutine. If you prefer, you can give the DRAW statement arguments and transformations in the form of variables or expressions as well as constants.

Figure 13–15 lists all of the DRAW statement transformations available to you and explains how they can affect the drawings in your graphics subroutines.

You can specify more than one transformation in a DRAW statement, by separating each one with an asterisk (*). The statement

```
DRAW FORT WITH SHIFT(2,4) * SCALE(5)
```

moves the picture over 2 positions on the X axis and up 4 on the Y axis according to the coordinates of the current window. It also enlarges the drawing to five times the original size.

Once a DRAW statement executes, the graphics subroutine runs to completion. Finally, control returns to the line following the DRAW statement in the calling routine.

Figure 13–15. The DRAW statement transformation functions

Function	*Transformation*
SCALE(S)	Change the size of the picture. Every point (X,Y) in the drawing moves to location (X∗S,Y∗S).
SCALE(S,T)	Change the size of the picture. Every point (X,Y) in the drawing moves to location (X∗S,Y∗T).
SHEAR(L)	Tilt all vertical lines forward by L radians or degrees. Every point (X,Y) in the drawing becomes (X + Y∗ TAN(L),Y). Radians are used unless you first use the OPTION ANGLE DEGREES statement.
SHIFT(A,B)	Move the picture on the screen. Every point (X,Y) in the drawing moves to location (X+A,Y+B).
ROTATE(A)	Rotate the drawing A degrees or radians counterclockwise about the origin of the current window. Radians are used unless you first execute an OPTION ANGLE DEGREES statement.

The PICTURE, END PICTURE, and EXIT PICTURE statements

PICTURE

END
PICTURE

EXIT
PICTURE

The PICTURE statement, like the SUB statement, identifies the drawing routine (composed of PLOT statements) as a program module that you can invoke whenever you wish. Figure 13–16 illustrates the PICTURE statement being used as the first line of subroutine BUG, which creates a creature that will appear throughout the display of a program. Notice that the picture statement includes the name of the graphics routine as well as parameters within parentheses. Just as with other True BASIC subroutines, the parameters serve as place holders for arguments passed by the calling routine. The arguments and parameters must agree in number and type and be given in the same order. Graphics modules with parameters that are a list of two strings and a number, such as (eye$, nose$, height) must be invoked by a DRAW statement with arguments that are also two strings and a number, such as (I$,E$,H).

The END PICTURE statement marks the end of the subroutine and the return of control to the calling routine. The statements in between make up the subroutine itself. True BASIC also includes an EXIT PICTURE statement for use within the body of a PICTURE subroutine. EXIT PICTURE returns control to the calling routine at the line following the DRAW statement that invoked the picture.

Picture subroutines include only statements pertaining to the drawing of a picture: the PLOT family of statements (if you use BOX statements, they will not be affected by transformations) and, perhaps, a statement to change the foreground color. While it is possible to execute an OPEN WINDOW statement or a SET WINDOW statement within a graphic subroutine, it is not a good idea. Nor should you use SET BACKGROUND COLOR or other globally effective graphics statements in the subroutine. These belong in the main routine, not only for reasons of program documentation, but also as a way of preventing your graphics subroutines from conflicting with one another.

Figure 13–16 combines the BUG subroutine with the main routine that calls it. Try running it on your computer to see how the color parameter is passed and how the DRAW statement and the ROTATE and SCALE transformations produce a bug lying on its side.

Figure 13-16. A PICTURE subroutine that draws a bug

```
REM *********MAIN Routine *******************
OPTION ANGLE DEGREES                           *
SET MODE "GRAPHICS"      (on the IBM PC only)   *
SET WINDOW -10,10,-10,10                        *
DRAW BUG("blue") WITH ROTATE(90) * SCALE(2)     *
END                                             *
REM *********Subroutine*********************
PICTURE BUG(COLOR$)
    LIBRARY "b:creature"
    SET BACKGROUND COLOR "red"
    SET COLOR COLOR$
    PLOT LINES: 0,1;0,-1              !body
    PLOT LINES: -.5,1;.5,1;.5,1.5;-.5,1.5;-.5,1!head
    PLOT POINTS: -.3,1.2;.3,1.2    !eyes
    PLOT LINES: .5,1.5;1,2           !right whisker
    PLOT LINES: -.5,1.5;-1,2         !left whisker
    PLOT LINES: 0,0;.5,0;1,-.25      !right arm
    PLOT LINES: 0,0;-.5,0;-1,.25     !left arm
    PLOT LINES: 0,-1;.5,-2;1,-1.75      !right leg
    PLOT LINES: 0,-1;-.5,-2;-1,-1.75   !left leg
END PICTURE
```

PICTURE libraries

PICTURE subroutines, like other subroutines, really belong in a subroutine library. The library can contain subroutines that draw complete designs and subroutines that draw components of a design. The subroutines that work on the grander scale can themselves call upon the other graphics subroutines to produce their component designs. The BUG subroutine, for example, can call upon HEAD, ARMS, LEGS, and WHISKER routines.

Your goal is to create design components that you can put together as suits each graphics project and call upon as needed. Figure 13-17 shows a subroutine library that includes the bug design rewritten as a series of routines that each create a component of an insect body. It shows that subroutine BUG calls upon each component as it is needed. Another subroutine—FLY, perhaps—might use these design building blocks in a different configuration.

As a subroutine library, the statements of Figure 13-17 begin with the EXTERNAL statement. Once the library is created, it can be permanently stored on the disk by using the SAVE command. For example, the statement

```
save CREATURE
```

stores the BUG subroutine and its components in a disk file named CREATURE.

Figure 13-18 illustrates how a main routine that uses the BUG routine needs only to invoke the CREATURE library and execute DRAW BUG( ) statements. By doing so, the example program randomly scatters 10 bugs on the screen.

Figure 13–17. A PICTURE subroutine library

```
▌ EXTERNAL
▌ PICTURE BUG(COLOR$)
▌     SET COLOR COLOR$
▌     PLOT LINES: 0,1;0,-1
▌     DRAW HEAD
▌     DRAW LEGS
▌     DRAW ARMS
▌     DRAW WHISKER
▌ END PICTURE
▌ PICTURE HEAD
▌     PLOT LINES: -.5, 1;.5,1;.5,1.5;-.5,1.5;-.5,1        !head
▌     PLOT POINTS: -.3,1.2;.3,1.2                         !eyes
▌ END PICTURE
▌ PICTURE WHISKER
▌     PLOT LINES: .5,1.5;1,2                              !right whisker
▌     PLOT LINES: -.5,1.5;-1,2                            !left whisker
▌ END PICTURE
▌ PICTURE ARMS
▌     PLOT LINES: 0,0;.5,0;1,-.25                         !right arm
▌     PLOT LINES: 0,0;-.5,0;-1,.25                        !left arm
▌ END PICTURE
▌ PICTURE LEGS
▌     PLOT LINES: 0,-1;.5,-2;1,-1.75                      !right leg
▌     PLOT LINES: 0,-1;-.5,-2;-1,-1.75                    !left leg
▌ END PICTURE
```

```
True BASIC here.
Ok. save CREATURE
Ok.
```

Figure 13–18. Using a graphics library

```
▌ RANDOMIZE
▌ SET MODE "GRAPHICS"        (on the IBM PC only)
▌ OPTION ANGLE DEGREES
▌ SET BACKGROUND COLOR "RED"
▌ SET WINDOW -10,10,-10,10
▌ LIBRARY "CREATURE"            !Invoke the CREATURE disk file
▌ FOR INSECT = 1 TO 10
▌     LET ANGLE = INT((180-1+1)*RND +1)
▌     LET OVER = INT ((7-(-7)+1)*RND-7)
▌     LET UP = INT((7-(-7)+1)*RND-7)
▌     DRAW BUG("GREEN") WITH ROTATE(ANGLE) * SHIFT(OVER,UP)
▌ NEXT INSECT
▌ END
```

Random values for the DRAW statement transformations set the angle and location of the bugs on the screen. The ROTATE angle is in the range of 1 to 179 degrees. In order to keep the bug in the current window, the SHIFT locations range from -7 to 7 on the X axis and from -7 to 7 on the Y axis.

Summary

The True BASIC graphics statements minimize the necessity to think about the hardware you are working with and allow you to concentrate on the concepts you are illustrating.

Programming skills

The SET WINDOW statement
The PLOT POINTS: statement
The PLOT LINES: statement
The PLOT AREA: statement
The PLOT TEXT, AT X,Y: statement
The GET POINT: statement
The BOX statements
The FLOOD statement
The OPEN #n: SCREEN statement
The WINDOW #n statement
The CLOSE #n statement
The DRAW statement
The PICTURE, END PICTURE, and EXIT PICTURE statements

Computer concepts

Graphics windows
Animated displays
Graphics subroutines
Graphics libraries

Review questions

1. Use PLOT TEXT and PLOT LINE to draw a graph of the function:

$$Y = (X + 7)^2 + 2$$

where:
a. $X = 0$
b. $Y = 83$
c. $X = 4$
d. $X = 6$
e. $Y = 227$
f. $X = 10$

Along with the graph be sure to display a table of all X and Y values obtained.

2. Here comes Fred the happy cat. He can do all sorts of tricks, right? Make the computer show Fred and a few tricks (at least three).

3. Store in a library a small zoo of at least four different animals. Create a display in which the animals are shown in various poses.

4. Embellished Computer Zoo: Write a program that asks the user which animal he or she wishes to see and then draws that animal in a nice cage. As a source of animals use the animal picture library of Problem Three.

5. Show and Tell: Write a program that shows, using two graphics mini-screens, a piece of poetry and at the same time a picture illustrating the verse.

## Chapter 14

File processing concepts

Disks are the library of a computer system. During a computing session, the computer's random access memory (RAM) is alive with your program code and data. With disks or other similar storage devices, such things can be permanently recorded. Without storage devices, all that you have done during the session will be forgotten when you shut off the computer.

You store a program on a disk by typing the program into the computer and giving the SAVE command. You store data on the disk by running a program that tranfers data across an input/output (I/O) channel to the disk.

True BASIC provides three types of disk files: text, record, and byte. The type you use depends upon how you plan to use the data stored within the file. The last three chapters describe how and when to use each of these kinds of files.

This chapter gives the background you need to use any type of True BASIC file. It presents disk-file processing concepts and some True BASIC file processing statements. These concepts include the computer processes and programming tasks that must occur in order to manipulate disk files. The True BASIC statements include the ones you need to use with all three True BASIC file types: OPEN, CLOSE, ASK, SET, ERASE, and UNSAVE.

The computer "worldview"

If the computer you are using had a worldview, the central processing unit (CPU) would be at the center, surrounded by the random-access memory (RAM). Every computer system includes these two components. All other devices are peripheral to these, and in fact are known by the term *peripheral devices*. Display screen, printer, disk, tape, keyboard, and mouse are all examples of peripheral devices. All computer systems have some, but usually not all, of these devices. Some devices, such as the keyboard, are for input only; others, such as printers, are for output. Data storage devices, such as disks and tapes, are for both input and output. Information can be stored on them and retrieved at a later time.

Disk storage devices provide fast, reliable access to data and allow random access to the files stored on them. *Random access* means the computer can access any part of any particular file by looking up its disk address in the disk directory rather than by searching the disk from start to finish. In contrast, tapes are neither as fast nor reliable as disks, and they provide only *sequential access* to data. In order to access the tenth file on the tape, the computer must read past the preceding nine files. Tapes are less expensive than disks, however.

Computer disks and tapes are magnetic storage devices. That is, the data are coded as spots magnetized clockwise or counterclockwise, with each spot representing one bit. (One of the most rapidly changing aspects of computer systems is the improvements in disk storage technology. As a result, each year sees more and more data being encoded in smaller and smaller areas.) Once you have stored valuable data on a disk, be sure to keep it away from magnetic fields, such as those created by electric motors and magnets.

Computer processes

Figures 14–1 and 14–2 show the path that data travel when they are being written to or read from a disk file. Notice that, in coming into or going out of RAM, data are collected in regions known as *buffers*. Usually, it is more efficient for the computer to wait until a buffer is full before actually completing a data transfer. As a programmer, you rarely need to be concerned with buffers, and with True BASIC you can proceed as though they do not exist.

Opening channels

Notice also that a communications channel exists between the RAM and the peripheral devices. If your computer is capable of it, True BASIC allows you to have up to ten open channels at one time between various files and various buffers. The *True BASIC User's Guide* for your type of computer tells how many channels can be open at once on your system.

One channel is always open — channel #0, between the RAM and the display or keyboard. This channel is *not* counted in the number of channels opened by your program.

Reading (input) and writing (output)

For the computer,

> *Input* means from a device to the RAM.
> *Output* means from the RAM to the device.

As Figure 14–1 shows, when reading from a disk file, data flow from the file, across a channel, to the RAM buffer and then to your program. If your program displays the data it reads, the information traverses channel #0 from RAM to the display screen. As Figure 14–2 shows, when writing to a disk file, data follow the reverse path: from your program to a RAM buffer and then across a channel to your disk file. If the data originate at an input device like the keyboard, they first traverse channel #0, from the device to your program.

Figure 14–1. Reading (input) from a disk file

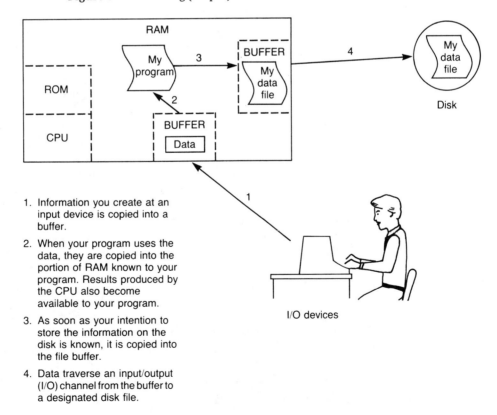

1. Data traverses the I/O channel *from* the disk *to* the file buffer in RAM.
2. Data are copied from the buffer to your program.
3. Data are sent *from* your program *to* the display screen buffer.
4. Data traverse channel O to the display.

Figure 14–2. Writing (output) to a disk file

1. Information you create at an input device is copied into a buffer.
2. When your program uses the data, they are copied into the portion of RAM known to your program. Results produced by the CPU also become available to your program.
3. As soon as your intention to store the information on the disk is known, it is copied into the file buffer.
4. Data traverse an input/output (I/O) channel from the buffer to a designated disk file.

Programming tasks

Programs that access file data must accomplish five important tasks:

1. Open a channel by associating a file name with a channel number.
2. Declare the type of data transfer: input, output, or both.
3. Declare the type of file organization: text, record, or byte.
4. Transfer the data.
5. Close the channel to the file.

The OPEN statement (programming tasks 1, 2, and 3)

OPEN

The OPEN statement takes care of the first three tasks. It allows for programmer-supplied arguments that describe the file in detail. For example, the statement

```
OPEN #4:NAME"b:book",CREATE new,ACCESS output,ORGANIZATION record,RECSIZE 16
```

is a complete True BASIC OPEN statement that tells the computer to set up a channel, known to this program as channel 4, to a disk file named "b:book". It also says that the file is a new one and that the program will be writing data out to the file. Finally, this OPEN statement instructs the computer to organize the file according to the True BASIC record file format. Each data item in this file will contain 16 bytes.

The capitalized words in the example are parts of the OPEN statement. You supply the words in lowercase letters. Even if your arguments are string constants, you do not need quotation marks for any of them except the file name.

The channel number can range from 1 to 1000. If you use a decimal, the computer rounds to the nearest integer. A particular channel number has meaning only within the run of the program. It serves to distinguish this channel from others that may be open in the same program. Thus, if file ADDRESS is opened on channel #3, file NAMES must be open on a different number channel, such as channel #5. Any transfers over channel #3 in this program affect ADDRESS; all transfers on channel #5 affect NAMES.

The relationship between a channel number and a file remains only during the current run of a program. Thus, another program can use channel #3 and channel #5 to refer to files other than ADDRESS or NAMES. Similarly, another program can refer to these two files by using different channel numbers.

For the NAME parameter, the computer permanently records the file name. In the example, the b: portion of the name "b: book" is the way to indicate on the IBM PC that the file resides on the disk inserted in drive b:. Figure 14–3 shows all of the possible entries you can give for each of the OPEN statement parameters.

True BASIC requires that you supply a channel number and the file name every time you open the file, but lets you omit the other parameters and rely on default values if you wish. Good programming style, however, requires that you supply all of the OPEN statement parameters every time you open the file. Spelling out all of the options makes it clear what is happening to the file.

True BASIC also allows you to open and close data files in subroutines and functions, although doing so is contrary to one of the most important rules of

Figure 14–3. The OPEN statement parameters

Parameter	Allowable arguments
#n	*n can be:* Any single number, numeric expression, or numeric variable. There can be no more than 10 different channels open at one time in a True BASIC program.
NAME N$	*N$ can be:* Any combination of string characters (or a string variable that represents any combination of string characters) acceptable to your computer. To ensure portability of your program from computer type to computer type, use the universally acceptable file name format of eight uppercase string characters.
CREATE T$	*T$ can be:* Any of the following three strings (or a string variable that represents one of these choices): *new* — to indicate the file does not yet exist. *old* (default) — to indicate that the file exists on the disk. *newold* — to indicate that the computer should use an existing file of the same name if it exists or create a file with this name if it does not exist.
ACCESS T$	*T$ can be:* Any of the following three strings (or a string variable that represents one of these choices): *input* — during this OPEN the file can only be read from, not written to. *output* — during this OPEN the file can only be written to, not read from. *outin* (default) — during this OPEN the file can either be read from or written to.
ORGANIZATION T$	*T$ can be:* Any of the following three strings (or a string variable that represents one of these choices): text (default). record. byte.
RECSIZE n	*n can be:* A single number, numeric expression, or numeric variable that tells how many bytes to read in a byte file or how many bytes are allowed for an item in a record file. For byte files the RECSIZE may change every time you open the file. For record files the RECSIZE never changes.

structured programming. This is, that the main routine, as the driver, opens and closes all data files used by the program.

Structured programming allows subroutines to read from and write to the data files that have been opened, however, and True BASIC makes it possible to pass file channel numbers as arguments to subroutines.

Use a dummy channel number in the SUB statement and give a real channel number in the CALL statement. If, for example, the main routine opens a file on channel #4, the CALL statement would be:

```
CALL READER (#4)
```

The channel designations in the READER subroutine would be:

```
SUB READER (#999)
PRINT #999: "Types of Cats"
```

#999 is a dummy channel number that holds a place for the real one passed by the main routine.

Transferring data (programming task 4)

You already know two statements that transmit data over a channel to a device: PRINT and INPUT. Variations of PRINT and INPUT transmit data between RAM and text files. Variations of READ and WRITE statements transfer data between RAM and Byte or Record files.

The CLOSE statement (programing task 5)

CLOSE

The CLOSE statement, which must appear in the main routine, cancels the relationship between a file and the program in RAM. CLOSE is another True BASIC statement that is not required, but whose use is recommended as a good means of documenting the status of the file that has previously been opened. CLOSE files when you are finished using them. Reopen them later if you need them.

To close access to the file opened on channel #4, write:

```
CLOSE #4
```

If you fail to use a CLOSE statement the channel is effectively closed by default when the program completes. No access to the file occurs unless it is opened by another program.

File design: Files, records, and fields

For the computer, a file is a collection of data transmitted under one name. The computer views a program as a file just as it views lists of names and addresses as files. In fact, in practical terms the computer considers the stream of output to the display or the input from the keyboard as files. Check the *True BASIC User's Guide* for your computer type to find the exact names, but you will see that the printer has a file name something like PTR: or LPT: (a carryover from the days when printers were line printers). The keyboard has a file name like KBD: By default, if these devices are part of your system, channel #0 is open to these devices when the computer power is turned on.

For people, however, the term *file* has a narrower meaning — file is a collection of related data stored under one name. A *file* is composed of records. *Records* are conceptual units of information. Each record contains all the information about a file item, and is composed of *fields,* units of data that pertain to the item. In a grocer's file, for instance, where the items are foods, one file record contains all the information for one food, and might be composed of several fields: a name field, a price field, a supplier field, and a quantity-on-hand field.

True BASIC data types

As you design a file, you need to know what type of data the computer recognizes and how many bytes the computer uses to store each type of data. True BASIC recognizes two types of data:

ASCII characters = 1 byte

Numbers = 8 bytes

True BASIC considers all data as one of these two types, numeric or character. No matter what the actual values the numbers in your files have, True BASIC stores them according to an internationally accepted Institute of Electrical and Electronic Engineers (IEEE) format that requires 8 bytes. The algorithm that governs this format is an ingenious one that makes it possible to represent in only 8 bytes all numbers in the range (-1×10^{99}) to (1×10^{99}), with ten digits of precision. For character data, True BASIC uses the 8-bit American Standard Code for Information Interchange (ASCII) code. This code varies somewhat from computer to computer, and the *True BASIC User's Guide* for your computer type gives the code used by True BASIC on your computer. Appendix B gives an example of the ASCII code available on the IBM PC.

The file record layout

Before beginning to use any type of file you must think about — and write down — what is to be included in one file record and how the information will be organized. For communicating with people, you must show the scope of a record (one patient, one company, or, perhaps, one item in inventory) and the data fields that will make up the record (name, price, quantity). For communicating with the computer, you must note the length and data type of each field in the record and estimate the overall size of the file.

The document you create, often called the *file record layout,* will be referenced time and again during the life of the file. Because it maps the bytes in one file record, you can use it to calculate in advance how many bytes on the disk the file will require. It specifies the type of data involved, string or numeric, so you know what variables you can use. What is more important, a file record layout allows you or other programmers, at a future time, to use the file in another program. If you cannot remember how a file is organized you cannot retrieve its data.

Figure 14–4 shows a file record layout designed for a file of computer software in the inventory of the Speedy Service Software Store (over 1 billion programs sold). It describes the layout for one file record and summarizes the file dimensions. Each file record contains a name field, quantity field, price field, and date field. The length and type of each field are listed, along with the variables in the computer programs that use this file. There is no programming need to use the same variables in all of the programs that access the file. But having such consistency makes it easy to keep track of what these programs do with the file information.

The file record layout also shows that 1024 fields of 88 bytes each require 90,112 bytes of storage. Actually, the file will take up somewhat more disk space, since every file contains file header information used by the computer in identifying the file and locating file records. (Remember, one character = 1 byte and one number = 8 bytes for True BASIC.)

Figure 14–4. Software inventory: File record layout

File name: Invent   File type: Record   File size: 1024 records

Variable name	Field description	Field length (in bytes)	Data type
Progr$	Product name	64	string
Q_O_H	quantity on hand	8	numeric
Price	current price	8	numeric
Date$	date of last order (mm/dd/yy)	8	string
	Total bytes per record	88	

Total bytes per file (88 × 1024) = 90,112

File types: sequential and random access

Notice the heading "File type" in the file record layout of Figure 14–4. This refers to the type of organization used by the computer to store the file data. Over the years, numerous forms of organizing file data have been tried, as computer scientists have sought to find the most efficient means of retrieving data. As commonly happens with computer attributes, there are trade-offs between speed and simplicity that distinguish one file type from another. These trade-offs make it impossible to establish a form of file organization that is best for all applications.

Generally speaking, all types of computer file organization can be divided into those that provide sequential access to data and those that provide random, or direct, access to data. For True BASIC, text files provide sequential access and record files provide random access. Text files are useful when you use almost all data in the file every time it is opened. Store mailing lists (for which every name is printed on a label) in text files. Record files are useful if you frequently update file records and want to look at them out of sequence. Theater seat reservations that change for each performance should reside in random-access record files.

The third type of True BASIC file, byte, purposely has no particular organization. A file opened as a byte file is viewed as a stream of bytes with no mechanism for distinguishing between logical file records or data fields. The byte file type exists primarily as a means of transporting file data from another computer application for use by True BASIC programs. Most likely you will not design a file in the byte format, but you may want to open a file created in another format as a byte file in order to read and recopy it.

Regardless of the type of file you are using, you will find you need information about the file or need to change the status of a file during the run of your program. True BASIC gives you this control with the following file manipulation statements:

> ASK (about file attributes)
> SET (file attributes)
> ERASE (part or all of a file)
> UNSAVE (a complete file)

The ASK statement

ASK

ASK provides information about files opened on a channel number you have designated in your OPEN statement or on channel #0 that communicates with the display for output and the keyboard for input. For example, the statement

```
ASK #4: ACCESS mode$
```

stores in the mode$ variable the ACCESS mode of the file opened on channel 4. The ACCESS mode can be input, output, or outin. Figure 14–5 lists the ASK statement parameters available to you, and describes the purpose of each.

Figure 14–5. The ASK statement parameters

ASK statement	*Result*
ASK #n: ACCESS m$	m$ contains the access mode of file #n: "input," "output," or "outin."
ASK #n: FILESIZE s	s contains the size of file #n: text files: s = number of bytes record file: s = number of records byte file: s = number of bytes
ASK #n: MARGIN m	m contains the current margin for the text file #n. MARGIN has no meaning for record and byte files, so m = 0 if #n is either of these file types.
ASK #n: NAME n$	n$ contains the name of file #n: or n$ is a null string if #n: is a channel to the display.
ASK #n: ORGANIZATION O$	O$ contains the file type for file #n: "text," "record," "byte," or, if #n: is a channel to the screen "window."
ASK #n: POINTER p$	p$ contains the position of the file pointer for file #n: "begin," "middle," "end." If #n: is a channel to the screen, p$ is always "middle."

(continued)

Figure 14–5. *Continued*

ASK statement	*Result*
ASK #n: RECORD r	r contains the location indicated by the file pointer for file #n:. Counting begins with 1 for the first byte or record in the file and increases sequentially: text file: r = which byte in the file record file: r = which record in the file byte file: r = which byte in the file
ASK #n: RECSIZE r	r contains the number of bytes in a record for record file #n:. RECSIZE has no meaning for text and byte files, so r = 0 for these file types.
ASK #n: ZONEWIDTH z	z contains the current zone width for text file #n:. ZONEWIDTH has no meaning for record and byte files, so z = 0 for these file types.

The SET statement

SET

SET allows you to change file attributes. Thus, the statement

```
SET #4: RECSIZE 32
```

sets a new record size of 32 for the empty file opened on channel #4. Unlike the ASK #n: you cannot use all SET #n: statements for all three True BASIC file types, and fatal program errors occur if you use a SET #n: statement for the wrong type of file. The chapters that follow describe the SET #n: statements that have meaning for each file type and show you how to use them.

The ERASE statement

ERASE

The ERASE statement erases the contents of a file and the organizational type of the file, and sets the file pointer to the beginning of the file. ERASE does not erase the file name from the disk file directory, however. A file that has been completely erased still exists as an empty file and can still be opened for output. Its organizational type can be redefined to the same or a new file organization when the file is next used. To erase file #4 for example, enter:

```
ERASE #4
```

The file on channel #4 can be either a text, record, or byte file.

The ACCESS mode of a file being erased must be output or outin. The computer considers erasing a file to be changing its contents. You can only change files opened for output or outin ACCESS modes.

The UNSAVE statement

| UNSAVE |

UNSAVE deletes a file from the disk directory so that it is no longer accessible by a program. Since the UNSAVE statement only works for files that are closed, you have no channel number designation to use in the UNSAVE statement. Rather, specify the file name, or a string variable or string expression representing the name in an UNSAVE statement. To UNSAVE the file named "pay," include the statement

```
UNSAVE "pay"
```

in your program. A file need not be empty before you UNSAVE it.

Summary

Disks are the library of a computer system. With disks or other similar storage devices, your program code and data can be permanently stored. True BASIC provides three types of disk files: text, record, and byte.

Programming skills

The OPEN statement
The CLOSE statement
The ASK statement
The SET statement
The ERASE statement
The UNSAVE statement

Computer concepts

Designing a file record layout

Fields
Records
Files
Data types

Computer processes

Writing to a file (output)
Reading from a file (input)

File types

Text
Record
Byte

File organization

Sequential access
Random access

Review questions

1. Is the transfer of data from a program in RAM to a disk file known as input or output?
2. Is the transfer of data from a program in RAM to a display known as input or output?
3. What are the five programming tasks necessary for accessing disk file data?
4. Give examples of True BASIC statements that accomplish the five programming tasks.
5. List the data types known to True BASIC, and give the number of bytes used by each.
6. What is a data field?
7. What is a file record?
8. What does a file record layout describe?
9. What are the two basic types of file organization?
10. List the three types of True BASIC files, and give an example showing when using each type is preferable to using others.

## Chapter 15

Text files

The computer views text files as a collection of data fields separated by a marker such as the comma or *enter* key codes. You, as the programmer, must give structure to these data fields.

When you write into the file, use the file record layout to remind yourself of the sequence of data fields that belong in one file record. Write out the fields for one file record, and then begin again for another record until all of the information is in the file.

Read the file with a programming routine that parallels the writing routine. In fact, it is a good idea to make them match exactly. If the write routine includes a line like

```
PRINT #4: "DAFFODILS"; 4.50 ; "PER DOZEN"
```

the read routine should look something like

```
INPUT #4: FLOWER$,PRICE,QUAN$
```

That is, the number of fields and their data type for the PRINT # are matched by the number of fields and their type in the corresponding INPUT # statement (a character string, a number, a character string). It is also a good idea to work with one complete file record in each read operation. You may only use part of the information you have accessed, but you will have an easy time keeping track of your place in the file.

Writing into a text file

Figure 15-1 sets up a mailing list for a fund-raising campaign. It prompts for a donor's name and the amount of the contribution and writes them into a disk file called FUNDS.ONE.

Figure 15–1. Writing into a text file

```
OPEN #1: NAME "FUNDS.ONE", ACCESS output, CREATE new, ORGANIZATION text
PRINT "Enter END to stop"
PRINT
DO
        INPUT PROMPT "Enter name: ": NAME$
        IF NAME$<> "END" THEN
           INPUT PROMPT "Enter amount: ": AMOUNT
           PRINT #1: NAME$;",";AMOUNT   !write data and field separator
        ELSE
           EXIT DO
        END IF
LOOP
CLOSE #1
END
```

```
Ok. run
Enter END to stop

Enter name: Whithers
Enter amount: 45.00
Enter name: Filmore
Enter amount: 100.00
Enter name: Smythwick
Enter amount: 75.00
Enter name: END
Ok.
```

The OPEN statement sets up a channel for data transfer from the program to the FUNDS.ONE. file. The channel designator, the #1 in the example, distinguishes this channel from others that might be open at the same time in the same program.

The PRINT #n: statement

PRINT
#n

The PRINT #n: statement does the file writing. When you use PRINT to write to a file, you must specify the channel number associated with the file. If you do not, the computer assumes you mean default channel #0, and it transfers data from your program to the display screen.

If you want to be able to retrieve each data field in the record later on, you must write into the file record a comma or semicolon between each data field as though it were a data item itself. These separators become part of the file record. They are used by the INPUT # statement that reads the data to tell where one data field begins and another one ends.

You must also include punctuation in the PRINT #n: statement to indicate whether the information going to the file should be closely packed on the disk or spaced according to the current print-line zone width. Do this as you usually do in a PRINT statement: Separate with semicolons those items you want closely packed.

Separate with commas those items that are to be spaced by zone widths. In the example of Figure 15–1 the items going into the file are separated by semicolons. On the disk the data will look like:

> S. Whithers, 45
> D. Filmore, 100
> R. Smythwick, 75

The numbers are printed with leading spaces, but otherwise, the data fields and the commas that distinguish one from another are stored on the disk in a closely packed format.

The SET #n: MARGIN function

The default PRINT #: zone widths for a text file are the same as for the PRINT zones on the display screen. Each line, or text file record, contains 80 characters (Margin = 80) and is made up of five zones with 16 characters each. If you wish to change these parameters, use the SET function. To increase the file record length (or line length) for the text file opened on channel #1 to 132 characters, type

```
SET #1: MARGIN 132
```

To decrease the PRINT # zones for the records in the text file opened on channel #1 to 10 characters, execute the statement

```
SET #1: ZONEWIDTH 10
```

The ASK #n: MARGIN function

When the channel to a file is open, you can inquire about the record length and field widths by means of the ASK functions. For example, the statement

```
ASK #1: MARGIN reclen
```

specifies in the "reclen" variable the number of characters in a file record for the file opened on channel #1.

You can also ask about the current zone width. Use the statement

```
ASK #1: ZONEWIDTH field
```

to retrieve in the "field" variable the current number of character positions in a zone of the file opened on channel #1.

The PRINT #n, USING: statement

```
PRINT
#n
USING
```

Sometimes you don't need to access the data fields in the records of text files. When, for example, the text file contains lines of text designed to be printed as a report, all you need to do is write out and read in whole records, or lines of text, at one time.

The PRINT #n, USING: statement writes out whole lines for you. You can use it to format a file record just as you use PRINT USING to format a print line. Figure 15–2 is a version of the fund-raising program that formats the names and dollar amounts for each donor. Because of the PRINT #1, USING: statement, the file record on the disk has the same format as a print line on paper or the screen.

Figure 15–2. Writing into a text file

```
REM The name "B:FUNDS.FMT" will open a file, FUNDS.FMT, on the B disk
REM Use "FUNDS.FMT" if you only have one disk drive
OPEN #1: NAME "B:FUNDS.FMT", ACCESS output, CREATE new, ORGANIZATION text
PRINT "Enter END to stop"
PRINT
LET F$="<########       $###.##"
DO
      INPUT PROMPT "Enter name: ": NAME$
      IF NAME$<> "END" THEN
         INPUT PROMPT "Enter amount: ": AMOUNT
         PRINT #1, USING F$: NAME$,AMOUNT
      ELSE
         EXIT DO
      END IF
LOOP
CLOSE #1
END
```

```
Ok. run
Enter END to stop

Enter name: Smith
Enter amount: 45.00
Enter name: Hodges
Enter amount: 100.00
Enter name: Rodgers
Enter amount: 75.00
Enter name: END
Ok.
```

Regardless of whether you use PRINT #n: or PRINT #n, USING: , when a record is written to the disk, the last characters are the ones produced by the *enter* key (carriage return and line feed). The computer uses these to separate one file record from another.

The CLOSE #n statement ensures that the entire file is written to the disk and releases the connection between the channel number and the file.

Reading from a text file

Figure 15–3 reads the data entered into the FUNDS.ONE file by the PRINT #n: statement. The OPEN #3: statement permits data transfer from the FUNDS.ONE file over the channel known to the program as #3. Notice that there is no need to use the same channel number to read the file that you used in writing to the file.

The INPUT #n: statement

INPUT #n:

INPUT #3: reads the FUNDS.ONE file data. Since the INPUT #3: statement contains one variable for each field in one file record, the INPUT #3: statement in Figure 15–3 reads the entire record. Even if you only intend to use the name field or the amount field, read the entire record with each INPUT #n: statement. Your program is clearer and you will have no trouble keeping track of your place in the file.

Figure 15–3. Reading from a text file

```
OPEN #3: NAME "FUNDS.ONE", ACCESS input, CREATE old, ORGANIZATION text
PRINT "Campaign Contributors"
PRINT
DO WHILE MORE #3
    INPUT #3: NAME$,AMOUNT        !read from the file
    PRINT NAME$,AMOUNT            !write on the screen
LOOP
CLOSE #3
END
```

```
Ok. run
Campaign Contributors

Whithers        45
Filmore         100
Smythwick       75
Ok.
```

The LINE INPUT #n: statement

LINE INPUT #n:

The LINE INPUT #n: statement is the counterpart to the PRINT #n, USING: statement. It reads whole records at a time from a text file into a character string variable. Use it anytime you wish to read a record without accessing a particular data field.

Figure 15–4 reads the FUNDS.FMT file, which has been formatted by PRINT #n, USING: statements. There are no field-separating commas in the file records, but there are dollar signs and decimal points, which are all lined up. The LINE INPUT #3: statement reads lines with the same format that they will have in the final report. To actually print the formatted report, two files must be opened – the printer and the disk file. Each has a different channel number so that the computer knows where to find the data to read and where to send the data it writes.

Figure 15–4. Reading a text file, one file record at a time

```
■ OPEN #1: PRINTER
■ OPEN #3: NAME "B:FUNDS.FMT", ACCESS input, CREATE old, ORGANIZATION text
■ PRINT "Campaign Contributors"
■ PRINT
■ DO WHILE MORE #3
■    LINE INPUT #3: DETAIL$    !read a complete file record
■    PRINT #1: DETAIL$           !print a complete report line on printer
■ LOOP
■ CLOSE #3
■ END
```

```
Smith      $ 45.00       (on printer)
Hodges     $100.00
Rodgers    $ 75.00
```

Updating a text file

Once you have written data into a text file, you cannot change the data in it directly. To update existing data in a text file you must open two files: the one to be updated and a new one that will become the revised version of the old file. Ultimately, you may want to erase your original file.

Figure 15–5 illustrates changing the donation of a contributor in the FUNDS.ONE file to reflect a last-minute increase in his generosity. The first two

Figure 15–5. Updating a text file

```
■ OPEN #1: NAME "FUNDS.ONE", ACCESS input, CREATE old, ORGANIZATION text
■ OPEN #2: NAME "FUNDS.TWO", ACCESS output, CREATE new, ORGANIZATION text
■ PRINT
■ INPUT PROMPT "Enter name, additional donation: ": DONOR$, GIFT
■ PRINT
■ DO WHILE MORE #1
■    INPUT #1: NAME$,AMOUNT
■    IF NAME$=DONOR$ THEN
■       LET AMOUNT = AMOUNT + GIFT     !add new gift to old total
■    ELSE
■    END IF
■    PRINT #2: NAME$;",";AMOUNT         !write data to new file
■ LOOP
■ ERASE #1
■ CLOSE #2
■ END
```

```
Ok. run

Enter name, additional donation: Filmore,50.00

Ok.
```

lines of the program open the original file, FUNDS.ONE, and a new, empty file, FUNDS.TWO. The create mode for the files reflects their current status; for the existing file it is OLD, for the new file it is NEW. The access mode for the old file is INPUT; for the new file it is OUTPUT.

The DO loop reads each file record in the old file and writes out to the new file. It copies the data into the new file without change unless the name stored in NAME$ matches the name entered for DONOR$. In that special case, file updating occurs. The computer adds the value entered for GIFT to the existing value in AMOUNT and, when control falls to the PRINT #2: statement, writes this updated version of AMOUNT into the new file. After all of the records in the original file have been read, the original file is erased and the new file closed.

Notice that the old and new files must have different names. It is good programming practice to name your files with a short first name that indicates the subject matter of the file and a three-letter extension (after the dot (.)) that indicates the version of the file. In the example the files have the names FUNDS.ONE and FUNDS.TWO to reflect their relative dates of creation.

Depending upon your project, you may or may not want to erase the original file after you create a newer version. If you do want to erase the old file, use the ERASE #n statement, as in the example. If you do not wish to erase the original file, use a CLOSE #n statement for each file.

Appending data to a text file

You cannot write over data in an existing text file, but you can add data to the end of one. All you need to do is move the file pointer to the end of the file and begin writing. The computer appends the new data after the last file record.

The program of Figure 15–6 adds three more names to the FUNDS.TWO file. The OPEN statement describes the file as an old file open for output. The SET #1: POINTER END statement makes appending data possible. It tells the computer to move the file pointer past the last record in the file. The writing occurs where the pointer is positioned so that there is no problem of attempting to write over existing data.

Figure 15–6. Appending data to a text file

```
OPEN #1: NAME "FUNDS.TWO", ACCESS output, CREATE old, ORGANIZATION text
SET #1: POINTER END        !start writing at end of file
FOR INDEX = 1 TO 3
    INPUT PROMPT "Enter name, donation: ": NAME$,AMOUNT
    PRINT #1: NAME$;",";AMOUNT
NEXT INDEX
CLOSE #1
END
```

```
Ok. run
Enter name, donation: Rodney, 80.00
Enter name, donation: Atwood, 100.00
Enter name, donation: Hershy, 50.00
Ok.
```

Be sure that you add new data with the same format of data fields and separators in each file record as exist in the original file. The computer will let you do otherwise, but you will surely confuse yourself and your fellow programmers if you change the format of the records in your text file in mid-stream.

When the formats of the new and the previous data match, the original file reading routine can read all of the data in the larger file. Figure 15–7 uses the same program to read the larger file as was used to read the original file.

Figure 15–7. Reading an appended text file

```
OPEN #1: NAME "FUNDS.TWO", ACCESS input, CREATE old, ORGANIZATION text
PRINT "Campaign Contributors"
PRINT
DO WHILE MORE #1
    INPUT #1: NAME$,AMOUNT          !read from the file
    PRINT NAME$,AMOUNT              !write on the screen
LOOP
CLOSE #1
END
```

```
Ok. run
Campaign Contributors

Whithers    45
Filmore     150
Smythwick   75
Rodney      80
Atwood      100
Hershy      50
Ok.
```

The SET #n: POINTER function

The True BASIC SET #n: POINTER function has two important uses for text files. As the previous examples illustrate, it makes it possible to append data to the end of a text file by moving the pointer to the end of a file with a statement like

```
SET #1: POINTER END
```

The SET #n: POINTER function also makes it possible to read data in a file when the pointer is set beyond the item you wish to see. The statement

```
SET #1: POINTER BEGIN
```

moves the pointer back to the beginning of the open file. You can then read one record after another until you find the one that interests you.

Because text files are sequential files, the SET #n: POINTER function cannot skip the pointer around in text files, retrieving one record here and one record there. These random-access capabilities are reserved for the record files, which are described in the next chapter.

Summary

The computer views text files as a collection of data fields separated by a marker such as the comma or *enter* key codes. You, as the programmer, must give structure to these fields.

Programming skills

The PRINT #n: statement

The SET #n: MARGIN function

The ASK #n: MARGIN function

The PRINT #n, USING: statement

The INPUT #n: statement

The LINE INPUT #n: statement

The SET #n: POINTER function

Computer concepts

Writing a text file
Reading a text file
Updating a text file
Appending data to a text file

Review questions

1. The Alumni Office uses a text file.
   a. Create a text file that will be useful for the Director of Alumni Affairs. Store the name, graduating class, favorite sport, and current occupation of each alumnus. (Use a sample of 10 alumni.)
   b. Use the file to print a letter of invitation to the State Swimming Championships to all of the alumni who are recorded as having swimming as their favorite sport.
2. The Computer Company keeps a sequential file of its 20 employees.
   a. Create a text file that contains their names, street addresses, cities, and states.
   b. Use the computer to print mailing labels for their weekly paychecks.
3. The Weather Bureau keeps the snowfall statistics for each county in a separate text file. Each file contains three pieces of information: the weather reporter's name, the county name, and the number of inches of snow for the season.
   a. First write the program, and then enter the data for three counties.
   b. Draw upon all three files to get the data to calculate the average snowfall for the three counties. Print the average on the screen.

4. The Internal Revenue Service has surprise refunds for all taxpayers who paid before the April 15 deadline.
   a. Create a file with the names, payment dates, and amount of tax paid for each citizen. (Use a sample of 6.)
   b. Have the computer read the file and calculate a 10% refund for all pre–April 15 payers. Print their names and the amounts of their refunds on the screen.
5. All of the retail stores that are customers of the Junk Jewelry Manufacturing Company are listed in the company's customer master file, which contains their names and cities, and designations of their credit standings. (P = poor, G = good).
   a. Write a program that creates this text customer master file.
   b. Write a program that creates two new text files, GOOD.DAT and POOR.DAT, each containing the list of customers with good or poor ratings.
   c. Ask the bookkeeper whether he wishes to see the list of good customers or poor customers and print out the names and cities of everyone in the appropriate file.
6. Kenneth Bedford, prominent Metropolitan City attorney, uses a computer to keep track of his clients and their legal problems.
   a. Write a program that allows him to enter the following names, charges, and court decisions into a text file:

Name	Charge	Decision
Prof. Prune	Libel	Won!
Miss Rouge	Slander	Lost
Tom Tough	Arson	????
General Spice	Theft	Won!
Mrs. Knight	Bribery	Lost

   b. Tom Tough has gone from the frying pan into the fire. Write the program that updates this file and change the "????" decision to "Lost" for him.
   c. Write a program that prints out the updated file.
7. The Mighty Metropolitan baseball team and the Sluggin' Scouts use a computer to store in the team text files the names, at bats, and hits of each of the nine players on their teams.
   a. Create the METRO file and the SCOUT file with this information.
   b. Draw from the data in these files to create another file, ALLSTAR, which contains the names, teams, and batting averages of the players from either team with the best batting average. ALLSTAR includes only the nine best batters. Print their names and batting averages on the screen as well.
8. By some well-kept secret, the names on the mailing lists from catalog sales companies always become part of the Master Junk Mail mailing list.
   a. Create a larger (10-name) MASTER TEXT file and a smaller (5-name) FAMILY TEXT file to represent the names for the junk mail list and the Family Mail Order Catalog file.
   b. Append the FAMILY mailing list to the MASTER list.
   c. Write the program that randomly picks one name from this MASTER file and sends a letter telling the person that she has won the $10 million sweepstakes.
9. Use the computer to assign jobs to the campers at Camp Jolly Good Fun.
   a. Make sure that no one repeats a job until he has done all of the other jobs. Set up five text files—MON, TUES, WED, THURS, and FRI—to store the duty roster for each day of the week. Use a sample of five campers and five jobs for this exercise.
   b. Ask the camp director which day's duty roster he wishes to see and print the duty roster that has been stored in the file for that day.
10. The school registrar uses a computer to store student academic records.
   a. Create and fill a text file with the name, course, and grade point average of students in the courses at Highpoint High. Use the sample names below:

Name	Course	Average
Smith	French	98
Jones	English	45

Ocker	Math	56
Bell	French	87
Moral	English	98
Hawkins	English	91
Tremont	Math	99
Bosting	Math	78
Helms	Math	90
Goodie	English	78

b. Select those students with averages above 89 to be stored in a special file: SMART.

c. Allow the registrar to create advanced courses from the information in the SMART file. Have her enter the name of the course she is interested in, and have the computer list the students in the file who are enrolled in the course she has requested.

Chapter 16

Record files

True BASIC record files provide random access to file data. By allowing you to move the file pointer forward and backward through your file, they make it possible for you to locate each record in order to read and modify the contents. The price of this flexibility in accessing file data is a certain measure of inflexibility in the organization of the file. To make random access possible every data field in the file must have the same number of bytes. The computer uses this field length to calculate the location of any one item you request.

Usually, data files are thought of as being made up of records that each contain all the information about one item in the file. Each record, in turn, is made up of fields containing data pertaining to the particular item. In a dentist's file, for example, a complete file record contains all of the information describing a patient. It is made up of a name field, a payment field, and a number-of-cavities-filled field.

If you think of files in this way, then the name "field" files, rather than "record" files, best describes this type of True BASIC file. The computer views a True BASIC record file as a collection of fields rather than as a collection of records. Using record files for the dentist you can refer and point to each field in every record of the file. But there is no True BASIC statement or function that automatically gives access to a complete file record. It is up to you, the programmer, to provide this logic in your file-accessing routines.

As Figure 16–1 illustrates, True BASIC record files store the dentist's file information simply as a name field, followed by a cavity field, followed by a dollar field, followed by a name field, a cavity field, a dollar field, and so on. The computer considers each field to be a record, and it numbers them sequentially. You can retrieve information from any field by referring to its number. In so doing, you must remember that fields 1, 4, and 7 mark the beginning of the data for a patient and therefore write your program to access the data according to this structure.

This chapter explains the True BASIC statements that allow you to create, read, and update record files and explains how to give a structure to the fields in the file. It makes use of a file record layout to design and document the file organization for yourself and future file users.

Figure 16–1. Record file data/programmer's file structure

Computer's view of a file record	File contents	Programmer's view of a file record	
Record #1	Lee	field #1	
Record #2	6	field #2	Record #1
Record #3	66.00	field #3	
Record #4	Collins	field #1	
Record #5	3	field #2	Record #2
Record #6	33.33	field #3	
Record #7	Talbott	field #1	
Record #8	4	field #2	Record #3
Record #9	45.75	field #3	

Designing a record file

Your first step in creating a True BASIC record file is to design a file record layout. This allows you to visualize a complete file record and its data fields and forces you to select and document the RECSIZE for the file.

The RECSIZE is the file attribute that tells the computer how many bytes to allow for each field in the record file. The RECSIZE is the same for all fields in the file, regardless of differences among the data within the various fields.

True BASIC has no practical limit to the RECSIZE (about 16 million bytes); so, you must choose a size that makes sense for your project. Be sure to make the RECSIZE long enough for the longest data item in the file. Once a file's RECSIZE is established, the computer gives an error message if you attempt to store items longer than the RECSIZE you have specified. Storing shorter items causes no problem. Short data items are written into fields of your specified length and padded with blanks. If your file is composed of only numeric data, you need a RECSIZE of 8 bytes, since True BASIC always stores numbers in the 8-byte IEEE format.

The file record layout helps keep track of whether a particular field contains string or numeric data. You need this information in order to determine which variables to use in programs that manipulate the file.

Figure 16–2 illustrates the file record layout for the payroll file. It is a useful example because, as in real life, the file contains string and numeric data of varying lengths, yet the data are stored in a record file with fixed field lengths in order to make random access possible. Notice that the file record layout includes file header information. At the beginning of each record file, True BASIC inserts five header bytes that tell the computer the file is a record file and that indicate the record size. At the beginning of each record within the file, True BASIC inserts four header bytes that tell how many bytes in the record are filled with meaningful data and whether the data are string or numeric.

First names are usually shorter than fifteen characters, or bytes, and numbers are always stored in 8 bytes in True BASIC, yet the field length for the payroll file is 16. This is to accommodate last names and job titles that might take up to 16 bytes.

Once you've decided upon the layout, use the OPEN statement to specify the record file organization and a RECSIZE. These attributes remain with a record file until it is ERASEd or UNSAVEd.

Figure 16-2. Payroll file record layout

File name: Pay   File type: Record   File size: 9 records

Variable name	Field description	Field length (in bytes)	Data type
Record__header 1	length of real data	3	numeric
Record__header 2	type of data	1	string
Last$	last name	16	string
Record__header 1	length of real data	3	numeric
Record__header 2	type of data	1	string
First$	first name	16	string
Record__header 1	length of real data	3	numeric
Record__header 2	type of data	1	string
Job$	job title	16	string
Record__header 1	length of real data	3	numeric
Record__header 2	type of data	1	string
Rate	wage	16	numeric
	Total bytes per record	80	

Bytes used by all records (80 × 9)   720
Bytes used for file header   5
Total bytes in file   725

Writing into a record file

Figure 16-3 creates the payroll file described by the file record layout in Figure 16-2. It takes file information from DATA statements and writes it out to the disk. The computer begins with the first position in the file, reads or writes an item, and moves the pointer to the next position in the file. The next reading or writing occurs at this file position, and the pointer moves to the next field in the file, and so on. When you are entering data for the first time, you can let the computer move the pointer through the file in this manner for you.

Figure 16-3. Creating a record file

```
OPEN #1: NAME "pay", ACCESS output, CREATE new, ORGANIZATION record, RECSIZE 16
DO WHILE MORE DATA
    READ LAST$,FIRST$,JOB$,RATE
  WRITE #1: LAST$,FIRST$,JOB$,RATE
LOOP
DATA Skoville, Clarence, Plumber, 489.39
DATA Bostwick, Hermon, Carpenter, 435.25
DATA Kohler, David, Painter, 491.21
CLOSE #1
END
```

```
Ok. run
OK.
```

The "record" option for the ORGANIZATION parameter in the OPEN statement tells the computer that this file is a record file. The value "16" for the RECSIZE parameter tells the computer that each data field within the file records has 16 bytes.

You can set the RECSIZE of the file only when the file is empty. If you are creating a new file, use the RECSIZE parameter in the OPEN statement. If you are recreating a file that has been opened and erased, use the statement

```
SET #1: RECSIZE 16
```

to set the True BASIC record length to 16 bytes for each data field in the file open on channel #1. The new RECSIZE setting overrides the previous setting for the file.

Notice that the statement

```
WRITE #1: LAST$,FIRST$,JOB$,RATE
```

in the example program represents a complete logical file record, since it writes all of the information for one employee each time it executes. It is important to organize the WRITE #n: statement this way in order to document the logic of the file processing for those who will use your program or the file it creates. But remember, the logical grouping of variables in the WRITE #n: statement has no effect on the organization of the file on the disk. Since this is a record file with a RECSIZE of 16, the computer stores one 16-byte field after another, with no indicators to show where one person's complete payroll record (one logical file record) ends and another's begins. From the computer's point of view, the data could just as well have been written with the following WRITE #n: statements

```
WRITE #1: LAST$
WRITE #1: FIRSTS$
WRITE #1: JOB$
WRITE #1: RATE
```

Regardless of the format of the WRITE #n: statements, the pay file is organized on the disk according to the representation in Figure 16–4. Each data field consumes 16 bytes and is preceded by 4 headerbytes.

Reading a record file

There are two things to keep track of when you read a record file: the type of data you are reading (numeric or string) and the position of the file pointer. As usual, you must read numeric data with numeric variables and use string variables to read character data. If you read the entire file from beginning to end, you can take advantage of the default progression of the pointer from data field to data field. If you take advantage of the random-access capabilities of record files to read a specific data field or group of fields, then you must use the SET #n: statement to move the pointer.

The program of Figure 16–5 randomly accesses the file and looks up the information for whichever employee the user requests. The OPEN statement that reads the record file almost matches the OPEN statement that created the file. The only difference is that the CREATE mode in the first instance is "new"; in the second instance it is "old." The ORGANIZATION parameter is "record" and the RECSIZE is 16. Once you create a record file with a particular RECSIZE, you must always OPEN it with the same RECSIZE value.

Figure 16–4. The pay file disk organization

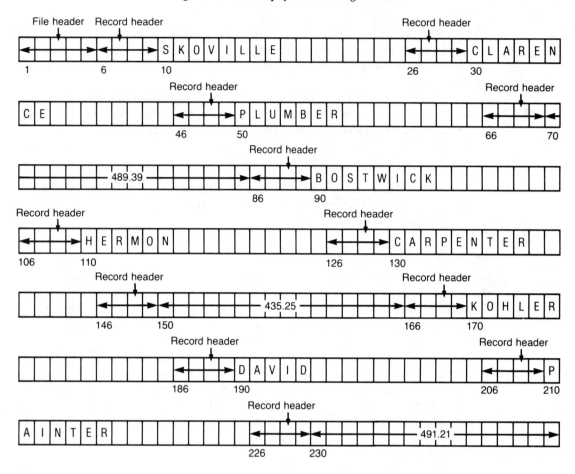

Figure 16–5. Reading a record file

```
■ OPEN #1: NAME "pay", ACCESS input, CREATE old, ORGANIZATION record, RECSIZE 16
■ INPUT PROMPT "Enter employee number ": NUM
■ SET #1: RECORD ((NUM - 1)*4) + 1
■ READ #1: LAST$,FIRST$,JOB$,RATE
■ PRINT
■ PRINT "The file information on employee number";NUM;"is:"
■ PRINT
■ PRINT "NAME ";LAST$;", ";FIRST$
■ PRINT "JOB TITLE ";JOB$
■ PRINT "WAGE";RATE
■ CLOSE #1
■ END
```

```
Ok. run
Enter employee number 2

The file information on employee number 2 is:

NAME Bostwick, Hermon
JOB TITLE Carpenter
WAGE 435.25
Ok.
```

The SET #n: statement controls the pointer. You can give the True BASIC record number for a specific field or for general locations such as "END" to move the pointer throughout the file. The example gives a specific field address. The expression

```
((num - 1)*4) + 1
```

tells the computer to move the pointer past each of the four data fields (the last and first names, the job title, and the wage rate) in the complete payroll records that precede the one of interest, payroll record number 2.

Once you position the pointer to the data field you wish to manipulate, the next READ #n: or WRITE #n: statement acts upon the data field located at the current file pointer position. The READ #n: or WRITE #n: operation takes place and the pointer advances to the next field in the file.

Retrieving the data in the file is not enough; you must PRINT them on the screen or paper. The PRINT statements in the example illustrate that you must concern yourself to some extent with how to present the file data. At the very least, precede the display of information with an introductory statement that explains what the data represent.

Figure 16-6 lists the possible SET #n: statement parameters appropriate for record files and explains their use.

Figure 16-6. The SET #n: parameters for record files

SET statement	*Function*
SET #n: POINTER BEGIN	Directs the file pointer to the first byte of the first field in file #n.
SET #n: POINTER END	Directs the file pointer to the first byte of the last field in file #n.
SET #n: POINTER SAME	Directs the file pointer back to the first byte of the field most recently accessed in file #n.
SET #n: POINTER NEXT	Directs the file pointer ahead to the first byte of the field following the current file pointer position.
SET #n: RECORD num	Directs the file pointer to the first byte of the field in position "num" in file #n. Note that "num" can be a number constant, a numeric variable, or an arithmetic expression.
SET #n: RECSIZE num	Sets the field length for file #n to "num" number of bytes.

Of course, you are not required to view the data in your record file as a collection of logical file records. If, for example, you simply want to read the third surname in the file, and you know by reading the file record layout that this field is the ninth data field, you can set the pointer to this particular field and read the single data item stored there. The program of Figure 16-7 reads a single data field in this manner.

Figure 16-7. Reading a data field in a record file

```
▌ OPEN #1: NAME "pay", ACCESS input, CREATE old, ORGANIZATION record, RECSIZE 16
▌ SET #1: RECORD 9
▌ READ #1: LAST$
▌ PRINT
▌ PRINT "The third name in the file is:"
▌ PRINT
▌ PRINT LAST$
▌ CLOSE #1
▌ END
```

```
Ok. run

The third name in the file is:

Kohler
Ok.
```

Updating a record file

As long as your new information fits within the RECSIZE of the record file, you can write over any field you wish. All you need to do is keep track of the file pointer and, if necessary, control it by means of the SET #n: statements.

Figure 16-8 uses the SET #n: statement to give someone in the "pay" file a raise. The OPEN statement specifies the same ORGANIZATION (record) and

Figure 16-8. Updating a record file

```
▌ OPEN #1: NAME "pay", ACCESS outin, CREATE old, ORGANIZATION record, RECSIZE 16
▌ INPUT PROMPT "Enter employee number and new wage ": NUM, RAISE
▌ SET #1: RECORD NUM*4
▌ READ #1: WAGE
▌ PRINT
▌ PRINT "The previous wage was";WAGE
▌ SET #1: POINTER SAME
▌ WRITE #1: RAISE
▌ PRINT "The new wage is";RAISE
▌ CLOSE #1
▌ END
```

```
Ok. run
Enter employee number and new wage 2, 457.57

The previous wage was 435.25
The new wage is 457.57
Ok.
```

RECSIZE (16 bytes) as all other OPEN statements that use this file. The ACCESS parameter is outin, since before writing to the file the program reads the old file information. The statement

```
SET #1: RECORD NUM*4
```

moves the pointer to tne wage rate data field for the employee whose number is represented by the NUM variable. Use the file record layout to work out the arithmetic expression in your SET #1: RECORD statement that moves the pointer to the data field you intend to update. Once the pointer indicates the correct data field, the statement

```
READ #1: WAGE
```

retrieves the existing file data and moves the pointer to the next field in the file. For this reason, you need to use the statement

```
SET #1: POINTER SAME
```

to return the file pointer back one field to the data you intend to overwrite. The statement

```
WRITE #1: RAISE
```

does the updating for you. If you wish, you can use variables or actual constant values to represent the new information.

The computer does not require that you replace strings with strings and numbers with numeric data, but mixing data types may cause more problems than it solves. Remember, the file record layout describes the file for you and other programmers. If you change the data types of any fields, be sure to document the change in a new file record layout.

Appending data to a record file

Appending data to a record file is a straightforward process. Be sure the file is open for output, move the pointer to the end of the file, and begin writing new file information according to the specifications in the file record layout.

The program of Figure 16-9 adds new employees to the payroll file. In the append data portion of this example, the statement

```
SET #1: POINTER END
```

positions the file pointer past the last data field in the file. The next WRITE statement,

```
WRITE #1: LAST$,FIRST$,JOB$,RATE
```

extends the file as it writes the contents of each variable into new data fields. When the writing is completed, the pointer aims at the new end of file.

Figure 16-9. Appending data to a record file

```
OPEN #1: NAME "pay", ACCESS outin, CREATE old, ORGANIZATION record, RECSIZE 16
REM----------append routine------------
SET #1: POINTER END
INPUT PROMPT "Last Name ": LAST$
INPUT PROMPT "First Name ":FIRST$
INPUT PROMPT "Job Title ":JOB$
INPUT PROMPT "Wage Rate ":RATE
WRITE #1: LAST$,FIRST$,JOB$,RATE
REM----------check file routine-------
PRINT
SET #1: POINTER BEGIN
DO WHILE MORE #1
   READ #1:LAST$,FIRST$,JOB$,RATE
   PRINT LAST$,FIRST$,JOB$,RATE
LOOP
CLOSE #1
END
```

```
Ok. run
Last Name Laurelson
First Name Darryl
Job Title Architect
Wage Rate 565.84

Skoville      Clarence    Plumber      489.39
Bostwick      Hermon      Carpenter    457.57
Kohler        David       Painter      491.21
Laurelson     Darryl      Architect    565.84
Ok.
```

The second half of the sample program proves that data have been appended to the file. The statement

```
SET #1: POINTER BEGIN
```

repositions the pointer to indicate the first data field in the file. The DO loop, governed by the WHILE MORE #1 check, runs until there is no more file data to be read. It accesses a complete file record with each READ #1: statement and displays the record across a screen line. The new employee appears at the end of the list.

Summary

True BASIC record files provide random access to file data. The price of this flexibility is inflexibility in the organization of the file: each data field in the file must have the same number of bytes.

Programming skills

The RECSIZE attribute
The WRITE #1: statement
The READ #1: statement
The SET #n: statement

Computer concepts

Data field
Programmer's file record
True BASIC file record
Writing a record file
Reading a record file
Updating a record file
Appending data to a record file

Review questions

1. a. Write a program that allows the accountant in the dentist's office to keep track of the name, number of cavities, and amount owed for each patient. Use a random-access file that stores the information for each patient in one file record. Run the program and enter sample data for a few patients.
   b. Write a program that allows the accountant to enter a patient's ID number, and have the computer select that record and print how much money the patient owes. The ID number and the file record number will match. Have the computer accept a payment amount and update the patient's file record to reflect the payment.

2. The high school uses a computer to keep track of the number of unexcused absences taken by its students.
   a. Write the program that is run in September to initialize a record file. Associate each student's name with his student ID number, and enter a zero as the starting total of cuts taken by each.
   b. Write the program that is run throughout the year to update the file. The Attendance Officer enters a student's ID number and receives a report of the name and number of cuts so far. New cuts are then added, and the file tally is incremented accordingly.

3. The bank uses a random-access file to keep track of its customers' checking accounts.
   a. Write a program that initializes the file for 10 customers. It will associate each account number with a customer name and a checking account balance. Set the starting balances to zero.
   b. Write a program to be run thereafter to accept checking account transactions. Each time the teller enters the bank account number, the customer's name and current balance are presented. Deposits are accepted and added to the current balance, and the new total is reported. Before withdrawals are made, the computer checks to see if an overdraft will occur. If so, the transaction is not allowed.

4. The computer class takes its final exam using the computer. The instructor receives a report on the students' scores from the computer as well.
   a. Write the set-up program that stores the questions and answers (10 of them) in a random-access file.
   b. Write a test program that asks questions and stores the tally of correct answers for

each student in the student ANSWER file. This is a random-access file in which the answers are stored according to a student's ID number.

   c. Write the program that the instructor uses to receive a report of the test results. The computer uses the ANSWER file to calculate the score as a percent and prints out the student ID number and score in chart form.

5. Piper Cub Airways uses a computer to keep track of reservations on its three flights (numbers 001, 002, and 003). Each plane accommodates 15 passengers in 5 rows with 3 seats each.

   a. Write a program that sets up all three flights in three different random-access files and initializes the reservations records to blanks.

   b. Write the program that the ticket agent uses to make reservations. A passenger may choose which row and which seat she prefers. If the seat is available, her name is stored in the reservations file for that flight, along with the seat designation. Allow the agent to see a list of available seats for any of the flights whenever it is necessary.

   c. Write the program that accesses the file for each flight and prints a seating chart for the flight attendant.

6. The Department of Water Quality uses a computer to record the monthly changes in water quality in the Houwonscoponic River.

   a. Write the program that initializes a random-access file with readings of zero for each of the 12 months. (Readings will be integers from 1 to 10.)

   b. Write a program that the department limnologist uses each month to enter the quality reading (as 1 for the poorest quality to 10 for the highest). The limnologist types in the month and the computer stores the reading in the appropriate file record.

   c. Write a program that the director uses to write the annual report. Have the computer draw upon the file to print a graph of the readings for each month. Split the screen to display the data along with a line graph.

## Chapter 17

Byte files

True BASIC byte files give you complete control over the data in a file by making it possible to access one byte at a time. Effective use of this control requires careful planning and organization. You must know exactly what each byte of your file represents — whether a particular byte represents an ASCII character or part of the internal format for a number. Because of this need for detail, a file record layout, or an equivalent chart, that defines each byte in a file is an essential tool for manipulating byte files.

Since byte files do not require record length or data field definitions, you can also use them to receive data created on other computers in formats unknown to True BASIC but known to yourself. By opening the foreign file as a byte file and reading it as a stream of characters, you can rewrite the data into a new True BASIC byte file. Later, using your description of how the file was originally organized, you can write programs that access the bytes in the new True BASIC file in a meaningful way.

This chapter shows how to create, update, and read bytes files. It explains how to use True BASIC conversion functions and the file record layout in byte file processing. There is an example of the use of byte files to receive text data created on another computer and an example of using byte file processing to read a file created in a non-byte-file format.

Designing a byte file

Since the unit of transfer into a byte file is one byte, you are the one who must keep track of how many bytes together really have meaning. When you read from a byte file you can direct the computer to take groups of bytes at a time. Thus, one of your first tasks is to complete a file record layout.

Figure 17–1 gives the layout for a file of famous characters and some dollar amounts associated with each one.

Figure 17–1. Friends file record layout

Filename: Friends   File type: Byte   Contents: 24 records

Variable name	Description	Field length (in bytes)	Data type
Name$	Name	15	Character
Amount$	Dollars	8	Numeric
	Total record length	23 bytes	

Total bytes per file (23 × 24)552 bytes

Notice that the variables are string variables. Notice also that the AMOUNT$ variable represents numeric data. This is because all data in a byte file, even numeric data, must be string data. You must convert a number into string data before writing it into a byte file, and you must convert it back to a number after you read it from the file. In this converted-string representation, each number requires 8 bytes.

The True BASIC NUM and NUM$ functions perform these conversions for you:

Function	Result	Example
NUM$(X)	An 8-byte string	LET STRNUM$ = NUM$(X)
NUM(X$)	A number stored in the 8-byte IEEE format	LET X = NUM(STRNUM$)

Writing into a byte file

Before writing the program that creates the "Friends" file with both names and numbers, take a minute to observe how to write names into a byte file.

The program of Figure 17–2 uses a byte file to store names. When you are not storing numbers the process is quite straightforward.

Figure 17–2. Writing into a byte file

```
OPEN #1: NAME "Guys", ORGANIZATION byte, CREATE new, ACCESS output
DO WHILE MORE DATA
   READ NAME$
   WRITE #1: NAME$
LOOP
DATA "Rumpelstiltskin", "Red Riding Hood"
CLOSE #1
END
```

```
Ok. run
Ok.
```

The OPEN statement performs its usual function of defining the name (Guys), type (byte), status (new), and activity (output) for the file. With byte files, you never need to give a file RECSIZE. The computer always writes out one byte at a time, moving the file pointer as it does so. In this example of a new file, the pointer begins at the first byte of the file. The statement

```
WRITE #1: NAME$
```

writes the 15 bytes of Rumpelstiltskin one after another and finally moves the pointer to the sixteenth byte in the file. When Red Riding Hood is written, the first character is stored at byte 16, and the remaining characters are stored in successive bytes. The file appears as diagrammed in Figure 17–3.

Figure 17–3. Byte file data

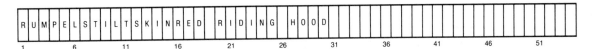

Because of the need to convert numbers to strings, the programming steps for storing numbers in a byte file are slightly more complex than those for storing characters. Figure 17–4 creates a byte file for the "Friends" file described by the file record layout in Figure 17–1 (page 236). It stores the friends' names as well as dollar amounts, and uses the NUM$ function to convert the numeric data to an 8-byte string format.

Figure 17–4. Writing numbers into a byte file

```
OPEN #1: NAME "Friends", ORGANIZATION byte, CREATE new, ACCESS output
DO WHILE MORE DATA
   READ NAME$,AMOUNT
   WRITE #1: NAME$
   LET AMOUNT$ = NUM$(AMOUNT)
   WRITE #1: AMOUNT$
LOOP
DATA "Rumpelstiltskin",45.75,"Red Riding Hood",35.56
CLOSE #1
END
```

Ok. run

Figure 17–5 shows the result of the WRITE #1: statements in the program of Figure 17–4. Each written name is followed by an 8-byte string representation of the numeric amounts.

Figure 17–5. Byte file data that include numbers

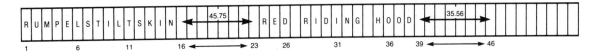

Reading a byte file

For byte files, you specify in each READ #: statement exactly how many bytes to read into a variable. For files of any complexity, this means the file record layout is your key to successful reading of a byte file. Since it tells you how the file is laid out, you can use it as a guide to accessing the file bytes in meaningful groups.

The program of Figure 17–6 reads the names and numbers in the Friends file created by Figure 17–4 (page 237). As the example program shows, you specify

Figure 17–6. Reading a byte file

```
OPEN #1: NAME "Friends", ORGANIZATION byte, CREATE old, ACCESS input
PRINT "The Friends File:"
PRINT
DO WHILE MORE #1
   READ #1, BYTES 15: NAME$
   READ #1, BYTES 8: AMOUNT$
   LET AMOUNT = NUM(AMOUNT$)
   PRINT NAME$," ";AMOUNT
LOOP
CLOSE #1
END
```

```
Ok. run
The Friends File:

Rumpelstiltskin   45.75
Red Riding Hood   35.56
Ok.
```

the number of bytes to read by adding a "BYTES" modifier to a READ #n: statement. This modifier tells the computer how many bytes the READ #n: statement should read. The bytes given in the READ #n, BYTES n: statement override any RECSIZE specifications given previously in your program.

Notice that the statements

```
READ #1, BYTES 15: NAME$
READ #1, BYTES 8: AMOUNT$
```

mirror the file record layout. Each complete record in the Friends file has 15 bytes followed by 8 bytes. Similarly, each pass of the DO loop that reads the file brings in 15 bytes, followed by 8 bytes. The example also shows that the easiest way to read a byte file is to make each READ #n, BYTES n: statement match each field definition in the file record layout.

There is no requirement in True BASIC byte file processing to make the data in one complete file record match the layout of data in the other file records. However, doing so is helpful. When all the names take up 15 bytes and the amounts take up 8 bytes, for example, the same READ #n, BYTES n: statement can be used in a loop to process all of the file records. If the names were all of varying lengths, you would need a different READ #n, BYTES n: statement to read each one. Your program would be harder to write and more difficult to understand.

Updating a byte file

You can rewrite any byte in a byte file. Usually, you open the file for outin access in order to first READ #n: and verify your place in the file. Then, you rewrite the bytes that need updating.

The program of Figure 17-7 changes the *amount* field for one of the members of the Friends file.

Figure 17-7. Updating a byte file

```
OPEN #1: NAME "Friends", ORGANIZATION byte, CREATE old, ACCESS outin
INPUT PROMPT "Enter the name and the new amount:":N$,A
DO WHILE MORE #1
   READ #1, BYTES 15: NAME$
   IF NAME$ = N$ THEN
      PRINT "You are, indeed, updating the file record for ";NAME$
      WRITE #1: NUM$(A)
      SET #1: POINTER END
   ELSE
      READ #1, BYTES 8: AMOUNT$
   END IF
LOOP
CLOSE #1
END
```

```
Ok. run
Enter the name and new amount? Rumpelstiltskin, 99.99
You are, indeed, updating the file record for Rumpelstiltskin
Ok.
```

The updating process works because, once again, the file record layout guides the programming routine. The computer sequentially accesses the bytes of the file from beginning to end, taking bytes in groups of 15 when names are being read and groups of 8 when numbers are being read or written. The computer first reads a name and moves the pointer to the byte following the name — that is, the first byte of the amount string. The IF statement checks to see whether the name just read matches the one entered in response to the prompt. If the names match, the computer converts the amount entered into a string format and writes it into the file. Writing occurs beginning with the byte indicated by the file pointer. The new amount replaces the previous file amount; you have updated the file. All that remains is to exit the search loop and close the file. The statement

```
SET #1: POINTER END
```

advances the pointer to the end of the file and forces the MORE #1 check on the DO statement to terminate the loop.

If the name read does not match the name entered, control falls to the ELSE clause. The pointer moves to the next name simply by having the program read the amount field and taking no action. When the next iteration of the loop occurs, the pointer has moved to the next name in the file.

When you update a file you must work within the original file structure. If you are changing names in the Friends file, for example, you must remember that the file has been designed with 15 bytes for each name. Truncate longer names and pad shorter ones with blanks. This ensures that the names provided by the update neither write over an amount string nor end with characters from longer, previous names.

There are as many ways to update a byte file as there are byte files. Since you can access each byte and set the pointer backward and forward in the file, you can create a complex series of checks and updates if you wish. But as with all other aspects of programming, clarity is the goal. Using the sequential approach outlined above and following the dictates of the file record layout make the updating process manageable and understandable.

Appending data to a byte file

The SET #1: POINTER END statement makes it possible to expand a byte file. The program of Figure 17–8 adds names and amounts to the Friends file.

Figure 17–8. Appending data to a byte file

```
OPEN #1: NAME "Friends", ORGANIZATION byte, CREATE old, ACCESS output
SET #1: POINTER END
DO WHILE MORE DATA
   READ NAME$,AMOUNT
   WRITE #1: NAME$
   LET AMOUNT$ = NUM$(AMOUNT)
   WRITE #1: AMOUNT$
LOOP
DATA "Snow White     ",25.80,"Humpty Dumpty ",80.66
CLOSE #1
END
```

```
Ok. run
Ok.
```

To append data to a byte file, open it as an old file for output processing. Use the statement

```
SET #1: POINTER END
```

to move the pointer to the end of the file, and subsequent WRITE #1: statements to append data to the previous end of the file.

Notice the DATA statements that contain the new names for the Friends file. The names are surrounded by quotation marks and actually include trailing blanks. The extra blanks ensure that the new names occupy 15 bytes, just as the previously stored names do. The file keeps to the plan spelled out in the file record layout.

Transferring raw data

Byte files make it easy to access data in a file created on your computer in formats not known to True BASIC. All you need to do is open the existing file as a byte file, read the data as a stream of bytes, and, if you wish to keep a copy, write them into a new byte file in your True BASIC system.

The program of Figure 17–9 opens a file for input, creates a new one for output, and thereby brings a data base into the system. Notice that, regardless of its original format (as a text file, a record file, or other type of file), the file providing data is defined as a byte file by the True BASIC program that does the transfer. Similarly, the transfer program defines the receiving file as a byte file.

Figure 17–9. Transferring data between files

```
OPEN #1: NAME "Datab", ORGANIZATION byte, CREATE old, ACCESS input
OPEN #2: NAME "Lists", ORGANIZATION byte, CREATE new, ACCESS output
DO WHILE MORE #1
   READ #1, BYTES 64: RECORD$
   WRITE #2: RECORD$
LOOP
CLOSE #1
CLOSE #2
End
```

Ok. run

Bringing data from a foreign file may be more trouble than it is worth if you do not also have the old file record layout or its equivalent. Not only do you need to know how the bytes are organized in order to use the data, but, for the transfer process, you ought to know how many bytes to read in each READ #n: statement. An error occurs if an end-of-file is reached during a READ operation. If necessary, you can protect against this by using an error-handling routine. But it is preferable to be able to organize your READ #n: statement so that there is no attempt to reach beyond the file's end. You should also know how long the file is. Then you can be sure to have a target disk with enough free space to accommodate the new file.

Reading data from a foreign file

If you have the file record layout, you can read any file as a byte file regardless of how it was created on your computer system. The program of Figure 17–12 accesses the information in the payroll file created in the previous chapter as a True BASIC record file. Before running it, review the Pay file's file record layout below.

Figure 17–10. Payroll file record layout

File name: Pay   File type: Record   File size: 9 records

Variable name	Field description	Field length (in bytes)	Data type
Record__header 1	length of real data	3	numeric
Record__header 2	type of data	1	string
Last$	last name	16	string
Record__header 1	length of real data	3	numeric
Record__header 2	type of data	1	string
First$	first name	16	string
Record__header 1	length of real data	3	numeric
Record__header 2	type of data	1	string
Job$	job title	16	string
Record__header 1	length of real data	3	numeric
Record__header 2	type of data	1	string
Rate	wage	<u>16</u>	numeric (8 bytes of data)
	Total bytes per record	80	

Bytes used by all records (80 × 9)	720	
Bytes used for file header	5	
Total bytes in File	725	

With three sample employees, the Pay file appears on the disk as in Figure 17–11. Remember, as the diagram shows, True BASIC record files begin with 5 bytes of file-header information, and each record in the file begins with 4 bytes of record-header information. The size of each data field in this record file is 16 bytes, as determined by the RECSIZE parameter used in the program that created the file. The RECSIZE is the same for all data fields, even though some contain character strings and some contain numeric information. The number fields fill only the first 8 bytes in the field with meaningful information.

Figure 17–12 is a program that reads the file. Notice that it uses the same techniques for this file as it would for reading files originally created as byte files, except that it takes into account the header bytes included in all True BASIC record files.

Even though the Pay file was created as a record file, this program opens it with a byte-file organization. The first step in reaching the file data is to move the pointer past the five file-header bytes. The statement

```
READ #1, BYTES 5: FILEHEADS
```

accomplishes this by simply reading the bytes into the FILEHEAD$ variable. FILEHEAD$ has no other use for this program.

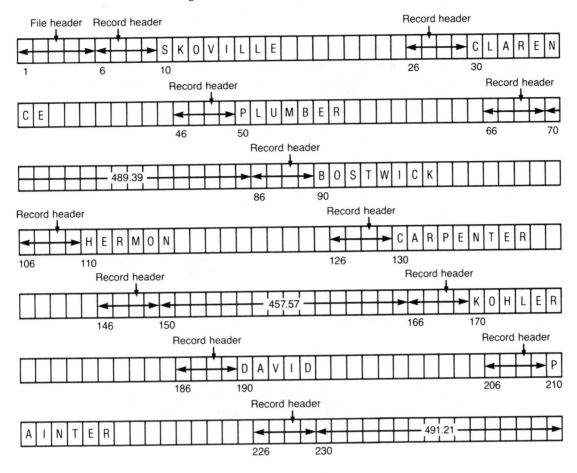

Figure 17-11. The Pay file

Figure 17-12. Reading data created as a record file in byte-file mode

```
OPEN #1: NAME "Pay", ORGANIZATION byte, CREATE old, ACCESS input
READ #1, BYTES 5: FILEHEAD$
FOR EMPLOYEE = 1 TO 3      !there are 3 employees in the file
    FOR FIELD = 1 to 3     !there are 3 16-character fields in each record
        READ #1, BYTES 4: RECORDHEAD$  !every field has a record header
        READ #1, BYTES 16: DATA$        !actual data
        PRINT DATA$;" ";
    NEXT FIELD
    READ #1, BYTES 4: RECORDHEAD$
    READ #1, BYTES 8: WAGE$
    PRINT NUM(WAGE$)
    READ #1, BYTES 8: UNUSEDBYTES$
NEXT EMPLOYEE
CLOSE #1
```

```
Ok. run
Skoville    Clarence    Plumber      489.39
Bostwick    Hermon      Carpenter    457.57
Kohler      David       Painter      491.21
Laurelson   Darryl      Architect    565.84
Ok.
```

After this first read operation the pointer aims at the first byte of the payroll record for the first employee in the file. Since the information for all employees has the same format, the statements that read a complete payroll record can be used repeatedly. The EMPLOYEE loop reads all of the information for a single employee with each iteration.

Within an employee's payroll record, there are three character string fields — last name, first name, and job title — that have the same format. These are read by repeating the statements that read a single 16-byte character string field three times:

```
READ #1, BYTES: 4:RECORDHEAD$ !every field has a record header
READ #1, BYTES: 16:DATA$       !actual data
```

This repetition occurs within the FIELD loop.

The *number* field for each record has 4 header bytes, 8 bytes of numeric information, and 8 bytes of meaningless information. The statements

```
READ #1, BYTES 4:  RECORDHEAD$
READ #1, BYTES 8:  WAGES$
READ #1, BYTES 8:  UNUSEDBYTE$$
```

divide and access the bytes devoted to the numeric field.

The run of the program produces the same results as the program of Figure 16–5 (page 228), which reads this file as a record file (Bostwick's record has been updated by Figure 16–8). It illustrates that, by means of byte files, you can access file data created in another format. All you need to guide you is the information within a file record layout.

Summary

True BASIC byte files give you complete control over the data in a file by making it possible to access one byte at a time.

Programming skills

The NUM and NUM$ functions
The READ #n, BYTES: statement

Computer concepts

Writing a byte file
Reading a byte file
Updating a byte file
Appending data to a byte file
Transferring raw data
Reading data from a foreign file

Review questions

1. a. Write a byte file that contains sequential floating-point values of 1 to 512.
   b. Show that you have succeeded.
   c. Modify the file to replace the entries 170, 234, and 300 with the words SKILLERY, SKALLERY, and ALIGATOR, respectively.
   d. Show that you have succeeded.
2. a. Store the name and ID number of each employee of the Central Bank in a byte file.
   b. Use the computer to allow the security guard to check workers as they arrive. When the guard enters the employee's name, have the computer print the matching ID number.
3. Use the computer to keep track of the inventory of ladies' shoes for the Cinderella Shoe Company. In a byte file store the style number and the quantity on hand for each style. There are 64 styles numbered from 1001 to 1064. Follow the steps below:
   a. Begin by putting initial quantity values in the file for each style.
   b. Tie the file into a cash register that subtracts from the quantity on hand each time a pair of shoes is sold.
4. You are an official of the United States Olympic Committee. The Winter Olympics are finished and the data have been stored in a byte file. Your job is to read the data about the medal winners and print out a chart like:

```
MEN'S DOWNHILL SKIING
GOLD: IGGY PIGGY          USA
SILVER: OLAF TOLSTOY      USSR
BRONZE: ALRED MINCINI     ITAL
```

   etc. for all 12 Olympic events. Allow 26 bytes for the name of each event and 30 bytes for the names of each medal winner and 4 bytes for the initials of their country. Write a program so that historians may inquire about any single event and see the gold, silver, and bronze medal winners. Break the project into 3 parts.
   a. Write a program to enter the names of the medalists and their countries for each event.
   b. Write a program to print out a list of each event with the name and country of each medalist.
   c. Write a program that allows historians to inquire about any one event.
5. Use a byte file to store bibliographic information on articles concerning computers. The first record of the file is an index. The remaining records contain abstracts of the contents of each article. Allow space for 16 entries in the index. Each entry is composed of a 12-character abbreviated title and a number indicating which file record (not counting the index) contains the abstract of the article. The records containing abstracts are each 64 bytes long. They are appended to the index and are numbered from 1 to 16.
   Write four programs:
   a. Initialize the index with blanks for each title and a zero for each record number.
   b. Accept from the keyboard the abbreviated title and abstract for an article. Store the title in the index and the abstract information in the next available file record.
   c. Print out all of the index entries and abstracts in the file.
   d. Let the librarian enter a record number and see the abstract stored in that record.

Appendix A

The binary number system and computer codes

The binary number system is the link between the world of humans and the world of machines that makes computing possible. This number system is so fundamental to computing that it is worthwhile to take time to review its characteristics.

Binary vs. decimal

Like the familiar decimal system, the binary number system is a code for expressing numerical amounts. And like all place-value number systems, it requires two steps: selecting the correct digit and placing that digit in the appropriate column.

The decimal system uses ten digits: 0, 1, 2, 3, 4, 5, 6, 7, 8, and 9. The binary system uses two digits: 0 and 1. The columns of the decimal system represent powers of 10. The columns of the binary system represent powers of 2. From left to right, the first four columns of these systems are compared in Figure A-1.

Figure A-1. Place values in the decimal and binary number systems

Placing a digit in a column declares how many times you intend to count the quantity represented by that column. Figure A–2 compares the way one dozen is expressed in each system. In the decimal system there is a 1 in the tens column and a 2 in the ones column: 12. In the binary system there is a 1 in the eights column, a 1 in the fours column, a 0 in the twos column, and a 0 in the ones column: 1100. The right-hand zeros hold column places in order to show which columns are represented with ones, the significant digits. Knowing what the column positions and the digits stand for in each system, you know that 12 in decimal is the equivalent of 1100 in binary.

Figure A–2. Expressing "one dozen" in decimal and binary

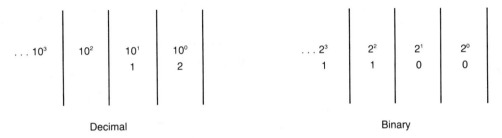

Decimal   Binary

Binary codes

Bit is the computer term for "binary digit." The two possible binary digits (0 and 1) are easily expressed electrically because electric circuits can be viewed as having two states: ON and OFF. Computer scientists have adopted the convention that a circuit ON represents 1 and a circuit OFF represents 0. When circuits are presented as columns of the binary number system, numbers are represented. In Figure A–3, "one dozen" is signaled by the energizing (closing) of the proper circuits.

Figure A–3. Expressing "one dozen" electrically

2^3	2^2	2^1	2^0
8	4	2	1
ON	ON	OFF	OFF
1	1	0	0

Imagine that you had millions of circuits, as some computers do. If each circuit represented a column of the binary system, you could express any quantity you would ever want. In reality, computers do not use millions of circuits to represent a number. Computer scientists view bits in units of eight, called *bytes,* and set arbitrary limits as to the number of bytes a particular language will reserve for representing a number. These limits determine both the range of numbers and the number of significant digits by which a number is represented on any particular system.

    True BASIC reserves 8 bytes for storing a number. However, numbers are packed into the 8 bytes according to a variation of the Institution of Electrical and Electronic Engineers (IEEE) format, which does such things as eliminate zeros in order to compress many significant digits. Thus, for True BASIC, 8 bytes can store a number far greater than can be represented by 64 bits in the binary number system: any number in the range of $1\,E-99$ to $1\,E+99$. True BASIC computes each number to a precision of at least 10 significant digits.

ASCII codes

To greatly expand the binary code's usefulness, and to create high-level languages, scientists developed a code known as the American National Standard Code for Information Interchange (ASCII) that gives letter and character equivalents for the numbers 0 through 127. Each of these can be expressed in one byte. Actually, the code varies from computer to computer, and True BASIC recognizes the code established for the computer system on which it runs. When True BASIC runs on an IBM PC, for example, it recognizes the extended ASCII character set listed in Appendix B.

    Computer scientists have also defined binary equivalents for many concepts, such as *true* and *false, larger* and *smaller, addition* and *subtraction.* In fact, computer languages use such ingenious adaptations of the binary code that you will be able to code almost anything you wish to express.

The extended ASCII Code for the IBM PC

ASCII value	Character	Control character	ASCII value	Character	Control character
000	(null)	NUL	024	↑	CAN
001	☺	SOH	025	↓	EM
002	☻	STX	026	→	SUB
003	♥	ETX	027	←	ESC
004	♦	EOT	028	(cursor right)	FS
005	♣	ENQ	029	(cursor left)	GS
006	♠	ACK	030	(cursor up)	RS
007	(beep)	BEL	031	(cursor down)	US
008	◘	BS	032	(space)	(none)
009	(tab)	HT	033	!	
010	(line feed)	LF	034	''	
011	(home)	VT	035	#	
012	(form feed)	FF	036	$	
013	(carriage return)	CR	037	%	
014	♫	SO	038	&	
015	☼	SI	039	'	
016	►	DLE	040	(	
017	◄	DC1	041	)	
018	↕	DC2	042	*	
019	‼	DC3	043	+	
020	¶	DC4	044	,	
021	§	NAK	045	-	
022	▬	SYN	046	.	
023	↨	ETB	047	/	

ASCII value	Character	Control character	ASCII value	Character	Control character
048	0	(none)	094	∧	(none)
049	1		095	—	
050	2		096	`	
051	3		097	a	
052	4		098	b	
053	5		099	c	
054	6		100	d	
055	7		101	e	
056	8		102	f	
057	9		103	g	
058	:		104	h	
059	;		105	i	
060	<		106	j	
061	=		107	k	
062	>		108	l	
063	?		109	m	
064	@		110	n	
065	A		111	o	
066	B		112	p	
067	C		113	q	
068	D		114	r	
069	E		115	s	
070	F		116	t	
071	G		117	u	
072	H		118	v	
073	I		119	w	
074	J		120	x	
075	K		121	y	
076	L		122	z	
077	M		123	{	
078	N		124			
079	O		125	}	
080	P		126	~	
081	Q		127	⌂	
082	R		128	Ç	
083	S		129	ü	
084	T		130	é	
085	U		131	â	
086	V		132	ä	
087	W		133	à	
088	X		134	å	
089	Y		135	ç	
090	Z		136	ê	
091	[		137	ë	
092	\		138	è	
093	]		139	ï	

ASCII value	Character	Control character	ASCII value	Character	Control character
140	î	(none)	186	‖	(none)
141	ì		187	╗	
142	Ä		188	╝	
143	Å		189	╜	
144	É		190	╛	
145	æ		191	┐	
146	Æ		192	└	
147	ô		193	┴	
148	ö		194	┬	
149	ò		195	├	
150	û		196	─	
151	ù		197	┼	
152	ÿ		198	╞	
153	Ö		199	╟	
154	Ü		200	╚	
155	¢		201	╔	
156	£		202	╩	
157	¥		203	╦	
158	Pt		204	╠	
159	ƒ		205	═	
160	á		206	╬	
161	í		207	╧	
162	ó		208	╨	
163	ú		209	╤	
164	ñ		210	╥	
165	Ñ		211	╙	
166	ª		212	╘	
167	º		213	╒	
168	¿		214	╓	
169	⌐		215	╫	
170	¬		216	╪	
171	½		217	┘	
172	¼		218	┌	
173	¡		219	█	
174	«		220	▄	
175	»		221	▌	
176	░		222	▐	
177	▒		223	▀	
178	▓		224	α	
179	│		225	β	
180	┤		226	Γ	
181	╡		227	π	
182	╢		228	Σ	
183	╖		229	σ	
184	╕		230	µ	
185	╣		231	τ	

ASCII value	Character	Control character	ASCII value	Character	Control character
232	☿	(none)	244	⌠	(none)
233	⊖		245	⌡	
234	Ω		246	÷	
235	δ		247	≈	
236	∞		248	°	
237	∅		249	•	
238	ε		250	·	
239	∩		251	√	
240	≡		252	ⁿ	
241	±		253	²	
242	≥		254	■	
243	≤		255	(blank 'FF')	

Solutions to selected chapter exercises

Chapter 1

1. Enter the FILES and the RUN commands:

   `Ok.FILES`   (Press the enter key.)

   `Ok.RUN HANOI`   (Press the enter key.)

3. Enter NEW, type in the following program, and then enter RUN:

   ```
   ▌PRINT "   True BASIC Keys on the IBM PC"
   ▌PRINT "F1 - sends the cursor to the edit window"
   ▌PRINT "F2 - sends the cursor to the command window"
   ▌PRINT "F4 - marks a line"
   ▌PRINT "F5 - copies marked lines"
   ▌PRINT "F6 - moves marked lines"
   ▌PRINT "F9 - runs the program in the edit window"
   ▌END
   ```

   ```
   Ok.NEW
   Ok.RUN    (The list of function keys appears.)
   ```

8. See Appendix A. Binary digits can be represented electrically: a closed circuit that is ON represents a one; an open circuit that is OFF represents zero. Collections of binary digits form codes that represent human-readable characters and numbers. As a result, human concepts are represented, stored, and processed electronically in computer systems.

9.

Component	*Historical Reason*
Central processing unit	The need for a fast calculating machine
Magnetic storage devices	The need to store vast amounts of data
Stored computer programs	The need for automation in data processing

Chapter 2

1. *Structured programming* means writing a program in such a way that its structure, its logic and flow of control, is patently clear. Structured programs are made up of program modules. Program modules, in turn, are made up of control structures.

5. Your problem definition must show input, process, and output. Your top-down design diagram must include at least four modules:
   a. The driver that will call the other modules.
   b. At least one module to perform input processing.
   c. At least one module to process the data and implement necessary procedures or formulae.
   d. At least one module to perform output processing.
6. Flowcharts and pseudocode show the sequence of events that occur within one program module. Design diagrams show how various modules in a complete program relate to one another; specifically, they show which module controls (calls) another module.
10. Eight steps in program development are:
   a. Problem definition
   b. Top-down design
   c. Flowcharting or pseudocode writing
   d. Desk-checking
   e. Module writing
   f. Module testing
   g. Program testing
   h. Real-world testing

Chapter 3

2. ▌ PRINT "Darwin's On the Origin of Species was published in 1859"
   ▌ PRINT "and Einstein's general theory of relativity"
   ▌ PRINT "was proven in 1922."
   ▌ PRINT "The time span separating these two events is "
   ▌ PRINT 1922 - 1859;"years."
   ▌ END

```
Ok. run
Darwin's On the Origin of Species was published in 1859
and Einstein's general theory of relativity
was proven true in 1922.
The time span separating these two events is
 63 years.
Ok.
```
4. a. correct
   b. PRINT Y; "is not the solution."
   c. correct
   d. OK DO FORMAT
   e. PRINT "Your age"
   f. END
   g. PRINT "YOUR ANSWER"
   h. OK RUN
   i. REM This is a number averaging program
   j. PRINT X; "is the solution."
5. ▌ PRINT "The age of Mickey Mouse was: "
   ▌ PRINT 1969 - 1929
   ▌ PRINT "When I was born."
   ▌ END

```
Ok. run
The age of Mickey Mouse was:
 40
When I was born.
Ok.
```

8. ▮ PRINT "Jimmy must pay";
   ▮ PRINT 24.50 + 6.38 + 1.80;"dollars."
   ▮ END

```
Ok. run
Jimmy must pay 32.68 dollars.
Ok.
```

Chapter 4

1. a. $(4^2 \times 2^3)^{.5} = \sqrt{4^2 \times 2^3} = \sqrt{128}$

   c. $\dfrac{\left(\dfrac{.3}{.9} \times 3 - 9\right)}{3} = -2.67$

   e. $[3(4 - 2^4)]^2 = 1296$

2. a. PRINT (2+4^2)/(5*8)
   c. PRINT 3*(6.2+5)/(4.5-2.3)
   e. PRINT 3.14*R^2
   g. PRINT ((3+12)/4)^2
   i. PRINT (4+34*15-4^2)/(7+8)

5. ▮ OPEN #1: printer
   ▮ PRINT #1:"-------------------------------------"
   ▮ PRINT #1:
   ▮ PRINT #1: "Number","Square","Cube"
   ▮ PRINT #1:
   ▮ PRINT #1:"-------------------------------------"
   ▮ PRINT #1: 2,2^2,2^3
   ▮ PRINT #1: 3,3^2,3^3
   ▮ PRINT #1: 4,4^2,4^3
   ▮ PRINT #1: 5,5^2,5^3
   ▮ PRINT #1:
   ▮ PRINT #1:"-------------------------------------"
   ▮ END

```
-------------------------------------
Number          Square          Cube
-------------------------------------
  2               4               8
  3               9              27
  4              16              64
  5              25             125
-------------------------------------
```

7. ▮ PRINT "Sold: $1.99 for 6 eating oranges."
   ▮ PRINT "Mr. Blackstone gets $"; TRUNCATE(1.99,0);"."
   ▮ PRINT "Charity gets";1.99 - TRUNCATE(1.99,0);"cent(s)."
   ▮ END

```
Ok. run
Sold: $1.99 for 6 eating oranges.
Mr. Blackstone gets $ 1 .
Charity gets .99 cent(s).
Ok.
```

Chapter 5

2. a. ∎ READ A,X,B
   ∎ PRINT A,X
   ∎ DATA 12
   ∎ DATA 4,5
   ∎ END

   ```
   Ok. run
    12              4
   Ok.
   ```

   b. ∎ READ A,X,B
   ∎ PRINT A,B
   ∎ DATA SUE,9,20
   ∎ END

   ```
   Ok. run
   Data item isn't a number.
   ```

   c. ∎ READ ADD,ADD2,ADD3
   ∎ PRINT ADD2
   ∎ DATA 12, 3
   ∎ END

   ```
   Ok. run
   Reading past end of data.
   ```

   d. ∎ READ CAT$,X
   ∎ PRINT CAT$,X
   ∎ DATA HENRY,"6",5
   ∎ END

   ```
   Ok. run
   HENRY           6
   Ok.
   ```

   e. ∎ LET A = 12
   ∎ PRINT A
   ∎ READ D,B
   ∎ PRINT A + B
   ∎ DATA 8,10
   ∎ END

```
Ok. run
 12
 22
Ok.
```

f. ∎ READ A
   ∎ READ B
   ∎ DATA 4,5,6,7,8,9
   ∎ RESTORE
   ∎ READ X,Y
   ∎ PRINT X;" PLUS ";Y;
   ∎ PRINT " IS ";X + Y
   ∎ END

```
Ok. run
 4 PLUS 5 IS 9
Ok.
```

g. ∎ LET R$ = "MELANIE"
   ∎ LET X = 21
   ∎ PRINT "IS"
   ∎ PRINT R$
   ∎ PRINT X
   ∎ PRINT R$;" IS "; X
   ∎ END

```
Ok. run
IS
MELANIE
 21
MELANIE IS 21
Ok.
```

h. ∎ PRINT "SALES OF MILK"
   ∎ PRINT
   ∎ READ A$,A,B$,B,C$,C,D$,D,E$,E
   ∎ PRINT A$,A
   ∎ DATA MONDAY,TUESDAY,WEDNESDAY, THURSDAY, FRIDAY
   ∎ DATA 25,26,32,42,38
   ∎ END

```
Ok. run
SALES OF MILK

Data item isn't a number
```

i. ∎ READ M$
   ∎ READ B$
   ∎ DATA SHE
   ∎ RESTORE
   ∎ READ F$,J$,L$
   ∎ READ X$,Y$,Z$
   ∎ DATA "IS"," THE",WRITER
   ∎ READ P$,Q$,R$
   ∎ DATA NOT, "THE", " TYPE"
   ∎ DATA " HERE"
   ∎ DATA ANYMORE

```
▌ PRINT J$;L$;P$;X$;Q$
▌ END
```

```
Ok. run
IS THE TYPEWRITER HERE
Ok.
```
j. ▌ LINE INPUT PROMPT "LIST 3 OF YOUR FAVORITE FOODS ":FOODS$
```
  ▌ LET AGE1$,AGE2$,AGE3$ = "AGED"
  ▌ READ AGE1,AGE2,AGE3
  ▌ READ NAM1$,NAM2$,NAM3$
  ▌ PRINT NAM2$;" ";AGE1$;AGE1
  ▌ PRINT NAM1$;" ";AGE3$;AGE1
  ▌ PRINT NAM3$;" ";AGE2$;AGE3
  ▌ PRINT "ALL LIKE ";FOODS$
  ▌ DATA 12,25,26,JIM, MARTY, LARRY
  ▌ END
```

```
Ok. run
LIST 3 OF YOUR FAVORITE FOODS MILK,CHEESE,BREAD
MARTY AGED 12
JIM AGED 12
LARRY AGED 26
ALL LIKE MILK,CHEESE,BREAD
Ok.
```
4. ▌ LET P = 2*2
```
  ▌ LET A = 2*25
  ▌ LET C = 2*35
  ▌ LET I = 2*8
  ▌ PRINT "Percent of Nutrients Still Needed Today:"
  ▌ PRINT
  ▌ PRINT "Protein",100 - P
  ▌ PRINT "Vitamin A",100 - A
  ▌ PRINT "Vitamin C",100 - C
  ▌ PRINT "Iron",100 - I
  ▌ END
```

```
Ok. run
Percent of Nutrients Still Needed Today:

Protein        96
Vitamin A      50
Vitamin C      30
Iron           84
Ok.
```
6. ▌ INPUT PROMPT "Hello! Tell me your name, please. ":NAME$
```
  ▌ PRINT "Let's have some fun, ";NAME$
  ▌ PRINT "Type in a noun, a verb, an adverb, and an adjective in
    that order."
  ▌ INPUT NOUN$,VERB$,ADVERB$,ADJ$
  ▌ PRINT "The enormous ";NOUN$;" is always ";ADJ$
  ▌ PRINT "even when it ";VERB$;" after the cook talks
    ";ADVERB$;"."
  ▌ END
```

```
Ok. run
Hello! Tell me your name, please. Jim
Let's have some fun, Jim
Type in a noun, a verb, an adverb, and an adjective in that order.
? horse,chews,roughly,greasy
The enormous horse is always greasy
 even when it chews after the cook talks roughly.
Ok.
```

11. ▮ REM convert time since 1900 to birth into days
    ▮ REM sample birth date is November 16, 1970
    ▮ LET DAYS1 = 69*365   !days through 1969
    ▮ LET DAYS2 = 31+28+31+30+31+30+31+31+30+31   !days Jan. -Oct., 1970
    ▮ LET DAYS3 = 16   !the 16 days in November
    ▮ LET TOTAL1 = DAYS1 + DAYS2 + DAYS3
    ▮ REM
    ▮ REM convert time since 1900 to present into days
    ▮ REM present date is February 11, 1985
    ▮ Let DAYS4 = 84*365   !days through 1984
    ▮ Let DAYS5 = 31   !days in Jan., 1985
    ▮ LET DAYS6 = 11   !the 11 days in February
    ▮ LET TOTAL2 = DAYS4 + DAYS5 + DAYS6
    ▮ LET ALIVE = TOTAL2 - TOTAL1 !the number of days alive
    ▮ REM
    ▮ REM convert days alive to years, months, and days
    ▮ LET YEARS = INT(ALIVE/365)   !computing number of years alive
    ▮ LET ALIVE = ALIVE - YEARS*365 !the days alive that are less
      than a whole year
    ▮ LET MONTH = INT(ALIVE/30.4167)   !computing the number of months
      alive
    ▮ LET ALIVE = ALIVE - INT(MONTH*30.4167)   !computing the number
      of days alive
    ▮ PRINT YEARS;"years";MONTH;"months";ALIVE;"days"
    ▮ END

```
Ok. run
 14 years 2 months 27 days
Ok.
```

Chapter 6

2. a. ▮ LET H = 1
   ▮ PRINT H + H^2
   ▮ LET H = (H + 1)^2
   ▮ IF H>=10 THEN
   ▮   PRINT "You have exceeded the limit."
   ▮ ELSE
   ▮   PRINT "You are under the limit. Proceed."
   ▮ END IF
   ▮ END

```
Ok. run
 2
You are under the limit. Proceed.
Ok.
```

b. ▪ INPUT PROMPT "Enter your final score: ":SCORE
   ▪ PRINT "Your adjusted score is: "
   ▪ SELECT CASE ROUND((SCORE*2 + SCORE*1.677)/3.677)
   ▪ CASE 0 TO 60
   ▪   PRINT "NOT SO HOT!"
   ▪ CASE 60 to 80
   ▪   PRINT "BETTER"
   ▪ CASE 80 TO 90
   ▪   PRINT "MUCH BETTER"
   ▪ CASE ELSE
   ▪   PRINT "SUPERIOR"
   ▪ END SELECT
   ▪ END

```
Ok. run
Enter your final score: 45
Your adjusted score is:
NOT SO HOT!
Ok.
```

c. ▪ LET TO = 24
   ▪ LET TE = 20
   ▪ IF TO > TE OR NOT TE <= 3^5 THEN
   ▪   PRINT "You may move on to the next round."
   ▪ ELSE
   ▪   PRINT "You are required to play this one again."
   ▪ END IF
   ▪ END

```
Ok. run
You may move on to the next round.
Ok.
```

d. ▪ READ A$,B$
   ▪ IF A$ = "-1" THEN
   ▪   PRINT "That's all folks."
   ▪ ELSE
   ▪   RESTORE
   ▪   READ Q$
   ▪ END IF
   ▪ IF Q$ = "-1" THEN
   ▪   READ A$,B$
   ▪ ELSE
   ▪   PRINT Q$
   ▪ END IF
   ▪ PRINT A$
   ▪ DATA "The duck family"
   ▪ DATA -1, Huey, Looey, Duey
   ▪ END

```
Ok. run
The duck family
The duck family
Ok.
```

```
e. ▌ LET T = 23
   ▌ IF " Christmas" <= "christmas" THEN
   ▌     LET T = T + 3
   ▌ ELSE
   ▌     LET T = T + 15
   ▌ END IF
   ▌ PRINT T^2
   ▌ END
```

```
   Ok. run
    676
   Ok.
```

5.
```
   ▌ PRINT "Enter the times in minutes and seconds for each of the
     following."
   ▌ INPUT PROMPT "GOLD: "GOLDM,GOLDS
   ▌ INPUT PROMPT "SILVER: ":SILM,SILS
   ▌ INPUT PROMPT "BRONZE: ":BRONM,BRONS
   ▌ LET GOLDS = GOLDM*60 + GOLDS
   ▌ LET SILS = SILM*60 + SILS
   ▌ LET BRONS = BRONM*60 + BRONS
   ▌ IF SILS - GOLDS < 1 THEN
   ▌     PRINT "There is a tie for the GOLD MEDAL."
   ▌ ELSE IF BRONS - SILS < 1 THEN
   ▌     PRINT "There is a tie for the SILVER MEDAL."
   ▌ ELSE
   ▌     PRINT "There are no ties."
   ▌ END IF
   ▌ END
```

```
   Ok. run
   Enter the times in minutes and seconds for each of the following.
   GOLD: 2,30
   SILVER: 2,45
   BRONZE: 2,45.5
   There is a tie for the SILVER MEDAL.
   Ok.
```

6.
```
   ▌ INPUT PROMPT "Enter your first name in capital letters.":NAME$
   ▌ SELECT CASE NAME$
   ▌   CASE "FRED"
   ▌       PRINT "Please take a seat in the Royal Box!"
   ▌   CASE "A" TO "L"
   ▌       PRINT "Sit in the Balcony"
   ▌   CASE "M" TO "Z"
   ▌       PRINT "Sit in the Orchestra"
   ▌   CASE else
   ▌       PRINT "Enter your first name in capital letters."
   ▌ END SELECT
   ▌ PRINT "Enjoy the Show!"
   ▌ END
```

```
   Ok. run
   Enter your first name in capital letters. JIM
   Sit in the Balcony
```

```
Enjoy the Show!
Ok. run
Enter your first name in capital letters. FRED
Please take a seat in the Royal Box!
Enjoy the Show!
Ok.
```

9. ▮ PRINT "Enter today's weight."
   ▮ INPUT WEIGHT
   ▮ SELECT CASE WEIGHT
   ▮   CASE 121 TO 130
   ▮   PRINT "Wrestle as a Bantam today"
   ▮   CASE 131 TO 140
   ▮   PRINT "Wrestle as a Light Weight today."
   ▮   CASE 141 TO 150
   ▮   PRINT "Wrestle as a Middle Weight today."
   ▮   CASE 151 TO 160
   ▮   PRINT "Wrestle as a Heavy Weight today."
   ▮   CASE 161 TO 200
   ▮   PRINT "Wrestle in the Unlimited Class today."
   ▮   CASE else
   ▮   PRINT "Try another wrestling league."
   ▮ END SELECT
   ▮ PRINT "Good Luck, sport!"
   ▮ END

```
Ok. run
Enter today's weight.
? 135
Wrestle as a Light Weight today.
Good Luck, sport!
Ok. run
Enter today's weight.
? 185
Wrestle in the Unlimited Class today.
Good Luck, sport!
Ok.
```

Chapter 7

1. a. DO WHILE NAM$ <> "James"
   b. correct
   c. correct
   d. NEXT INDEX
   e. FOR DAY = 7 TO 1 STEP -1
   f. correct
   g. FOR P = 100 TO 1 STEP -2
   h. correct
   i. DO WHILE MORE DATA
   j. LOOP UNTIL X = 10
3. ▮ INPUT PROMPT "What is your age? ":AGE
   ▮ FOR X = 1 TO AGE
   ▮   PRINT "YOU ARE A SUPERSTAR!!"
   ▮ NEXT X
   ▮ END

```
Ok. run
What is your age? 4
YOU ARE A SUPERSTAR!!
YOU ARE A SUPERSTAR!!
YOU ARE A SUPERSTAR!!
YOU ARE A SUPERSTAR!!
Ok.
```

4. ■ DO while more data
   ■   READ QUESTION$, ANSWER$
   ■   PRINT "What is the capital of ";Question$
   ■   INPUT GUES$
   ■   IF GUES$ = ANSWER$ then
   ■   PRINT "Right on!"
   ■   ELSE
   ■   PRINT "Wrong."
   ■   END IF
   ■ LOOP
   ■ DATA Kansas, Topeka, Oregon, Salem, Maine,Augusta
   ■ END

```
Ok. run
What is the capital of Kansas
? Salem
Wrong.
What is the capital of Oregon
? Salem
Right on!
What is the capital of Maine
? Augusta
Right on!
Ok.
```

8. ■ LET CHAR, COUNT = 1
   ■ PRINT "Enter a sentence ending with a period."
   ■ INPUT SENTENCE$
   ■ DO while SENTENCE$(CHAR:CHAR) <> "."
   ■   IF SENTENCE$(CHAR:CHAR) = " " then LET COUNT = COUNT + 1
   ■   LET CHAR = CHAR + 1
   ■ LOOP
   ■ PRINT "There are";COUNT;"words in your sentence."
   ■ END

```
Ok. run
Enter a sentence ending with a period.
? The quick man jumped over the hedge.
There are 7 words in your sentence.
Ok.
```

10. ■ Let CC, H2O, STRAW = 128   ! (128 ounces = 1 gallon)
    ■ DO while CC >= 4 or H2O >= 4 or STRAW >= 4
    ■   input prompt "What kind of cone do you wish? ": FLAVOR$
    ■   select case FLAVOR$
    ■   case is = "chocolate chip"
    ■   if CC <> 0 then
    ■   print "Sold - one chocolate chip cone"
    ■   let CC = CC - 4
    ■   else
    ■   print "Sorry, all out. Try watermelon or strawberry."

```
          end if
    case is = "watermelon"
        if H2O <> 0 then
            print "Sold - one watermelon cone"
            let H2O = H2O - 4
        else
            print "Sorry, all out. Try chocolate chip or
            strawberry. "
        end if
    case is = "strawberry"
        if STRAW <> 0 then
            print "Sold - one strawberry cone"
            let STRAW = STRAW - 4
        else
            print "Sorry, all out. Try watermelon or chocolate chip. "
        end if
    case else
        print"We only sell chocolate chip, watermelon or
        strawberry."
    end select
Loop
Print "We're all out of ice cream but ordering more. Come
again soon."
End
```

```
Ok. run
What kind of cone do you wish? chocolate chip
Sold - one chocolate chip cone
What kind of cone do you wish? strawberry
Sold - one strawberry cone
What kind of cone do you wish? chocolate chip
Sorry, all out. Try watermelon or strawberry.
What kind of cone do you wish?
```

Chapter 8

```
3. DIM NAME$(50), SCORE(50)
   FOR GOLFER = 1 TO UBOUND(NAME$)
       INPUT PROMPT "Enter the name: ":NAME$(GOLFER)
       INPUT PROMPT "Enter the score: ":SCORE(GOLFER)
   NEXT GOLFER
   PRINT
   PRINT tab(10); "Gold Tournament Results"
   PRINT
   PRINT TAB(2);"Name";tab (16); "Score"; tab(27);"No. Players Beaten"
   PRINT
   FOR CURRENT = 1 TO UBOUND(NAME$)
       LET HIGHER = 0
       FOR OTHERS = 1 TO UBOUND(NAME$)
           IF SCORE(CURRENT) < SCORE(OTHERS) THEN LET HIGHER =
           HIGHER + 1
       NEXT OTHERS
       PRINT NAME$(CURRENT), SCORE(CURRENT),HIGHER
   NEXT CURRENT
   END
```

```
Ok. run
Enter the name: Jones
Enter the score: 78
Enter the name: Smith
Enter the score: 76
Enter the name: Andrews
Enter the score: 68
Enter the name: Bury
Enter the score: 69
Enter the name: Freeman
Enter the score: 70
```

```
                Golf Tournament Results
    _____

    Name        Score      No. Players Beaten

    Jones        78              0
    Smith        76              1
    Andrews      68              4
    Bury         69              3
    Freeman      70              2
Ok.
```

7.
```
REM set up section
RANDOMIZE
DIM COLOR$(10) !list of ten possible colors to wear
DIM CHOICE(3) !each one is the position in COLOR$ of a color to
be worn today
FOR POSITION = 1 TO 10
    READ COLOR$(POSITION)
NEXT POSITION

FOR POSITION = 1 TO 3
    LET CHOICE(POSITION) = 0
NEXT POSITION

LET REJECT = 0   ! 1 = color choice repeated, 0 = no repeats so far

REM   Select three different random numbers in the range of 1 to 10
FOR SELECTION = 1 TO 3 !get 3 numbers to be used as positions
in COLOR$ list

    LET RANDNUM = INT(RND * 10 + 1) !this number = position in
    list of colors

REM check to see if this random number has already been used
    FOR NOREPEAT = 1 TO SELECTION - 1
      IF RANDNUM = CHOICE(NOREPEAT) THEN
          LET REJECT = 1
          LET SELECTION = SELECTION - 1 !set loop back redo color
          choice
          EXIT FOR
      ELSE
          REM - look at next previously selected RANDNUM
      END IF
    NEXT NOREPEAT
REM decide whether we need to try again or we can go to next
color choice
    IF REJECT <> 1 THEN
        LET CHOICE(SELECTION) = RANDNUM !accept this random number
    ELSE
        LET REJECT = 0 !set flag back. We're going to try another
        RANDNUM
```

```
■      END IF
■
■ NEXT SELECTION
■
■ REM print the list of colors for the day
■ PRINT
■ PRINT tab(10);"The colors for today are:"
■ PRINT
■ FOR SELECTION = 1 TO 3
■    PRINT COLOR$(CHOICE(SELECTION))
■ NEXT SELECTION
■ DATA Red, Blue, Green, Yellow, Orange
■ DATA White, Pink, Purple, Black, Brown
■ END
```

```
Ok. run
         The colors for today are:
Red
Pink
Orange
Ok.
```

8.
```
■ DIM WORKER(5,5) !five employees, five days a week
■ DIM DAY$(5)
■ LET HIGH = 0
■ FOR DAY = 1 TO 5
■     READ DAY$(DAY)
■     PRINT DAY$(DAY)
■     PRINT
■     FOR EMPLOYEE = 1 TO 5
■       PRINT "Enter number of boxes for employee # ";EMPLOYEE
■       INPUT WORKER(DAY,EMPLOYEE)
■       LET TOTAL = TOTAL + WORKER(DAY,EMPLOYEE)
■
■ REM Search for most productive employee
■       IF WORKER(DAY,EMPLOYEE) > HIGH THEN
■         LET HIGH = WORKER(DAY,EMPLOYEE)
■         LET PERSON = EMPLOYEE
■         LET WHEN = DAY
■       ELSE
■         REM this person is not a candidate for the highest
■       END IF
■     NEXT EMPLOYEE
■ NEXT DAY
■ PRINT
■ PRINT "The average number of boxes packed this week was:
  "; TOTAL/25
■ PRINT "The most boxes packed by one person this week was:
  "; HIGH
■ PRINT "This number of boxes was packed by employee # ";PERSON
■ PRINT "on ";DAY$(WHEN)
■ PRINT "Keep it up!"
■ DATA Monday, Tuesday, Wednesday, Thursday, Friday
■ END
```

```
Ok. run
.
.
.
Tuesday
Enter number of boxes for employee # 1
? 15
Enter number of boxes for employee # 2
? 22
Enter number of boxes for employee # 3
? 16
Enter number of boxes for employee # 4
? 14
Enter number of boxes for employee # 5
? 15
.
.
.
The average number of boxes packed this week was:  15.92
The most boxes packed by one person this week was: 22
This number of boxes was packed by employee #      2
on Tuesday
Keep it up!
Ok.
```

9.
```
DIM TEAM$(2)
LET TEAM$(1) = "North High"
LET TEAM$(2) = "South High"
DIM NAME$(2,5) !names for two teams, five wrestlers each
DIM SCORE(2,5) !scores for two teams, five wrestlers each
DIM SELECT$(5), HOME$(5) !top five wrestlers and their teams
LET RANK = 1
FOR TEAM = 1 TO 2
    PRINT TEAM$(TEAM);":"
    PRINT
    FOR WRESTLER = 1 TO 5
      PRINT "Wrestler # ";WRESTLER
      INPUT PROMPT "Name, Score: ":NAME$(TEAM, WRESTLER),SCORE
      (TEAM, WRESTLER)
    NEXT WRESTLER
PRINT
NEXT TEAM

REM select the top five wrestlers

FOR HIGH = 100 TO 0 STEP - 1
  FOR TEAM = 1 TO 2
    FOR WRESTLER = 1 TO 5
      IF SCORE(TEAM,WRESTLER) = HIGH THEN
          LET SELECT$(RANK) = NAME$(TEAM,WRESTLER)
          LET HOME$(RANK) = TEAM$(TEAM)
          LET RANK = RANK + 1
      ELSE
          REM This wrestler not a candidate for the top five
      END IF
      IF RANK = 6 THEN EXIT FOR
    NEXT WRESTLER
  IF RANK = 6 THEN EXIT FOR
  NEXT TEAM
IF RANK = 6 THEN EXIT FOR
NEXT HIGH
REM print the results
PRINT
PRINT "The Top Five Wrestlers: "
PRINT
```

```
■ MAT PRINT SELECT$,HOME$
■ END
```

```
Ok. run
.
.
.
South High:

Wrestler #  1
Name, Score: Tiny,1
Wrestler #  2
Name, Score: Meany, 22
Wrestler #  3
Name, Score: Fireman,66
Wrestler #  4
Name, Score: Bruiser,73
Wrestler #  5
Name, Score: Sugar,33

The Top Five Wrestlers:

Gorgeous      Bruiser      Fireman      Honey        Mouseman

North High    South High   South High   North High   North High

Ok.
```

Chapter 9

```
2. a. LET HIGH = X * 4
   b. CALL PRINTER
   c. FUNCTION ACOUNT(MONEY)
   d. END SUB
   e. EXIT SUB
   f. correct
   g. correct
   h. EXIT DEF
   i. LET RESULT = (A + B + C) / Z
   j. FUNCTION WAGES(HOURS)
4. ■ REM *********************************
   ■ REM *                               *
   ■ REM *         One-Line Function     *
   ■ REM *                               *
   ■ REM *                               *
   ■ REM *********************************
   ■ FUNCTION TRANSFORM(A) = A^2 - 2*A - 1
   ■    PRINT "X", "TRANSFORM (X)"
   ■    FOR X = 1 TO 5
   ■        PRINT X, TRANSFORM(X)
   ■    NEXT X
   ■ END
```

```
Ok. run
X               TRANSFORM (X)
 1              -2
 2              -1
 3               2
 4               7
 5              14
Ok.
```

7.
```
REM ********************************
REM *                              *
REM *       Main Routine           *
REM *                              *
REM ********************************
LET CORRECT = 0
LET TRY = 0
FOR MULTIPLIER = 1 TO 12
   FOR MULTIPLICAND = 1 TO 12
      PRINT "What is ";MULTIPLIER; "times"; MULTIPLICAND
      INPUT GUESS
      IF GUESS = MULTIPLIER * MULTIPLICAND THEN
         CALL CHEERS
         LET TRY = 0
         LET CORRECT = CORRECT + 1
      ELSE
         IF TRY = 1 THEN
            CALL SORRY
            LET TRY = 0
         ELSE
            LET TRY = 1
            PRINT "Try again."
            LET MULTIPLICAND = MULTIPLICAND - 1
            LET TRY = 1
         END IF
      END IF
   NEXT MULTIPLICAND
   PRINT
NEXT MULTIPLIER
PRINT "You got ";CORRECT;"correct."
END
REM ********************************
REM *                              *
REM *     External Subroutine      *
REM *                              *
REM ********************************
SUB CHEERS
   RESTORE
   RANDOMIZE
   LET RANDNUM = INT(RND * 5 + 1)
   RESTORE
   FOR SKIP = 1 TO RANDNUM
      READ REPLY$
   NEXT SKIP
PRINT REPLY$
DATA Correct, Fine, Good, SWELL, Wow
END SUB
REM ********************************
REM *                              *
REM *     External Subroutine      *
REM *                              *
REM ********************************
SUB SORRY
   RANDOMIZE
```

```
■     RESTORE
■     LET RANDNUM = INT(RND * 5 + 1)
■     FOR SKIP = 1 TO RANDNUM
■        READ REPLY$
■     NEXT SKIP
■ PRINT REPLY$
■ DATA Sorry, BAD, Nope, No, Booo
■ END SUB
```

```
Ok. run
.
.
.
Fine
What is   12 times 7
? 84
Fine
What is   12 times 8
? 96
Good
What is   12 times 9
? 109
Try again.
What is   12 times 9
? 109
Sorry
What is   12 times 10
? 120
Fine
What is   12 times 11
? 132
Correct
What is   12 times 12
? 144
Good

You got   137 correct.
Ok.
```

```
9. ■ REM ********************************
   ■ REM *                              *
   ■ REM *         Main Routine         *
   ■ REM *                              *
   ■ REM ********************************
   ■ DECLARE DEF NAMECHK$
   ■ PRINT "Enter your name and I'll tell you if you are on the flight."
   ■ INPUT NAME$
   ■ LET NAME$ = UCASE$(NAME$)
   ■ IF NAME$ = NAMECHK$(NAME$) THEN
   ■     PRINT "You are on the list."
   ■ ELSE
   ■     PRINT "Sorry, no flight for you today."
   ■ END IF
   ■ END
   ■ REM ********************************
   ■ REM *                              *
   ■ REM *  External Function Definition *
   ■ REM *                              *
   ■ REM ********************************
   ■ FUNCTION NAMECHK$(PERSON$)
   ■ RESTORE
```

```
█ LET NAMECHK$ = " "
█ DO WHILE MORE DATA
█    READ LIST$
█    IF PERSON$ = LIST$ THEN
█       LET NAMECHK$ = PERSON$
█    ELSE
█       REM look at another name
█    END IF
█ LOOP
█ DATA JONES, SMITH, THOMAS, WILKS, AIMS, REED, RING, O'CONNELL,
  O'HARA
█ END DEF
```

```
Ok. run
Enter your name and I'll tell you if you are on the flight.
? O'HARA
You are on the list.
Ok. run
Enter your name and I'll tell you if you are on the flight.
? BOUCHE
Sorry, no flight for you today.
Ok.
```

Chapter 10

```
4. █ REM ********************************
   █ REM *                              *
   █ REM *        Main Routine          *
   █ REM *                              *
   █ REM *                              *
   █ REM ********************************
   █ WHEN EXCEPTION IN
   █    PRINT "Who are you looking for?"
   █    INPUT FRIEND$
   █    DO
   █       READ NAME$
   █       IF NAME$ = FRIEND$ THEN LET FOUND = 1
   █    LOOP
   █ USE
   █ REM ********************************
   █ REM *                              *
   █ REM *        Exception handler     *
   █ REM *                              *
   █ REM *                              *
   █ REM ********************************
   █    IF EXTYPE = 8001 THEN        !8001 is READing past end of DATA
   █       IF FOUND = 1 THEN
   █          PRINT "I know ";FRIEND$;" very well."
   █       ELSE
   █          PRINT "I do not know ";FRIEND$
   █       END IF
   █    ELSE
   █       EXIT  HANDLER             ! let True BASIC handle other errors
   █    END IF
   █ END WHEN
```

```
▌ DATA ABLE, BAKER, CHARLIE
▌ END
```

```
Ok. run
Who are you looking for?
? CHARLIE
I know CHARLIE very well.
Ok. run
Who are you looking for?
? ZOOEY
I do not know ZOOEY
Ok.
```

6.
```
▌ REM ********************************
▌ REM *                              *
▌ REM *          Main Routine        *
▌ REM *                              *
▌ REM *                              *
▌ REM ********************************
▌ DIM LIST$(10)
▌ FOR X = 1 TO 10
▌    READ LIST$(X)
▌ NEXT X
▌    INPUT PROMPT "Which list item interests you ": ITEM
▌ DO
▌    WHEN EXCEPTION IN
▌        PRINT LIST$(ITEM);" is my favorite!"
▌        LET FLAG$ = "no problem"
▌    USE
▌ REM ********************************
▌ REM *                              *
▌ REM *          Exception handler   *
▌ REM *                              *
▌ REM *                              *
▌ REM ********************************
▌    IF EXTYPE  = 2001 THEN        !2001 is subscript out of bounds.
▌          LET ITEM = 10
▌          PRINT "No doubt you meant 10. Now, to continue . . ."
▌          LET FLAG$ = "problem"
▌    ELSE
▌       EXIT  HANDLER              ! let True BASIC handle other errors
▌    END IF
▌    END WHEN
▌ LOOP WHILE FLAG$ = "problem"
▌ DATA Blue, Red, White, Green, Orange, Purple, Pink, Yellow,
  Brown, Gray
▌ END
```

```
Ok. run
Which list item interests you 6
Purple is my favorite!
Ok. run
Which list item interests you 56
No doubt you meant 10. Now, to continue . . .
Gray is my favorite!
Ok.
```

```
9. ▌ REM *********************************
   ▌ REM *                               *
   ▌ REM *        Main Routine           *
   ▌ REM *                               *
   ▌ REM *                               *
   ▌ REM *********************************
   ▌ DO
   ▌    WHEN EXCEPTION IN
   ▌         WHEN EXCEPTION IN
   ▌              READ NUM
   ▌         USE
   ▌              REM *********************************
   ▌              REM *                               *
   ▌              REM *       Exception handler       *
   ▌              REM *                               *
   ▌              REM *                               *
   ▌              REM *********************************
   ▌              IF EXTYPE = 8101 THEN    ! 8101 is data item isn't
   ▌              number
   ▌                 PRINT "The problem is not all data are numeric"
   ▌                 LET FLAG$ = "quit"
   ▌              ELSE
   ▌                 EXIT HANDLER
   ▌              END IF
   ▌         END WHEN
   ▌    USE
   ▌         REM *********************************
   ▌         REM *                               *
   ▌         REM *       Exception handler       *
   ▌         REM *                               *
   ▌         REM *                               *
   ▌         REM *********************************
   ▌         IF EXTYPE = 8001 THEN    ! 8001 reading past end of data
   ▌             PRINT "End of data. Let's stop."
   ▌             LET FLAG$ = "quit"
   ▌         ELSE
   ▌             EXIT HANDLER
   ▌         END IF
   ▌    END WHEN
   ▌ LOOP UNTIL FLAG$ = "quit"
   ▌ Data 12,h22,32,42,52,62,72,82,92,102
   ▌ END
```

```
Ok. run
The problem is that not all data are numeric
Ok.
```

Chapter 11

```
2. a. ▌ LET HO$ = "35"
      ▌ LET VALUE = VAL(ho$)
      ▌ PRINT 3*VALUE
      ▌ END
```

```
    Ok. run
     105
    Ok.
b. ▮ LET R$ = "R"
   ▮ LET T = ORD(R$)
   ▮ LET G = T^2 + T*5
   ▮ PRINT G *LEN(R$)
   ▮ END
```

```
    Ok. run
     7134
    Ok.
c. ▮ LET R$ = "Rumplestiltskins"
   ▮ LET P$ = "s"
   ▮ LET X =  POS(R$,P$,4)
   ▮ PRINT X^2
   ▮ END
```

```
    Ok. run
     49
    Ok.
d. ▮ LET V$ = "<########      $###.##"
   ▮ PRINT "REPORT ON WAGES"
   ▮ PRINT
   ▮ FOR X = 1 TO 3
   ▮    READ N$,W$
   ▮    PRINT USING V$:N$,W$
   ▮ NEXT X
   ▮ DATA Herpin,4.25,Bartram,4.75, Driscoll,3.85
   ▮ END
```

```
    Ok. run
    REPORT ON WAGES

    Herpin         4.25
    Bartram        4.75
    Driscoll       3.85
    Ok.
```

```
3. ▮ REM The limit of the FOR. . .NEXT matches the number of names
     in data
   ▮ FOR X = 1 TO 4
   ▮     READ NAM$,STRE$,CITY$,ZONE$
   ▮     PRINT TAB(32);NAM$
   ▮     PRINT TAB(32);STRE$
   ▮     PRINT TAB(32);CITY$
   ▮     PRINT TAB(32);ZONE$
   ▮     PRINT
   ▮     PRINT
   ▮     PRINT
   ▮     PRINT
   ▮ NEXT X
   ▮ DATA Hilda Doe, 124 E.56th Street,"New York, N.Y.", 10208
   ▮ DATA Fred Flint, 1 Long Lane, "Pineville, N.J.", 08761
```

▊ DATA Sally Smith, 5 Green Ave., "Middletown, Conn.", 06088
▊ DATA Frieda Jones, 87 Chip Road, "Hamberg, Mass.", 12332
▊ END

Ok. run

```
                              Hilda Doe
                              124 E.56th Street
                              New York, N.Y.
                              10208




                              Fred Flint
                              1 Long Lane
                              Pineville, N.J.
                              08761




                              Sally Smith
                              5 Green Ave.
                              Middletown, Conn.
                              06088




                              Frieda Jones
                              87 Chip Road
                              Hamberg, Mass.
                              12332
```

Ok.

7. ▊ LET FORM$ = "<#########   ###.#"
   ▊ READ PROT,VITA,VITC,IRON
   ▊ LET PROT = PROT*1.5
   ▊ LET VITA = VITA*1.5
   ▊ LET VITC = VITC*1.5
   ▊ LET IRON = IRON *1.5
   ▊ PRINT "OUNCES REQUIRED TO GROW"
   ▊ PRINT
   ▊ PRINT USING FORM$: "PROTEIN",PROT
   ▊ PRINT USING FORM$: "VIT. A",VITA
   ▊ PRINT USING FORM$: "VIT. C",VITC
   ▊ PRINT USING FORM$: "IRON",IRON
   ▊ DATA 2,10,15,9
   ▊ END

```
Ok. run
OUNCES REQUIRED TO GROW

PROTEIN          3.0
VIT. A          15.0
VIT. C          22.5
IRON            13.5
Ok.
```

8. ▇ REM
   ▇ DIM REPORT$(7)
   ▇ LET FORMAT$ = "<#### ####### ###############################"
   ▇ FOR DAY = 1 TO 7
   ▇   LET REPORT$(DAY) = "DAY: "   !initializing REPORT$( )
   ▇   PRINT "Enter the data for day: ";DAY
   ▇   INPUT DATA$
   ▇   LET D$ = TRIM$(DATA$)   !trimming blanks from the input
   ▇   LET CH = 1   !starting position for string
   ▇   search
   ▇   DO WHILE ORD (D$(CH:CH)) => 65 !adding day of week to
   ▇   REPORT$( )
   ▇   LET REPORT$(DAY) = REPORT$(DAY)&D$(CH:CH)
   ▇   LET CH = CH + 1
   ▇   LOOP
   ▇   LET REPORT$(DAY) = REPORT$(DAY)&"   TEMP(C): "   !adding
   ▇   temp label
   ▇   DO WHILE ORD(D$(CH:CH)) <57   !adding the temperature
   ▇   LET REPORT$(DAY) = REPORT$(DAY)&D$(CH:CH)
   ▇   LET CH = CH + 1
   ▇   LOOP
   ▇   LET REPORT$(DAY) = REPORT$(DAY)&" Cloud Percent: " !adding
   ▇   cloud % label
   ▇   DO WHILE ORD(D$(CH:CH)) >000   !adding the cloud percent
   ▇   amount
   ▇   LET REPORT$(DAY) = REPORT$(DAY)&D$(CH:CH)
   ▇   LET CH = CH + 1
   ▇   LOOP
   ▇ NEXT DAY
   ▇ FOR REPORT = 1 TO 7   !printing out the report for each day
   ▇   PRINT REPORT$(REPORT)
   ▇   PRINT
   ▇ NEXT REPORT
   ▇ END

```
Ok. run
Enter the data for day:  1
? Monday23cp50
Enter the data for day:  2
? Tuesday22cp75
Enter the data for day:  3
? Wednesday19cp80
Enter the data for day:  4
? Thursday17cp90
Enter the data for day:  5
? Friday10cp11
Enter the data for day:  6
? Saturday14cp15
Enter the data for day:  7
? Sunday20cp1

DAY:   Monday    TEMP(C): 23   Cloud Percent:  cp50

DAY:   Tuesday   TEMP(C): 22   Cloud Percent:  cp75

DAY:   Wednesday   TEMP(C): 19   Cloud Percent:  cp80

DAY:   Thursday   TEMP(C): 17   Cloud Percent:  cp90
```

```
DAY:    Friday      TEMP(C):  10   Cloud Percent:   cp11

DAY:    Saturday    TEMP(C):  14   Cloud Percent:   cp15

DAY:    Sunday      TEMP(C):  20   Cloud Percent:   cp1

Ok.
```

Chapter 12

```
1. ▌ LET style$="mf"
   ▌ LET first$="ms o4 13 b 18 a 14 g abb 12 b"
   ▌ LET second$="ms o4 14 aa 12 a 14 b o5 d 12 d"
   ▌ PLAY style$
   ▌ PLAY first$          !note no concatenation
   ▌ PLAY second$
   ▌ PRINT "THAT was good, wasn't it! How about another?"
   ▌ PRINT "(HIT any key to continue)"
   ▌ GET KEY a
   ▌ PRINT "TUNE B"    !begin second part
   ▌ LET style2$="mf"
   ▌ LET one$="o4 ms 14 g o5 c 18 cdc o4 b 14 aaa o5 d 18 dedc"
   ▌ LET two$="o4 ms 14 bgg o5 e 18 efed 14 c o4 a 18 gg"
   ▌ LET three$="14 ms o4 a o5 d o4 b o5 12 c p4"
   ▌ LET song$=style2$ & one$ & two$ & three$    !aha--concatenation
   ▌ PLAY song$
   ▌ PRINT"OO! That was even better! Bye for now!"
   ▌ END
```

```
Ok. run
Ok.

TUNE A
THAT was good, wasn't it! How about another?
(HIT any key to continue)
```

```
2. ▌ SET mode "graphics"
   ▌ LET style$="mb"              ! set background music
   ▌ LET first$="o4 13 b 18 a 14 gabb 12 b 14 aa 12 a 14 bd 12 d"
   ▌ LET song$= style$ & first$
   ▌ PLAY song$
   ▌ FOR q = 1 to 8    !begin loop to draw boxes of each color
   ▌     READ c$
   ▌     SET color c$
   ▌     LET x=rnd
   ▌     LET y=rnd
   ▌     LET n = x + .1
   ▌     LET m = y + .1
   ▌     PLOT AREA: x,y ; x,m ; n,m ; n,y
   ▌     SET cursor 1,1
   ▌     PRINT "PRESS any key"
   ▌     GET KEY a
   ▌     SET color "black"
   ▌     PLOT AREA: x,y ; x,m ; n,m ; n,y
   ▌ NEXT q
```

```
■ DATA red,green,magenta,yellow,blue     !color data
■ DATA cyan,brown,white
■ END
```

Ok.

5.
```
■ REM randomness and the set cursor command
■ CLEAR
■ FOR q= 1 to 20                !for loop to print name with sound
  random
■     LET x=int(rnd*24)+1
■     LET y=int(rnd*80)+1
■     SET color "white"
■     SET cursor x,y
■     PRINT "ALFALFA"
■     SOUND q*100,1
■     SET color "red"
■     SET cursor 1,1
■     PRINT "(PRESS a key)"
■     GET KEY a
■ NEXT q
■ END
```

Ok.

Chapter 13

1.
```
■ REM using plot commands to make a graph with data
■ SET mode "graphics"
■ SET window -5,10,0,300
■ PLOT LINES: 0,0;0,300                !draw the coordinate system
■ PLOT LINES: -5,0;10,0
■ PLOT TEXT, at -.5,1: "0"
■ PLOT TEXT, at -2,290:"300"
■ PLOT TEXT, at 9.2,1: "10"
■ PLOT LINES: -4,218;-2,218
■ PLOT LINES: -3,228;-3,150
■ PLOT TEXT, at -3.8,222: "x"          !draw the data table
■ PLOT TEXT, at -2.8,222: "y"
■ PLOT TEXT, at -3.8,201: "0"
■ PLOT TEXT, at -3.8,191:"2"
■ PLOT TEXT, at -3.8,181:"4"
■ PLOT TEXT, at -3.8,171:"6"
■ PLOT TEXT, at -3.8,161:"8"
■ PLOT TEXT, at -3.8,151:"10"
■ PLOT TEXT, at -2.8,201:"51"
■ PLOT TEXT, at -2.8,191:"83"
■ PLOT TEXT, at -2.8,181:"123"
■ PLOT TEXT, at -2.8,171:"171"
■ PLOT TEXT, at -2.8,161:"227"
■ PLOT TEXT, at -2.8,151:"291"
■ PLOT TEXT, at 2,290: "y= (x+7)^2 + 2"  !label the graph
■ PLOT LINES: 0,51;2,83;4,123;6,171;8,227;10,291    !draw the graph
■ END
```

Ok.

3.
```
■ REM     working with a picture library to make a display
■ LIBRARY "b:zoo"
■ OPTION ANGLE degrees
■ SET mode "graphics"
■ SET window -10,10,0,10
■ SET color "green/white"
```

```
▪ PRINT"IT'S been snowing"
▪ PRINT"AT the animal pound"
▪ PRINT"BUT a few creatures"
▪ PRINT"ARE still around."
▪ PRINT"(HIT any key)"
▪ GET KEY e
▪ DRAW giraffe("blue") !draw animals--call them from the library
▪ DRAW fish("red")
▪ DRAW fred("magenta")
▪ PRINT"HERE'S Freddy!!"
▪ DRAW fido("cyan")
▪ PRINT". . .AND his best friend, Fido!!"
▪ END
```

```
Ok.
▪ REM external library (b:zoo)
▪ external
▪ picture giraffe(color$)
▪ set color color$
▪ plot lines: 1.3,9.9 ; .3,8.9 ; .7,8.5 ; 1.7,9.5 ; 1.3,9.9
▪ plot lines:1.7,9.5 ; 2.7,6.5 ; 4.7,6.5 ; 4.7,5.5 ; 2.7,5.5 ; 2.7,6.5
▪ plot lines:4.7,6.2 ; 5.7,6.2
▪ plot lines: 2.7,5.5; 2,3.5
▪ plot lines: 3,5.5 ; 3.6,3.8
▪ plot lines: 4.4,5.5 ; 3.7,3.5
▪ plot lines: 4.7,5.5 ; 5.3,3.8
▪ plot lines: 1.4,9.7 ; 1.2,10 ; 1,9.8
▪ end picture
▪ picture fish(color$)
▪ set color color$
▪ plot area: 6.5,7.5 ; 7,8 ; 8,8 ; 8.5,7.8 ; 8.8,8 ; 8.8,7 ;
  8.5,7.2 ; 8,7 ; 7,7
▪ end picture
▪ picture fred(color$)
▪ set color color$
▪ plot lines:-5,5 ; -5.5,4.5 ; -5,4 ; -4.5,4.5 ; -5,5
▪ plot lines:-5,4.7 ; -5,4.3
▪ plot lines:-5.2,4.3 ; -4.8,4.3
▪ plot lines:-5.3,4.3 ; -6.3,2.3 ; -6.3,1.3 ; -3.7,1.3 ;
  -3.7,2.3 ; -4.7,4.3
▪ plot lines:-5.5,4.5; -5.3,5.3 ; -5.1,4.7
▪ plot lines:-4.5,4.5 ; -4.7,5.3 ; -4.9,4.7
▪ end picture
▪ picture fido(color$)
▪ set color color$
▪ plot area:3,3 ; 2.5,2.5 ; 2.8,2; 3.3,2.5
▪ plot area:3.3,2.5 ; 5.3,2.5 ; 5.3,2 ; 3.3,2
▪ plot lines:5.3,2.3 ; 5.8,2.3
▪ plot lines:3.3,2 ; 3,1.7
▪ plot lines:3.5,2 ; 3.7,1.8
▪ plot lines:5.1,2 ; 4.8,1.7
▪ plot lines:5.3,2 ; 5.5,1.8
▪ plot lines:2.7,2.3 ; 2.5,2
▪ plot lines:3,2.8 ; 2.8,3.3 ; 2.7,2.7
▪ end picture
```

```
Ok.
5. ▪ rem      using mini-screens for text and graphics
   ▪ SET mode "graphics"
   ▪ SET color "red/black"
   ▪ OPEN #1: screen 0,.5,0,1
   ▪ OPEN #2: screen .5,1,0,1
   ▪ WINDOW #1
```

```
■ SET window 0,10,0,10
■ PRINT"'THERE is no frigate "
■ PRINT"   like a book"
■ PRINT"TO take us lands"
■ PRINT"    away,"
■ PRINT"NOR any coursers"
■ PRINT"   like a page"
■ PRINT"OF prancing poetry.'"
■ PRINT
■ PRINT"         --Emily"
■ PRINT"       Dickinson"
■ WINDOW #2
■ SET window 0,10,0,10
■ PLOT LINES: 1,2 ; 1,8 ; 8,7 ; 8,1 ; 1,2
■ PLOT LINES: 1,8 ; 2,9 ; 9,8 ; 9,2 ; 8.1,2.1
■ PLOT LINES: 1,8 ; 8,7 ; 8,1
■ PLOT LINES: 2,9 ; 9,8 ; 9,2
■ PLOT LINES: 7.5,7.2 ; 8.5,8.1
■ PLOT LINES: 8,2 ; 8.5,2.5
■ PLOT LINES: 8.5,8.1 ; 8.5,2.5
■ END
```

Ok.

Chapter 14

1. output
6. A data field represents a unit of data within a larger file record. A worker's wage rate, for example, is a unit of data that pertains to the worker's employment record.
7. A file record (comprised of fields) is a conceptual unit of information that contains all of the information about one item in a file. A worker's employment record, for example, is a unit of information about one worker in a file of all the company's employees.
10. The three types of True BASIC files are:
    1. *Text*   for sequential access to lists such as mailing lists.
    2. *Record*   for random access to frequently updated items such as airplane seat reservations.
    3. *Byte*   for random or sequential access to data created in other data file formats.

Chapter 15

```
3. a. ■ INPUT PROMPT "Which station are you reporting? ": STATION
      ■ SELECT CASE STATION
      ■      CASE IS = 1
      ■         OPEN # 1: NAME"B:First.dat", ACCESS output, CREATE
                new, ORGANIZATION text
      ■      CASE IS = 2
      ■         OPEN # 1: NAME"B:Second.dat", ACCESS output, CREATE
                new, ORGANIZATION text
      ■      CASE IS = 3
      ■         OPEN # 1: NAME"B:Third.dat", ACCESS output, CREATE
                new, ORGANIZATION text
      ■ END SELECT
      ■ INPUT PROMPT "Enter Name, County, Snowfall ":NAME$, COUNTY$,
        SNOW
      ■ PRINT # 1: NAME$;",";COUNTY$;",";SNOW
      ■ CLOSE #1
      ■ END
```

```
OK. run
Which station are you reporting? 1
Enter Name, County, Snowfall Davidsen, Litchfield, 201
Ok.
```

b.
```
■ OPEN # 1: NAME"B:First.dat", ACCESS input, CREATE old,
  ORGANIZATION text
■ OPEN # 2: NAME"B:Second.dat", ACCESS input, CREATE old,
  ORGANIZATION text
■ OPEN # 3: NAME"B:Third.dat", ACCESS input, CREATE old,
  ORGANIZATION text
■ FOR SITE = 1 TO 3
■     INPUT # SITE: NAME$,COUNTY$,SNOW
■     LET TOTAL = TOTAL + SNOW
■ NEXT SITE
■ PRINT "The average snowfall was ";TOTAL/3;" INCHES."
■ CLOSE #1
■ CLOSE #2
■ CLOSE #3
■ END
```

```
Ok. run
The average snowfall was  115  INCHES.
Ok.
```

4. a.
```
■ rem Entering data into taxpayer file.
■ OPEN # 1: NAME"B:TAX.DAT", ACCESS output, CREATE new,
  ORGANIZATION text
■ DO WHILE MORE DATA
■    READ NAME$,PAY$,TAX
■    PRINT # 1: NAME$;",";PAY$;",";TAX
■ LOOP
■ DATA Fred Grey, Jan 01,404.00,Drew Smythe, Jan 23, 3562.00
■ DATA John Berry, Feb 28, 2011.00, Hillary Green, Mar 11, 989.00
■ DATA Carol Tiger, May 09, 123.00, Sue Travis, Apr 14, 56.00
■ CLOSE #1
■ END
```

```
Ok.
```

b.
```
■ rem Find tax payers who paid before April 15.
■ OPEN # 1: NAME"B:TAX.DAT", ACCESS input, CREATE old,
  ORGANIZATION text
■ DO WHILE MORE #1
■    INPUT #1: NAME$,PAY$,TAX
■    LET MONTH$ = PAY$(1:3)
■    LET DAY = VAL(PAY$(5:6))
■    SELECT CASE MONTH$
■    CASE IS = "Jan","Feb","Mar"
■        PRINT USING "<############# your refund is
         $###.##":NAME$,TAX*.10
■    CASE IS = "Apr"
■        SELECT CASE DAY
■        CASE IS < 16
■           PRINT USING "<############# your refund is
            $###.##":NAME$,TAX*.10
■        CASE ELSE
■        END SELECT
■    CASE ELSE
■    END SELECT
■ LOOP
■ CLOSE #1
■ END
```

```
Ok. run
Fred Grey          your refund is $ 40.40
Drew Smythe        your refund is $356.20
John Berry         your refund is $201.10
Hillary Green      your refund is $ 98.90
Sue Travis         your refund is $  5.60
Ok.
```

6. a. ■ OPEN #1: NAME "b:LAWYER",ACCESS output,CREATE new,
   ORGANIZATION text
   ■ DO
   ■ INPUT PROMPT "NAME (type STOP to finish) ": NAME$
   ■ IF NAME$ = "STOP" THEN EXIT DO
   ■ INPUT PROMPT "Offense charged ":CRIME$
   ■ INPUT PROMPT "Decision Rendered ":JUDGE$
   ■ PRINT #1: NAME$;",";CRIME$;",";JUDGE$
   ■ LOOP
   ■ CLOSE #1
   ■ END

```
Ok. run
.
.
.
NAME (type STOP to finish) Miss Rouge
Offense charged Slander
Decision Rendered Lost
NAME (type STOP to finish) Tom Tough
Offense charged Arson
Decision Rendered ?
NAME (type STOP to finish)
.
.
.
Ok.
```

b. ■ INPUT PROMPT "Whose case was decided? ":CLIENT$
   ■ INPUT PROMPT "What was the decision? ":CHANGE$
   ■ OPEN #1: NAME "b:LAWYER",ACCESS outin, CREATE old,
   ORGANIZATION text
   ■ OPEN #2: NAME "b:LAW2",ACCESS output,CREATE new, ORGANIZATION
   text
   ■ DO WHILE MORE #1
   ■ INPUT #1: NAME$, CRIME$, JUDGE$
   ■ IF NAME$ = CLIENT$ THEN
   ■   PRINT #2: NAME$;",";CRIME$;",";CHANGE$
   ■ ELSE
   ■   PRINT #2: NAME$;",";CRIME$;",";JUDGE$
   ■ END IF
   ■ LOOP
   ■ ERASE #1
   ■ CLOSE #2
   ■ END

```
Ok. run
Whose case was decided? Tom Tough
What was the decision? Lost
Ok.
```

c. ■ PRINT "NAME",,"CHARGE", "DECISION"
   ■ PRINT "____",,"_____", "_____"

```
▌ OPEN #1: NAME "b:LAW2",ACCESS input, CREATE old, ORGANIZATION
  text
▌  DO WHILE MORE #1
▌      INPUT #1: NAME$, CRIME$, JUDGE$
▌      PRINT NAME$,,CRIME$,JUDGE$
▌ LOOP
▌ CLOSE #1
▌ END
```

```
Ok. run
NAME                CHARGE        DECISION

----                ------        --------
Prof.Prune          Libel         Won!
Miss Rouge          Slander       Lost
Tom Tough           Arson         Lost
General Spice       Theft         Won!
Mrs. Knight         Bribery       Lost
Ok.
```

9. a.
```
▌ OPEN #1: NAME "B:Monday", ACCESS output, CREATE new,
  ORGANIZATION text
▌ OPEN #2: NAME "B:Tuesday", ACCESS output, CREATE new,
  ORGANIZATION text
▌ OPEN #3: NAME "B:Wednesday", ACCESS output, CREATE new,
  ORGANIZATION text
▌ OPEN #4: NAME "B:Thursday", ACCESS output, CREATE new,
  ORGANIZATION text
▌ OPEN #5: NAME "B:Friday", ACCESS output, CREATE new,
  ORGANIZATION text
▌ REM set up a list of names and a list of jobs
▌ DIM NAME$(5), JOB$(5)
▌ FOR PLACE = 1 TO 5
▌   READ NAME$(PLACE), JOB$(PLACE)
▌ NEXT PLACE
▌ REM set up matches for each day
▌ FOR DAY = 1 TO 5
▌   LET SWITCH = DAY
▌   FOR MATCH = 1 to 5
▌      PRINT #DAY: NAME$(MATCH);","; JOB$(SWITCH)
▌      LET SWITCH = SWITCH + 1
▌      IF SWITCH >5 THEN LET SWITCH = 1
▌   NEXT MATCH
▌ NEXT DAY
▌ CLOSE #1
▌ DATA Roger Drain, beds, Lilly Sweet, dishes, Sara Bee, garbage
▌ DATA Meryl Ice, cooking, Erin Taps, shopping
▌ END
```

```
Ok.
```

b.
```
▌ INPUT PROMPT " Which roster do you wish (Monday, Tuesday,
  etc.)? ": DAY$
▌ LET FILE$ = "b:" & DAY$              !set up file name by
  concatenation
▌ PRINT
▌ PRINT tab(3); "Duty Roster for ";DAY$
▌ PRINT
▌ OPEN #1: NAME FILE$, ACCESS input, CREATE old, ORGANIZATION text
▌ DO WHILE MORE #1
▌   INPUT #1: NAME$,JOB$
▌   PRINT tab (2);NAME$, JOB$
```

```
▪ LOOP
▪ CLOSE #1
▪ END
```

```
Ok. run
 Which roster do you wish (Monday, Tuesday, etc.)? Monday

  Duty Roster for Monday

 Roger Drain    beds
 Lilly Sweet    dishes
 Sara Bee       garbage
 Meryl Ice      cooking
 Erin Taps      shopping
Ok.
```

Chapter 16

3. a.
```
▪ OPEN #1: NAME "B:bank",ACCESS output,CREATE new,ORGANIZATION
  record,RECSIZE 16
▪ DO WHILE MORE DATA
▪    READ  NAME$
▪    WRITE #1: NAME$, 0
▪ LOOP
▪ DATA J. Allen, T. Dieber, K. Ginn, R. Macadoo, F. Switch
▪ DATA G. Kelly, T. Vallan, L. Pressen, S. Barker, J. Fowel
▪ CLOSE #1
▪ END
```

```
Ok.
```

b.
```
▪ OPEN #1: NAME "B:Bank", ACCESS outin, CREATE old, ORGANIZATION
  record,RECSIZE 16
▪ INPUT PROMPT "Enter Account Number ":ACNT
▪ LET FORMAT$ = "<###########################################
  ##> $#,###.##"
▪ LET NO$ = "Transaction not allowed. Overdraft would be "
▪ LET YE$ = "The Balance is now"
▪ LET REPT$= "The current balance is"
▪ SET #1: Record ((ACNT - 1) * 2 + 1)    !Each record has two
  fields
▪ READ #1: NAME$, BAL
▪ PRINT "Account number "; ACNT;" belongs to: ";NAME$
▪ PRINT USING FORMAT$ :REPT$, BAL
▪ PRINT
▪ INPUT PROMPT "Enter the transaction ":CHNG
▪ LET TR = BAL + CHNG
▪ IF TR < 0 THEN
▪    PRINT USING FORMAT$: NO$,TR
▪ ELSE
▪    PRINT USING FORMAT$: YE$, TR
▪    SET #1: RECORD (ACNT*2)
▪    WRITE #1: TR
▪ END IF
▪ CLOSE #1
▪ END
```

```
Ok. run
Enter Account Number 10
Account number  10  belongs to: J. Fowel
The current balance is                    $ 25.00


Enter the transaction -4
The Balance is now                        $ 21.00
Ok.



Ok. run
Enter Account Number 10
Account number  10  belongs to: J. Fowel
The current balance is                    $ 21.00

Enter the transaction -35
Transaction not allowed. Overdraft would be  $-14.00
Ok.
```

5. a.
```
    ■ FOR PLANE = 1 TO 3
    ■   LET PLANE$ = "B:00" & STR$(PLANE)
    ■   OPEN #PLANE: NAME PLANE$,ACCESS output,CREATE new,
        ORGANIZATION record,RECSIZE 32
    ■   FOR SEATS = 1 TO 15
    ■       WRITE #PLANE: " "
    ■   NEXT SEATS
    ■   CLOSE #PLANE
    ■ NEXT PLANE
    ■ END
```

```
    Ok.
```

b.
```
    ■ INPUT PROMPT "Which flight do you want? ":PLANE
    ■ LET PLANE$ = "B:00" & STR$(PLANE)
    ■ OPEN #PLANE: NAME PLANE$,ACCESS outin,CREATE old,ORGANIZATION
      record,RECSIZE 32
    ■ LET RETRY = 0
    ■ INPUT PROMPT "Do you want a list of available seats? ": LIST$
    ■ IF LIST$ = "YES" THEN
    ■    CALL CHART
    ■ ELSE
    ■    DO WHILE RETRY = 0
    ■        INPUT PROMPT "Which Row and which seat do you want?
             ":R, S
    ■        SET #PLANE: record ((R - 1) * 3 + S)
    ■        READ #PLANE: NAME$
    ■        IF NAME$ = " " THEN
    ■           INPUT PROMPT "Enter your name ":RESERV$
    ■           SET #PLANE: record ((R - 1) * 3 + S)
    ■           WRITE #PLANE: RESERV$
    ■           PRINT "You have a reservation! "
    ■           LET RETRY = 1
    ■        ELSE
    ■           PRINT "Sorry that seat is taken. Try again."
    ■        END IF
    ■    LOOP
    ■ END IF
    ■ SUB CHART
    ■ PRINT
    ■ PRINT "Seating chart for flight # ";PLANE
    ■ PRINT
    ■    FOR ROW = 1 TO 5
    ■       PRINT "Row ";ROW;":"
```

```
      FOR SEAT = 1 TO 3
          SET #PLANE: record ((ROW - 1) * 3 + SEAT)
          READ #PLANE: NAME$
          PRINT "#";SEAT;":";NAME$
      NEXT SEAT
      PRINT
   NEXT ROW
END SUB
CLOSE #PLANE
END
```

```
Ok. run
Which flight do you want? 3
Do you want a list of available seats? no
Which Row and which seat do you want? 2,3
Sorry that seat is taken. Try again.
Which Row and which seat do you want? 2,2
Enter your name Mr. Mouse
You have a reservation!
Ok.
```

c.
```
INPUT PROMPT "Which flight do you want? ":PLANE
LET PLANE$ = "B:00" & STR$(PLANE)
OPEN #PLANE: NAME PLANE$,ACCESS outin,CREATE old,ORGANIZATION
   record,RECSIZE 32
PRINT
PRINT "Seating chart for flight # ";PLANE
PRINT
   FOR ROW = 1 TO 5
      PRINT "Row ";ROW;":"
      FOR SEAT = 1 TO 3
          SET #PLANE: record ((ROW - 1) * 3 + SEAT)
          READ #PLANE: NAME$
          PRINT "#";SEAT;":";NAME$
      NEXT SEAT
      PRINT
   NEXT ROW
CLOSE #PLANE
END
```

```
Ok. run
Which flight do you want? 3

Seating chart for flight #  3

Row  1 :
# 1 :
# 2 :
# 3 :

Row  2 :
# 1 :
# 2 :Mr. Mouse
# 3 :Miss Wilbur

    .
    .
    .
```

```
Row  5 :
# 1 :
# 2 :
# 3 :Master Greenhouse

Ok.
```

6. a. ■ OPEN #1: NAME "B:water", ACCESS output,CREATE new,ORGANIZATION
   record,RECSIZE 8
   ■ FOR MONTH = 1 TO 12
   ■   WRITE #1: 0
   ■ NEXT MONTH
   ■ CLOSE #1
   ■ END

```
Ok.
```
   b. ■ OPEN #1: NAME "B:Water", ACCESS output, CREATE old,
   ORGANIZATION record,RECSIZE 8
   ■ INPUT PROMPT "Enter the month ": MNTH$
   ■ FOR MO = 1 TO 12
   ■   READ MONTH$
   ■   IF MONTH$ = MNTH$ THEN
   ■   SET #1:record MO
   ■   PRINT "Enter water quality rating for ";MNTH$;
   ■   INPUT RATING
   ■   WRITE #1: RATING
   ■   ELSE
   ■   END IF
   ■ NEXT MO
   ■ DATA January, February, March, April, May, June
   ■ DATA July, August, September, October, November, December
   ■ CLOSE #1
   ■ END

```
Ok. run
Enter the month February
Enter water quality rating for February? 5
Ok.
```
   c. ■ OPEN #1: NAME "B:Water", ACCESS input, CREATE old, ORGANIZATION
   record,RECSIZE 8
   ■ SET MODE "graphics"
   ■ SET COLOR "red/blue"
   ■ PLOT TEXT, AT .15,.85: "Annual Water Quality Report"
   ■ OPEN #2: SCREEN .5, .95, .25, .75
   ■ OPEN #3: SCREEN .05, .35, .25, .75
   ■
   ■ rem SET UP GRAPH WINDOW ON RIGHT OF DISPLAY
   ■
   ■ WINDOW #2
   ■ SET WINDOW 0,12,-1,10
   ■ BOX LINES 1,12,1,10
   ■
   ■ rem SET UP CHART ON LEFT OF DISPLAY
   ■
   ■ WINDOW #3
   ■ SET WINDOW 0,13,0,13
   ■ PLOT TEXT, AT 0,13: "MONTH"
   ■ PLOT TEXT, AT 6,13: "QUALITY"
   ■ PLOT TEXT, AT 2,12: "J"
   ■ PLOT TEXT, AT 2,11: "F"
   ■ PLOT TEXT, AT 2,10: "M"

```
PLOT TEXT, AT 2,9:  "A"
PLOT TEXT, AT 2,8:  "M"
PLOT TEXT, AT 2,7:  "J"
PLOT TEXT, AT 2,6:  "J"
PLOT TEXT, AT 2,5:  "A"
PLOT TEXT, AT 2,4:  "S"
PLOT TEXT, AT 2,3:  "O"
PLOT TEXT, AT 2,2:  "N"
PLOT TEXT, AT 2,1:  "D"

rem LABEL GRAPH

WINDOW #2
PLOT TEXT, AT 1,0:  "J"
PLOT TEXT, AT 2,0:  "."
PLOT TEXT, AT 3,0:  "."
PLOT TEXT, AT 4,0:  "."
PLOT TEXT, AT 5,0:  "."
PLOT TEXT, AT 6,0:  "J"
PLOT TEXT, AT 7,0:  "."
PLOT TEXT, AT 8,0:  "."
PLOT TEXT, AT 9,0:  "."
PLOT TEXT, AT 10,0: "."
PLOT TEXT, AT 11,0: "."
PLOT TEXT, AT 12,0: "D"
PLOT TEXT, AT 0,1:  "1"
PLOT TEXT, AT 0,2:  "."
PLOT TEXT, AT 0,3:  "."
PLOT TEXT, AT 0,4:  "."
PLOT TEXT, AT 0,5:  "5"
PLOT TEXT, AT 0,6:  "."
PLOT TEXT, AT 0,7:  "."
PLOT TEXT, AT 0,8:  "."
PLOT TEXT, AT 0,9:  "."
PLOT TEXT, AT 0,10: "10"

REM PLOT DATA

FOR MONTH = 1 TO 12
    SET #1:record MONTH
    READ #1: RATE
    PLOT LINES: MONTH, RATE;
    WINDOW #3
    PLOT TEXT, AT 9,(12 - MONTH + 1): STR$(RATE)
    WINDOW #2
NEXT MONTH
CLOSE #1
END
```

Ok.

Chapter 17

1. a.
```
OPEN #1: NAME "B:Data",ACCESS output,CREATE new,ORGANIZATION
byte
FOR NUMBER = 1 TO 512
    WRITE #1: NUM$(NUMBER)
NEXT NUMBER
CLOSE #1
END
```

b. ▮ `OPEN #1: NAME "B:Data",ACCESS input,CREATE old,ORGANIZATION`
   `byte`
   ▮ `FOR NUMBER = 1 TO 512`
   ▮ `    READ #1, BYTES 8: DAT$`
   ▮ `    PRINT NUM(DAT$);`
   ▮ `NEXT NUMBER`
   ▮ `CLOSE #1`
   ▮ `END`

Partial Screen Output

```
150 151 152 153 154 155 156 157 158 159 160 161 162 163 164 165
166 167 168 169 170 171 172 173 174 175 176 177 178 179 180 181
182 183 184 185 186 187 188 189 190 191 192 193 194 195 196 197
198 199 200 201 202 203 204 205 206 207 208 209 210 211 212 213
214 215 216 217 218 219 220 221 222 223 224 225 226 227 228 229
230 231 232 233 234 235 236 237 238 239 240 241 242 243 244 245
246 247 248 249 250 251 252 253 254 255 256 257 258 259 260 261
262 263 264 265 266 267 268 269 270 271 272 273 274 275 276 277
278 279 280 281 282 283 284 285 286 287 288 289 290 291 292 293
294 295 296 927 298 299 300 301 302 303 304 305 306 307 308 309
310 311 312 313 314 315 316 317 318 319 320 321 322 323 324 325
326 327 328 329 330 331 332 333 334 335 336 337 338 339 340 341
342 343 344 345 346 347 348 349 350 351 352 353 354 355 356 357
358 359 360 361 362 363 364 365 366 367 368 369 370 371 372 373
374 375 376 377 378 379 380 381 382 383 384 385 386 387 388 389
390 391 392 393 394 395 396 397 398 399 400 401 402 403 404 405
406 407 408 409 410 411 412 413 414 415 416 417 418 419 420 421
422 423 424 425 426 427 428 429 430 431 432 433 434 435 436 437
438 439 440 441 442 443 444 445 446 447 448 449 450 451 452 453
454 455 456 457 458 459 460 461 462 463 464 465 466 467 468 469
470 471 472 473 474 475 476 477 478 479 480 481 482 483 484 485
486 487 488 489 490 491 492 493 494 495 496 497 498 499 500 501
502 503 504 505 506 507 508 509 510 511 512
Ok.
```

c. ▮ `OPEN #1: NAME "B:Data",ACCESS outin,CREATE old,ORGANIZATION`
   `byte`
   ▮ `FOR NUMBER = 1 TO 169`
   ▮ `    READ #1, BYTES 8: DAT$`
   ▮ `NEXT NUMBER`
   ▮ `WRITE #1:"Skillery"`
   ▮ `FOR NUMBER = 171 TO 233`
   ▮ `    READ #1, BYTES 8: DAT$`
   ▮ `NEXT NUMBER`
   ▮ `WRITE #1:"Skallery"`
   ▮ `FOR NUMBER = 235 TO 299`
   ▮ `    READ #1, BYTES 8:DAT$`
   ▮ `NEXT NUMBER`
   ▮ `WRITE #1:"Aligator"`
   ▮ `CLOSE #1`
   ▮ `END`

```
Ok.
```

d. ▮ `OPEN #1: NAME "B:Data",ACCESS input,CREATE old,ORGANIZATION`
   `byte`
   ▮ `FOR NUMBER = 1 TO 512`
   ▮ `    READ #1, BYTES 8: DAT$`
   ▮ `    SELECT CASE NUMBER`
   ▮ `        CASE IS = 170`
   ▮ `            PRINT DAT$;`
   ▮ `        CASE IS = 234`

```
■              PRINT DAT$;
■        CASE IS = 300
■              PRINT DAT$;
■        CASE ELSE
■              PRINT NUM(DAT$);
■   END SELECT
■ NEXT NUMBER
■ CLOSE #1
■ END
```

Partial Screen Output

```
150 151 152 153 154 155 156 157 158 159 160 161 162 163 164 165
166 167 168 169 Skillery 171 172 173 174 175 176 177 178 179 180
181 182 183 184 185 186 187 188 189 190 191 192 193 194 195 196
197 198 199 200 201 202 203 204 205 206 207 208 209 210 211 212
213 214 215 216 217 218 219 220 221 222 223 224 225 226 227 228
229 230 231 232 233 Skallery 235 236 237 238 239 240 241 242 243
244 245 246 247 248 249 250 251 252 253 254 255 256 257 258 259
260 261 262 263 264 265 266 267 268 269 270 271 272 273 274 275
276 277 278 279 280 281 282 283 284 285 286 287 288 289 290 291
292 293 294 295 296 297 298 299 Aligator 301 302 303 304 305 306
307 308 309 310 311 312 313 314 315 316 317 318 319 320 321 322
323 324 325 326 327 328 329 330 331 332 333 334 335 336 337 338
339 340 341 342 343 344 345 346 347 348 349 350 351 352 353 354
355 356 357 358 359 360 361 362 363 364 365 366 367 368 369 370
371 372 373 374 375 376 377 378 379 380 381 382 383 384 385 386
387 388 389 390 391 392 393 394 395 396 397 398 399 400 401 402
403 404 405 406 407 408 409 410 411 412 413 414 415 416 417 418
419 420 421 422 423 424 425 426 427 428 429 430 431 432 433 434
435 436 437 438 439 440 441 442 443 444 445 446 447 448 449 450
451 452 453 454 455 456 457 458 459 460 461 462 463 464 465 466
467 468 469 470 471 472 473 474 475 476 477 478 479 480 481 482
483 484 485 486 487 488 489 490 491 492 493 494 495 496 497 498
499 500 501 502 503 504 505 506 507 508 509 510 511 512
Ok.
```

3. a.
```
■ OPEN #1: NAME "B:Cinder",ACCESS output,CREATE new,
  ORGANIZATION byte
■ LET STYLENUM = 1000
■ DO WHILE MORE DATA
■    READ INVENT
■    LET STYLENUM = STYLENUM + 1
■    WRITE #1: NUM$(STYLENUM), NUM$(INVENT)
■ LOOP
■ DATA 10,2,43,312,42,4,5,45,63,745,8,67,98,7,15
■ DATA 45,67,89,34,12,345,221,25,90,63,42,13,15,4,33
■ DATA 78,60,4,32,55,12,84,77,56,94,34,23,44,12,3
■ DATA 10,2,43,312,42,4,5,45,63,745,8,67,98,7,15
■ DATA 78,60,4,32
■ CLOSE #1
■ END
```

Ok.

b.
```
■ OPEN #1: NAME "B:Cinder",ACCESS outin,CREATE old,ORGANIZATION
  byte,RECSIZE 8
■ INPUT PROMPT "Which style are you selling? ":STYLE
■ INPUT PROMPT "How many pairs are you selling? ":QUANTITY
■ DO WHILE MORE #1
■    READ #1, BYTES 8: STYLENUM$
■    LET STYLENUM = NUM(STYLENUM$)
■    IF STYLENUM = STYLE THEN
```

```
■          READ #1, BYTES 8: INVENT$    !Quantity info follows style no.
■          LET INVENT = NUM(INVENT$)
■          PRINT "Current supply of ";STYLE;" is ";INVENT;"."
■          IF INVENT - QUANTITY < 0 THEN
■              PRINT "I do not have enough for you, sorry."
■          ELSE
■              LET INVENT = INVENT - QUANTITY
■              FOR BACKBYTE = 1 to 8 !can only move pointer back
■              one byte at a time
■                  SET #1: pointer same !in order to write over
■                  previous quantity
■              NEXT BACKBYTE
■              WRITE #1: NUM$(INVENT) !update the quantity field
■          END IF
■              SET #1: pointer end   !get out of the file
■      ELSE
■      END IF
■ LOOP
■ CLOSE #1
■ END
```

```
Ok. run
Which style are you selling? 1022
How many pairs are you selling? 10
Current supply of  1022  is  221 .
Ok. run
Which style are you selling? 1022
How many pairs are you selling? 0
Current supply of  1022  is  211 .
Ok.
```

4. a.
```
■ DECLARE DEF ADDBLANK$   !an internal function to control
  length of data fields
■ OPEN #1: NAME "B:Olymp",ACCESS output,CREATE new,ORGANIZATION
  byte
■ FOR WINNER = 1 TO 3    !just a sample
■    INPUT PROMPT "ENTER EVENT: ": EVENT$
■    WRITE #1: ADDBLANK$(EVENT$, 26) !give field data, and
  total field length
■    INPUT PROMPT "ENTER GOLD: ": GOLD$,GNATION$
■    WRITE #1: ADDBLANK$(GOLD$, 30) !give field data, and total
  field length
■    WRITE #1: ADDBLANK$(GNATION$,4) !give field data, and
  total field length
■    INPUT PROMPT "ENTER SILVER: ": SILVER$, SNATION$
■    WRITE #1: ADDBLANK$(SILVER$,30) !give field data, and
  total field length
■    WRITE #1: ADDBLANK$(SNATION$,4) !give field data, and
  total field length
■    INPUT PROMPT "ENTER BRONZE: ": BRONZE$, BNATION$
■    WRITE #1: ADDBLANK$(BRONZE$,30) !give field data, and
  total field length
■    WRITE #1: ADDBLANK$(BNATION$,4) !give field data, and
  total field length
■ NEXT WINNER
■ REM internal function to pad real data with blanks
■ DEF ADDBLANK$(ITEM$, LENGTH)
■    LET PAD = LEN(ITEM$) !how long is actual data item?
■    LET ADD = LENGTH - PAD !how many blanks are needed?
■    LET BLANK$ = REPEAT$(" ",ADD) !create a string of blanks
■    LET ADDBLANK$ = ITEM$ & BLANK$ !combine data and blanks
```

```
■ END DEF
■ CLOSE #1
■ END
```

```
Ok. run
ENTER EVENT: Men's Downhill Skiing
ENTER GOLD: Ingmar Eninger, AUS
ENTER SILVER: Bladivir Slotof, USSR
ENTER BRONZE: Olaf Geiger, NOR
ENTER EVENT: Ladies Downhill Skiing
ENTER GOLD: Trudy Belter, USA
ENTER SILVER: Maria Schwartz, SWSS
ENTER BRONZE: Tavia Zabrinski, YUG
ENTER EVENT: Men's Giant Slalom
ENTER GOLD: Kenneth Hatch, ENG
ENTER SILVER: Curtis Whaler, CAN
ENTER BRONZE: Eric Haydel, DEN
Ok.
```

b.
```
■ PRINT tab(20); "Winter Olympics"
■ PRINT
■ OPEN #1: NAME "B:Olymp",ACCESS input,CREATE old,ORGANIZATION
  byte
■ FOR WINNER = 1 TO 3    !just a sample
■     READ #1, Bytes 26: EVENT$
■     PRINT tab(15); EVENT$
■     PRINT
■     READ #1, BYTES 30: GOLD$
■     PRINT tab(15); "Gold:   "; GOLD$;
■     READ #1, BYTES 4: GNATION$
■     PRINT GNATION$
■     READ #1, BYTES 30: SILVER$
■     PRINT tab(15); "Silver: "; SILVER$;
■     READ #1, BYTES 4: SNATION$
■     PRINT SNATION$
■     READ #1, BYTES 30: BRONZE$
■     PRINT tab(15); "Bronze: "; BRONZE$;
■     READ #1, BYTES 4: BNATION$
■     PRINT BNATION$
■     PRINT
■ NEXT WINNER
■ CLOSE #1
■ END
```

```
Ok. run
                    Winter Olympics

               Men's Downhill Skiing

               Gold:   Ingmar Eninger              AUS
               Silver: Bladivir Slotof             USSR
               Bronze: Olaf Geiger                 NOR

               Ladies Downhill Skiing

               Gold:   Trudy Belter                USA
               Silver: Maria Schwartz              SWSS
               Bronze: Tavia Zabrinski             YUG
```

```
                    Men's Giant Slalom

                    Gold:    Kenneth Hatch           ENG
                    Silver: Curtis Whaler            CAN
                    Bronze: Eric Haydel              DEN
      Ok.
c. ■ PRINT tab(20); "Winter Olympics Research"
   ■ PRINT
   ■ OPEN #1: NAME "B:Olymp",ACCESS input,CREATE old,ORGANIZATION
     byte
   ■ INPUT PROMPT "Which Event? ":WHICH$
   ■ LET WHICH$ = TRIM$(WHICH$) !get rid of surrounding blanks
   ■ FOR WINNER = 1 TO 3    !just a sample
   ■    READ #1, BYTES 26: EVENT$
   ■    LET EVENT$ = TRIM$(EVENT$) !get rid of surrounding blanks
   ■    READ #1, BYTES 30: GOLD$
   ■    READ #1, BYTES 4: GNATION$
   ■    READ #1, BYTES 30: SILVER$
   ■    READ #1, BYTES 4: SNATION$
   ■    READ #1, BYTES 30: BRONZE$
   ■    READ #1, BYTES 4: BNATION$
   ■    IF WHICH$ = EVENT$ THEN
   ■       PRINT
   ■       PRINT tab(20); EVENT$
   ■       PRINT
   ■       PRINT tab(15); "The winners were: "
   ■       PRINT
   ■       PRINT tab(15); "Gold:   "; GOLD$;
   ■       PRINT GNATION$
   ■       PRINT tab(15); "Silver: "; SILVER$;
   ■       PRINT SNATION$
   ■       PRINT tab(15); "Bronze: "; BRONZE$;
   ■       PRINT BNATION$
   ■    ELSE
   ■       REM read the next event
   ■    END IF
   ■ NEXT WINNER
   ■ CLOSE #1
   ■ END
```

```
   Ok. run
                    Winter Olympics Research

   Which Event? Ladies Downhill Skiing

                    Ladies Downhill Skiing

              The winners were:

                    Gold:    Trudy Belter            USA
                    Silver: Maria Schwartz           SWSS
                    Bronze: Tavia Zabrinski          YUG
   Ok.
```

```
5. a. ■ OPEN #1: NAME "B:Library",ACCESS output,CREATE new,ORGANIZATION
        byte
     ■ REM set up index with space for pointers to 16 articles
     ■ FOR ENTRY = 1 to 16
```

```
        WRITE #1: 0 ! Zero means the file position for abstract is
        not used
        LET TITLE$ = REPEAT$(" ",12)
        WRITE #1:TITLE$
NEXT ENTRY
CLOSE #1
END
```

```
Ok.
```

b.
```
OPEN #1: NAME "B:Library",ACCESS outin,CREATE old,ORGANIZATION
byte
REM ask for index info - then ask for an abstract describing
article
INPUT PROMPT "ENTER ABBREVIATED TITLE - 12 CHARACTERS OR
LESS: ":TITLE$
REM find an empty index entry
REM loop always go to 16 in order to end it with pointer past
index
FOR INDEXPOS = 1 TO 16
   READ #1, BYTES 8:ENTRY$
   LET ENTRY = NUM(ENTRY$) !convert string to a number
   IF ENTRY <> 0 THEN
        READ #1, BYTES 12:PREVTITLE$ !Skip this index position
   ELSE
        FOR BACKUP = 1 TO 8 !move pointer to first byte of this
        entry
            SET #1: pointer same
        NEXT BACKUP
        LET INDEXPOS$ = NUM$(INDEXPOS)
        WRITE #1:INDEXPOS$ !mark this file position in use
        WRITE #1:TITLE$ !write title in index
        EXIT FOR
   END IF
NEXT INDEXPOS
REM now move pointer in order to append a new abstract
SET # 1: pointer end
REM pointer now aims at position for writing current information
PRINT "ENTER ARTICLE ABSTRACT - 64 CHARACTERS: "
LINE INPUT ABSTRACT$
   LET PAD = LEN(ABSTRACT$)  ! how long is the abstract?
   LET ADD = 64 - PAD ! how many blanks must be added to
   maintain 64-byte field?
   LET BLANK$ = REPEAT$(" ",ADD) !create blank string of needed
   length
   LET ABSTRACT$ = ABSTRACT$ & BLANK$ !concatenate abstract and
   blanks
WRITE #1: ABSTRACT$ !64 bytes of data and blanks
CLOSE #1
END
```

```
Ok. run
ENTER ABBREVIATED TITLE - 12 CHARACTERS OR LESS: CPTRSJOKES
ENTER ARTICLE ABSTRACT - 64 CHARACTERS:
? Funny things computers do
Ok. run
ENTER ABBREVIATED TITLE - 12 CHARACTERS OR LESS: CPTRSMEDCIN
ENTER ARTICLE ABSTRACT - 64 CHARACTERS:
? Hiccups and heart beats of computers
```

```
Ok. run
ENTER ABBREVIATED TITLE - 12 CHARACTERS OR LESS: SPORTSCPTR
ENTER ARTICLE ABSTRACT - 64 CHARACTERS:
? Fatigue factors and running times
Ok.
```

c. ■ OPEN #1: NAME "B:Library",ACCESS input,CREATE old,ORGANIZATION
   byte
   ■ FOR ENTRY = 1 TO 16
   ■ PRINT "Index Information: ";
   ■   READ #1, BYTES 8:ENTRY$
   ■   PRINT "Entry Number : ";NUM(ENTRY$);" ";
   ■   READ #1, BYTES 12:TITLE$
   ■   PRINT "Title: ";TITLE$
   ■   PRINT
   ■ NEXT ENTRY
   ■ PRINT tab (20);"Abstracts"
   ■ LET ENTRY = 1
   ■ DO WHILE MORE #1
   ■   READ #1,BYTES 64:ABSTRACT$
   ■   PRINT "Entry number :";ENTRY
   ■   PRINT ABSTRACT$
   ■   LET ENTRY = ENTRY + 1
   ■   PRINT
   ■ LOOP
   ■ CLOSE #1
   ■ END

```
Ok. run
Index Information: Entry Number :   1  Title: CPTRSJOKES

Index Information: Entry Number :   2  Title: CPTRSMEDCIN

Index Information: Entry Number :   3  Title: SPORTSCPTR

Index Information: Entry Number :   0  Title:
  .
  .
  .
                    Abstracts
Entry number : 1
Funny things computers do

Entry number : 2
Hiccups and heart beats of computers

Entry number : 3
Fatigue factors and running times

Ok.
```

d. ■ OPEN #1: NAME "B:Library",ACCESS input,CREATE old,ORGANIZATION
   byte
   ■ FOR ENTRY = 1 TO 16
   ■ PRINT "Index Information: ";
   ■   READ #1, BYTES 8:ENTRY$
   ■   PRINT "Entry Number : ";NUM(ENTRY$);" ";
   ■   READ #1, BYTES 12:TITLE$
   ■   PRINT "Title: ";TITLE$
   ■   PRINT
   ■ NEXT ENTRY
   ■ INPUT PROMPT "Which entry do you wish to see? ":SEE

```
▌ PRINT tab (20);"Abstract # "; SEE
▌ PRINT
▌ FOR SEARCH = 1 TO SEE - 1
▌    READ #1,BYTES 64:ABSTRACT$
▌ NEXT SEARCH
▌    READ #1,BYTES 64:ABSTRACT$
▌    PRINT ABSTRACT$
▌ CLOSE #1
▌ END
```

```
Ok. run
Index Information: Entry Number :  1  Title: CPTRSJOKES

Index Information: Entry Number :  2  Title: CPTRSMEDCIN

Index Information: Entry Number :  3  Title: SPORTSCPTR

Index Information: Entry Number :  0  Title:
  .
  .
  .
Which entry do you wish to see? 3
                Abstract # 3

Fatigue factors and running times
Ok.
```

Index

Characters

& (ampersand operator), 142
* (asterisk), 37, 161
^ (caret), 37, 161
, (comma), 27, 28, 54–55, 118, 159,
    161, 214–215
. (decimal point), 161
/ (division), 37
$ (dollar sign), 48, 161
= (equal sign), 69, 71
! (exclamation point), 29–30
> (greater than), 69, 71, 162
>= or => (greater than or equal to), 69
< (less than), 69, 71, 162
<= or =< (less than or equal to), 69
■ (line tag), 4, 32
− (minus sign), 37, 161
<> or >< (not equal to), 69, 71
% (percent sign), 161
+ (plus sign), 37, 161
# (pound sign), 161
? (question mark), 53
; (semicolon), 26, 27, 28, 117, 159,
    214–215

Abbreviated commands, 7–8, 31
ABS() function, 44
ACCESS parameter, 205
Addition (+), 37
    matrices and, 123
American National Standards
    Institute. *See* ANSI
American Standard Code for
    Information Interchange. *See*
    ASCII

Ampersand operator (&), 142
AND logical operator, 72–74
ANGLE() function, 44
Animating graphics, 189–192
ANSI (American National Standards
    Institute), 19
Arguments, 132–134, 138
Arithmetic functions. *See* Numeric
    functions
Arithmetic operations, 37–38
Array functions, 115
    LBOUND(), 116
    SIZE(), 116
    UBOUND(), 116
Arrays, 106–115
    DIM statement and, 106–108
    subscripts and, 106, 109–115
    See also Matrices
ASCII (American Standard Code for
    Information Interchange), 10,
    207, 248, 249–252
    comparisons based on, 72
ASK #n: MARGIN function, 215
ASK CURSOR function, 177
ASK MAX COLOR function, 174–175
ASK statement, 209–210
Asterisk (*), 37
    PRINT USING statement and, 161
ATN() function, 44

Background color. *See* Color
Background music. *See* PLAY
    statement; SOUND statement
Binary digit. *See* Bit
Binary number system, 9–10, 246–248

Bit, 9, 10, 247–248
Blank lines, 31
Blocks, editing, 32
Booting. *See* Starting
BOX AREA statement, 190
BOX CIRCLE statement, 191
BOX CLEAR statement, 191
BOX ELLIPSE statement, 191
BOX LINES statement, 190
BREAK command, 6
Bubble sort, 109, 119
Buffers, 202
Built-in matrices, 125–127
BYE command, 6
Byte(s), 10, 247–248
   header, 225–226
Byte files, 208–209, 235–244

CALL statement, 31–32
Caret (^), 37
   PRINT USING statement and, 161
Case, 31
CASE clause, 79–80
   See also SELECT CASE statement
Case control structure, 15, 77–78
   See also SELECT CASE statement
CASE ELSE clause, 80
   See also SELECT CASE statement
CAUSE EXCEPTION statement,
   154–155
   See also EXIT HANDLER
     statement; WHEN
     EXCEPTION IN...USE...END
     WHEN statement
Central processing unit. *See* CPU
CHANGE command, 6
Channels, 202–203
   screen and, 192–194
   See also File(s)
Character-string data
   converting to numeric, 236
   format of, 207
   PRINT USING statement and, 164,
     166–169
Character-string functions
   CHR$(), 168
   DATE, 168
   LCASE()$, 168
   LEN(), 168
   LTRIM$(), 168
   NUM(), 168
   NUM$(), 168

ORD(), 168
POS(), 168
REPEAT$(), 168
RTRIM$(), 169
STR$(), 169
TIME, 169
TRIM$(), 169
UCASE(), 169
USING(), 169
VAL(), 48, 50–51, 169
Character-string variables
   quotation marks and, 51
   relational operators and, 71–72
   substrings and, 51–53
   user-defined functions and, 140–142
CHR$() function, 168
CLEAR statement, 175
CLOSE #n statement, 194
CLOSE statement, 206
COBOL, 9–10
Code
   ASCII, 10, 207, 248, 249–252
   executable, 11
   intermediate, 11
   source, 11
Color, 172–175
   ASK MAX COLOR function and,
     174–175
   BOX AREA statement and, 190
   changing screen, 2–3
   FLOOD statement and, 191–192
   PLOT AREA: statement and, 187
   SET BACKGROUND COLOR
     statement and, 173–174
   SET COLOR statement and, 173–
     174
   See also Graphics
Comma (,), 27, 28
   INPUT statement and, 54–55
   MAT READ statement and, 118
   PRINT #n: statement and, 214–215
   PRINT TAB statement and, 159
   PRINT USING statement and, 161
Command(s). *See specific command*
Command key (F2), 2
Command window, 2, 6
   cursor and, 3
   RUN command and, 4–5
   scrolling in, 6
   SPLIT command and, 3
Comments. *See* Exclamation point (!);
   REM statement

COMPILE command, 6
Compile-time errors, 148
Compiler, 11
Computer dating program, 16–18
Computer system, 8–10, 201–202
CON (constant) matrix, 127
Concatenation, 142
Constants, PRINT USING statement and, 162
CONTINUE command, 6
Control program, 10
Control structures, 14–15
    case, 15, 77–78
    leading decision loop, 15
    sequential, 15, 26, 27
    trailing decision loop, 15
    true-false, 15, 66–67
    See also Structured programming
Control variable, 96–99
Converting numbers to character strings, 236
COPY command, 6
Copy key (F5), 2, 32
COS() function, 44
CPU (central processing unit), 8, 9, 201
CREATE parameter, 205
CTRL-B (Background color key), 2–3
CTRL-E (Edge color key), 2–3
CTRL-F (Foreground color key), 2–3
Cursor, 3, 175–177
    ASK CURSOR function and, 177
    graphics, 188–189
    SET CURSOR function and, 175–176

DATA statement, 57–61, 91–93
    RESTORE statement and, 61
    See also READ statement
Data types, 207
DATE function, 168
DATE$ function, 168
Dating program, 16–18
Decimal number system, 246–247
Decimal point (.), PRINT USING statement and, 161
DECLARE DEF statement, 140
DEG() function, 44
DELETE command, 6
Delete key (Del), 2, 32
Descriptive flowcharts, 19, 21
Desk-checking, 23
DET() function, 127

DIM statement, 106–108
    See also Arrays; Matrices
DIR command, 144
Disk files. *See* File(s)
Display screen. *See* Screen
Division (/), 37
DO FORMAT command, 6
DO NUM command, 6
DO PAGE command, 6
DO RENUM command, 6
DO UNNUM command, 6
DO...LOOP statement, 86–91
    combining with FOR...NEXT statement, 101, 102
    EXIT DO statement and, 91
    nesting, 93–95
    UNTIL modifier and, 87–90
    WHILE modifier and, 87–90
    See also FOR...NEXT statement
Dollar sign ($), 48
    PRINT USING statement and, 161
DOT() function, 127
Double subscripts, 111–113
DRAW statement, 195–196
Driver. *See* Main routine

Edge color key (CTRL-E), 2–3
EDIT command, 6
Edit key (F1), 2
Edit window, 2, 5
    NEW command and, 4
    scrolling in, 5
    SPLIT command and, 3
Editing programs, 5, 32–33
Editor, 11, 32–33
ELSE IF clause, 76–77
    See also IF statement
END #n test, 92
END DATA test, 92
END DEF statement. *See* FUNCTION...END DEF statement
END PICTURE statement. *See* PICTURE...END PICTURE statement
END statement, 25–26
END SUB statement. *See* SUB...END SUB statement
END WHEN statement. *See* WHEN EXCEPTION IN...USE...END WHEN statement
Enter (Insert line key), 2

Entering programs, 3–4
EPS() function, 44
Equal sign (=)
    character-string variables and, 71
    numeric variables and, 69
ERASE statement, 210–211
Error codes, 150–151
    creating, 154–155
Errors
    compile-time, 148
    logical, 148
    run-time, 148–155
Exception-handler statements. *See*
    WHEN EXCEPTION
    IN...USE...END WHEN
    statement
Exclamation point (!), 29–30
Executable code, 11
EXIT DEF statement, 142
EXIT DO statement, 91
EXIT FOR statement, 100–101
EXIT HANDLER statement, 149
    percolation and, 152–154
    See also CAUSE EXCEPTION
    statement; WHEN
    EXCEPTION IN...USE...END
    WHEN statement
EXIT PICTURE statement, 196
EXIT SUB statement, 136
Exponential notation. *See* Scientific
    notation
Exponentiation (^), 37
Expressions, PRINT TAB statement
    and, 159–160
External functions, 140
EXTERNAL statement, 143–144
External subroutines, 131–136
EXTEXT$ variable, 150, 154–155
EXTYPE variable, 149, 154–155

F1 (Edit key), 2
F2 (Command key), 2
F3 (Find key), 2
F4 (Mark key), 2, 32
F5 (Copy key), 2, 32
F6 (Move key), 2, 32
F7 (Undelete key), 2, 32–33
F9 (RUN key), 2
F10 (Help key), 2
Fibonacci sequence, 36
Fibonacci, Leonardo, 36

Fields, 207
    See also File(s)
File(s), 201–211
    byte, 208–209, 235–244
    channels and, 202–203
    designing, 206–208
    foreign, 241–244
    library, 143–145, 197–199
    opening/closing in main routines,
        18, 142, 206, 236
    random access, 201
    record, 208–209, 224–232
    sequential, 202
    subroutines and, 204–206
    text, 208–209, 213–221
File pointer, setting. *See* SET #n:
    POINTER function
File record layout, 207–208, 226
FILES command, 6, 144
FIND command, 6
Find key (F3), 2
Flag(s)
    setting, 151–152
    testing. *See* SELECT CASE
    statement
FLOOD statement, 191–192
Flowcharts, 19–22
    desk-checking, 23
    See also Pseudocode; Structured
    programming
FOR...NEXT statement, 95–99
    combining with DO...LOOP
    statement, 101, 102
    control variable and, 96–99
    EXIT FOR statement and, 100–101
    nesting, 99
    STEP modifier and, 97–99
    See also DO...LOOP statement
Foreground color. *See* Color
Foreign files, byte files and, 241–244
Format program, 31
Formatting
    output. *See* PRINT USING
    statement
    programs, 30–32
FORTRAN, 9
Function(s). *See* Array functions;
    Character-string functions;
    Matrix functions; Numeric
    functions; Trigonometric
    functions; User-defined functions
    or specific function

FUNCTION...END DEF statement,
139–140
one-line functions and, 143
parentheses and, 140

GET KEY statement, 177–179
See also INPUT statement; KEY
INPUT statement
GET POINT statement, 188–189
GIGO (garbage in, garbage out), 148
Graphics, 184–199
animating, 189–192
BOX AREA statement and, 190
BOX CIRCLE statement and, 191
BOX CLEAR statement and, 191
BOX ELLIPSE statement and, 191
BOX LINES statement and, 190
CLOSE #n statement and, 194
cursor, 188–189
DRAW statement and, 195–196
EXIT PICTURE statement and, 196
FLOOD statement and, 191–192
GET POINT statement and,
188–189
OPEN #n: SCREEN statement and,
192–193
PICTURE...END PICTURE
statement and, 196–199
PLOT AREA: statement and, 187
PLOT LINES: statement and, 187
PLOT POINTS: statement and, 186
PLOT TEXT, AT X,Y: statement
and, 188
SET WINDOW statement and,
184–186
subroutines, 194–199
WINDOW #n statement and,
193–194
See also Color
Greater than (>)
character-string variables and, 71
numeric variables and, 69
PRINT USING statement and, 162
Greater than or equal to (>= or =>), 69

Hardware, 8–9
Header bytes, 225–226
Hello command, 2
Help key (F10), 2
Hierarchy
of logical operators, 74
of operations, 37–38

Higgins, David A., 14
High-level languages, 9–10
History window. *See* Command window
Hollerith, Herman, 47

I/O (input-output) channels. *See*
Channels
I/O (input/output) devices, 8, 202
IDN (identity) matrix, 126, 127
IEEE (Institute of Electrical and
Electronic Engineers) format, 10,
207, 248
IF statement, 67–77
ELSE IF clause and, 76–77
logical operators and, 72–74
null paths and, 74–75
one-line, 74–76
relational operators and, 68–72
Implicit redimensioning, 123, 124–125
INCLUDE command, 6
Indented lines, 31
Infinite loops, 86–87
Input, 202
INPUT #n: statement, 217
See also LINE INPUT #n: statement
INPUT PROMPT statement, 56
See also INPUT statement; LINE
INPUT statement; LINE
INPUT PROMPT statement
INPUT statement, 53–56
SET CURSOR function and,
175–176
See also GET KEY statement;
INPUT PROMPT statement;
KEY INPUT statement; LET
statement; LINE INPUT
statement; LINE INPUT
PROMPT statement
Insert key (Ins), 2
Insert line key (Enter), 2
Institute of Electrical and Electronic
Engineers format. *See* IEEE
format
INT() function, 39–40, 44
Intermediate code, 11
Internal subroutines, 142–143
Internal user-defined functions,
142–143
International Organization for
Standardization. *See* ISO
Interpreter, 11–12
INV() function, 127

Invoking. *See* Starting
ISO (International Organization for Standardization), 19

Justification. *See* PRINT USING statement

KEEP command, 6
KEY command, 6
KEY INPUT statement, 179
  See also GET KEY statement; INPUT statement
KEY INPUT test, 92
Keyboard
  file names and, 207
  GET KEY statement and, 177–179
  KEY INPUT statement and, 179
  See also specific key

Languages, high-level, 9–10
LBOUND() function, 116
LCASE$() function, 168
Leading decision loop, 15, 85, 86, 87–89, 95–99
LEN() function, 168
Less than (<)
  character-string variables and, 71
  numeric variables and, 69
  PRINT USING statement and, 162
Less than or equal to (<= or =<), 69
LET statement, 47–53
  user-defined functions and, 138
  See also INPUT statement; INPUT PROMPT statement; LINE INPUT PROMPT statement; LINE INPUT statement
Liber Abbaci (Pisano), 36
Library files, 143–145, 197–199
LIBRARY statement, 144–145
Light pen, GET POINT statement and, 188–189
LINE INPUT #n: statement, 217–218
  See also INPUT #n: statement
LINE INPUT PROMPT statement, 56–57
  See also INPUT statement; INPUT PROMPT statement; LINE INPUT statement
LINE INPUT statement, 56–57
  See also INPUT statement; INPUT PROMPT statement; LINE INPUT PROMPT statement
Line length, changing, 29, 215

Line tag (∎), 4, 32
Lines, program, 31, 32
LIST command, 6, 7
Lists, 106–109
Literal characters, PRINT USING statement and, 164–165
Local variables, 132, 138
LOCATE command, 6
LOG() function, 44
LOG2() function, 44
LOG10() function, 44
Logical errors, 148
Logical operators, 72–74
Long-term storage. *See* Disks; Tape, magnetic
Loop(s)
  combining, 101, 102
  DO...LOOP statement and, 86–91, 93–95
  FOR...NEXT statement and, 95–101, 102
  infinite, 86–87
  leading decision, 85, 86, 87–89, 95–99
  nesting, 93–95, 99
  testing, 91–93
  trailing decision, 85–86, 89–90
LOOP statement. *See* DO...LOOP statement
Lower window. *See* Command window
Lowercase, 31
LTRIM$() function, 168

Magnetic tape. *See* Tape, magnetic
Main routine, 130, 206
Main storage. *See* RAM
Margins, changing, 29, 215
Mark key (F4), 2, 32
MAT INPUT statement, 119–120
  redimensioning with, 121–122
MAT LINE INPUT PROMPT statement, 121–122
MAT LINE INPUT statement, 120–121
  redimensioning with, 121–122
MAT PRINT statement, 115–117, 119
  See also PRINT statement
MAT READ statement, 117–119
  redimensioning with, 121–122
  See also READ statement
Mathematic functions. *See* Numeric functions
Matrices, 115–127

adding, 123
built-in, 125–127
MAT INPUT statement and,
        119–120
MAT LINE INPUT PROMPT
        statement and, 121–122
MAT LINE INPUT statement and,
        120–121
MAT PRINT statement and,
        115–117, 119
MAT READ statement and, 117–119
multiplying, 124–125
redimensioning, 121–122
subtracting, 123
See also Arrays
Matrix functions
DET(), 127
DOT(), 127
INV(), 127
TRN(), 127
MAX() function, 44
MAXNUM() function, 44, 45, 52–53
Memory addresses, 47–48
        See also LET statement; Variables
Microprocessing unit. *See* CPU
MIN() function, 44
Mini-screen. *See* Window(s)
Minus sign (−), 37
        PRINT USING statement and, 161
MOD() function, 44
Modular programming. *See* Structured
        programming
Monitor. *See* Screen
MORE #n test, 92
MORE DATA test, 92, 93
Mouse, GET POINT statement and,
        188–189
MOVE command, 6
Move key (F6), 2, 32
MPU (microprocessing unit). *See* CPU
Multiple subscripts, 113–115
Multiplication (*), 37
        matrices and, 124–125
Music. *See* PLAY statement; SOUND
        statement

NAME parameter, 205
Nesting
        loops, 93–95, 99
        WHEN EXCEPTION
                IN...USE...END WHEN
                statement, 152, 153
NEW command, 4, 6, 32

NEXT statement. *See* FOR...NEXT
        statement
Not equal to (<> or ><)
        character-string variables and, 71
        numeric variables and, 69
NOT logical operator, 72–74
NUL$ (null string) matrix, 127
Null paths, 74–75
        See also IF statement
Null print statement, 27
NUM() function, 168, 236
NUM$() function, 168, 236
Numbering lines, 31
Numbers
        binary system, 246–248
        converting to character strings, 236
        decimal system, 246–247
        format of, 10, 44–45, 207, 247–248
        PRINT USING statement and,
                163–164
        printing, 26
        random. *See* RANDOMIZE
                statement; RND function
        scientific notation and, 43
Numeric functions, 39–42, 44
        ABS(), 44
        EPS(), 44
        INT(), 39–40, 44
        LOG(), 44
        LOG2(), 44
        LOG10(), 44
        MAX(), 44
        MAXNUM(), 44, 45, 52–53
        MIN(), 44
        MOD(), 44
        REMAINDER(), 44
        RND, 41–42, 44
        ROUND(), 40, 44
        SGN(), 44
        SQR(), 39, 44
        TRUNCATE(), 40–41, 44
Numeric variables, 48
        relational operators and, 69–70

Ok. prompt, 3
OLD command, 6, 7
One-line functions, 143
OPEN #n: SCREEN statement,
        192–193
OPEN statement, 204–206
Operating system, 12
OR logical operator, 72–74
ORD() function, 168

Order of operations, 37–38
ORGANIZATION parameter, 205
Orr, Ken, 14
Output, 202

Parameters, 132–134, 138, 140
Parentheses, 37–38
    FUNCTION...END DEF statement
        and, 140
PASCAL, 10
Percent sign (%), PRINT USING
    statement and, 161
Percolation, 152–154
Peripheral devices, 201–202
    See also specific peripheral device
PI function, 44
PICTURE...END PICTURE
        statement, 196–199
    EXIT PICTURE statement and, 196
    libraries and, 197–199
Pisano, Leonardo, 36
PLAY statement, 180–182
    See also SOUND statement
PLOT AREA: statement, 187
PLOT LINES: statement, 187
PLOT POINTS: statement, 186
PLOT TEXT, AT X,Y: statement, 188
Plus sign (+), 37
    PRINT USING statement and, 161
Pointer, setting. *See* SET #n:
        POINTER function
POS() function, 168
Pound sign (#), PRINT USING
        statement and, 161
PRINT #n, USING: statement,
        215–216
PRINT #n: statement, 214–215
PRINT statement, 26–29
    See also MAT PRINT statement
PRINT TAB statement, 159–160
PRINT USING statement, 161–166
    character-string data and, 164
    literal characters and, 164–165
    numeric data and, 163–164
Print zones, 27
    changing width of, 29, 215
    MAT PRINT statement and,
        116–117
    PRINT #n: statement and, 214–215
    PRINT TAB statement and, 159
Printer, file names and, 207
Problem definitions, 15–17
    See also Structured programming

Program(s), 8
    characteristics of, 25–26
    comments. *See* Exclamation point
        (!); REM statement
    computer dating, 16–18
    desk-checking, 23
    editing, 5, 32–33
    entering, 3–4
    functions and. *See specific function*
    Format, 31
    formatting, 30–32
    prologue, 30
    running, 4–5
    saving. *See* SAVE command
    structured. *See* Structured
        programming
    stubs, 23
    subroutines and. *See* Subroutines
    See also Software
Programmer-defined functions. *See*
        User-defined functions
Programming Design and Construction
        (Higgins), 14
Programming languages, 9–10
Prologue, 30
Pseudocode, 19–23
    desk-checking, 23
    See also Flowcharts; Structured
        programming

Question mark (?), 53
Quotation marks
    character-string variables and, 51
    DATA statement and, 58–59, 60
    OPEN statement and, 204

RAD() function, 44
RAM (random-access memory), 8, 9,
        201
Random-access files. *See* Record files
RANDOMIZE statement, 42–43
    See also RND function
READ statement, 57–61
    RESTORE statement and, 61
    See also DATA statement; READ
        statement
Read-only memory. *See* ROM
Record files, 208–209, 224–232
Records, 207
    See also File(s)
RECSIZE parameter, 205, 225–226
Redimensioning, 121–122
    implicit, 123, 124–125

Relational operators, 68–72
　character-string variables and,
　　71–72
　numeric variables and, 69–70
REM statement, 29–30
REMAINDER() function, 44
REPEAT$() function, 168
REPLACE command, 6, 7
RESTORE statement, 61
　See also DATA statement; READ
　　statement
RND function, 41–42, 44
　See also RANDOMIZE statement
ROM (read-only memory), 8
ROTATE() function, 196
ROUND() function, 40, 44
RTRIM$() function, 169
RUN command, 4–5
RUN key (F9), 2
Run-time errors, 148–155
　correcting, 151–152

SAVE command, 6, 7
SCALE() function, 196
Scientific notation, 43
Screen
　CLOSE #n statement and, 194
　color. *See* Color
　graphics. *See* Graphics
　OPEN #n: SCREEN statement and,
　　192–193
　splitting, 3
　WINDOW #n statement and,
　　193–194
　windows. *See* Window(s)
Scrolling
　command window and, 6
　edit window and, 5
SELECT CASE statement, 78–81
　CASE clause and, 79–80
　CASE ELSE clause and, 80
　testing with, 80–81
Semicolon (;), 26, 27, 28
　MAT PRINT statement and, 117
　PRINT #n: statement and, 214–215
　PRINT TAB statement and, 159
Sequential-access files. *See* Text files
Sequential control structure, 15, 26, 27
SET #n: MARGIN function, 215
SET #n: POINTER function, 220–221
SET #n: statement, 210, 227–229
SET BACKGROUND COLOR
　　statement, 173–174

SET COLOR statement, 173–174
SET CURSOR function, 175–176
SET MARGIN statement, 29
SET WINDOW statement, 184–186
SET ZONEWIDTH statement, 29
Setting flags, 151–152
SGN() function, 44
SHEAR() function, 196
SHIFT() function, 196
SIN() function, 44
SIZE() function, 116
Software, 9–10
　See also Program(s)
Sorting, 109, 119
SOUND statement, 180
　See also PLAY statement
Source code, 11
Spaces, 31
SPLIT command, 3
SPLIT n command, 6
SQR() function, 39, 44
Starting, 1–2
Statement(s). *See specific statement*
STEP modifier, 97–99
Storage
　long-term. *See* Disks; Tape,
　　magnetic
　main. *See* RAM
Storing programs. *See* SAVE command
STR$() function, 169
String
　data. *See* Character-string data
　functions. *See* Character-string
　　functions
　variables. *See* Character-string
　　variables
Structured programming, 14–24
　control structures and, 15, 27, 67,
　　78, 86
　flowcharts and, 19–22, 23
　problem definitions and, 15–17
　pseudocode and, 19–23
　top-down design and, 14–15, 17–18
Stubs, 23
SUB...END SUB statement, 134–136
　EXIT SUB statement and, 136
Subroutines, 130–136
　characteristics of, 134
　external, 131–136
　files and, 204–206
　graphics, 194–199
　internal, 142–143
　percolation and, 153

Subroutines *(continued)*
  SUB...END SUB statement and, 134–136
Subscript(s), 106, 109–115
  double, 111–113
  functions. *See* Array functions
  multiple, 113–115
Substrings, 51–53
  See also Character-string variables
Subtraction (−), 37
  matrices and, 123
Symbolic flowcharts, 19, 22

TAB function. *See* PRINT TAB statement
TAN() function, 44
Tape, magnetic, 8, 201–202
Testing loops, 91–93
Text files, 208–209, 213–221
TIME function, 169
TIME$ function, 169
Top-down design, 14–15, 17–18
  See also Structured programming
Trailing decision loop, 15, 85–86, 89–90
Trigonometric functions, 44
  ANGLE(), 44
  ATN(), 44
  COS(), 44
  DEG(), 44
  PI, 44
  RAD(), 44
  SIN(), 44
  TAN(), 44
TRIM$() function, 169
TRN() function, 127
.tru extension, 7, 144
True BASIC Language System, 10–12
True BASIC User's Guide, 1–2, 9, 172, 202
True-false control structure, 15, 66–67
  See also IF statement
TRUNCATE() function, 40–41, 44
TRY command, 6
Types. *See* Data types

UBOUND() function, 116
UCASE() function, 169
Undelete key (F7), 2, 32–33
UNSAVE command, 6
UNSAVE statement, 211

UNTIL modifier
  DO...LOOP statement and, 87–90
  testing with, 91–93
Upper window. *See* Edit window
Uppercase, 31
USE statement. *See* WHEN EXCEPTION IN...USE...END WHEN statement
User-defined functions, 136–142
  characteristics of, 139
  DECLARE DEF statement and, 140
  EXIT DEF statement and, 142
  external, 140
  EXTERNAL statement and, 143–144
  FUNCTION...END DEF statement and, 139–140, 143
  internal, 142–143
  LET statement and, 138
  LIBRARY statement and, 144–145
  one-line, 143
  percolation and, 153
USING() function, 169

VAL() function, 169
Variables, 48
  character-string, 48, 50–53, 71–72, 140–142
  control, 96–99
  local, 132, 138
  numeric, 48, 69–70
  PRINT TAB statement and, 159–160
  PRINT USING statement and, 162
  See also DATA statement; INPUT PROMPT statement; INPUT statement; LET statement; LINE INPUT PROMPT statement; LINE INPUT statement; READ statement

WHEN EXCEPTION IN...USE...END WHEN statement, 148–149
  nesting, 152, 153
  See also CAUSE EXCEPTION statement; EXIT HANDLER statement
WHILE modifier
  DO...LOOP statement and, 87–90
  testing with, 91–93

Window(s), 2
  changing size of, 3
  CLOSE #n statement and, 194
  command, 2, 3, 4–5, 6
  edit, 2, 3, 4, 5
  OPEN #n: SCREEN statement and,
    192–193
  SET WINDOW statement and,
    184–186
WINDOW #n statement and,
  193–194
  See also Color; Graphics; Screen
WINDOW #n statement, 193–194

ZER (zero) matrix, 127